Alejandro Lerroux and the Failure of Spanish Republican Democracy

Sussex Studies in Spanish History

General Editor: Nigel Townson, Universidad Complutense, Madrid
Consultant Editor: José Álvarez-Junco, Universidad Complutense, Madrid
Advisory Editors: Pamela Radcliff, University of California, San Diego
Tim Rees, University of Exeter

Ángel Alcalde, Foster Chamberlin, and Francisco J. Leira-Castiñeira (editors), *The Crucible of Francoism: Combat, Violence, and Ideology in the Spanish Civil War.*

José Álvarez-Junco, *The Emergence of Mass Politics in Spain: Populist Demagoguery and Republican Culture, 1890–1910.*

Avi Astor, *Rebuilding Islam in Contemporary Spain: The Politics of Mosque Establishment, 1976–2013.*

Pablo Bornstein: *Reclaiming al-Andalus: Orientalist Scholarship and Spanish Nationalism, 1875–1919.*

Tom Buchanan, *The Impact on the Spanish Civil War on Britain: War, Loss and Memory.*

Andrew Dowling, *Catalonia since the Spanish Civil War: Reconstructing the Nation.**

Ferran Gallego and Francisco Morente (eds), *The Last Survivor: Cultural and Social Projects Underlying Spanish Fascism, 1931–1975.*

Hugo García, *The Truth about Spain!: Mobilizing British Public Opinion, 1936–1939.*

Irene González González, *Spanish Education in Morocco, 1912–1956: Cultural Interactions in a Colonial Context .*

Aitana Guia, *The Muslim Struggle for Civil Rights in Spain: Promoting Democracy through Migrant Engagement, 1985–2010.*

Patricia Hertel, *The Crescent Remembered: Islam and Nationalism on the Iberian Peninsula.*

Silvina Schammah Gesser, *Madrid's Forgotten Avant-Garde: Between Essentialism and Modernity.*

David Messenger, *L'Espagne Républicaine: French Policy and Spanish Republicanism in Liberated France.*

Javier Moreno-Luzón, *Modernizing the Nation: Spain during the Reign of Alfonso XIII, 1902–1931.*

Inbal Ofer, *Señoritas in Blue: The Making of a Female Political Elite in Franco's Spain.*

Stanley G. Payne, *Alcalá Zamora and the Failure of the Spanish Republic, 1931–1936.*
Mario Ojeda Revah, *Mexico and the Spanish Civil War: Domestic Politics and the Republican Cause.*
Raanan Rein and Joan Maria Thomàs (eds), *Spain 1936: Year Zero.*
Elizabeth Roberts, *"Freedom, Faction, Fame and Blood": British Soldiers of Conscience in Greece, Spain and Finland.*
Julius Ruiz, *'Paracuellos': The Elimination of the 'Fifth Column' in Republican Madrid during the Spanish Civil War.*
Miguel Ángel Ruiz Carnicer (ed.), *From Franco to Freedom: The Roots of the Transition to Democracy in Spain, 1962–1982.*
Guy Setton, *Spanish–Israeli Relations, 1956–1992: Ghosts of the Past and Contemporary Challenges in the Middle East.*
Emilio Grandío Seoane, *A Balancing Act: British Intelligence in Spain during the Second World War.*
Manuel Álvarez Tardío, *José María Gil-Robles: Leader of the Catholic Right during the Spanish Second Republic.*
Manuel Álvarez Tardío and Fernando del Rey Reguillo (eds.), *The Spanish Second Republic Revisited.*
Nigel Townson, *The Crisis of Democracy in Spain: Centrist Politics under the Second Republic, 1931–1936.*
Nigel Townson (ed.), *Is Spain Different?: A Comparative Look at the 19th and 20th Centuries.*
Roberto Villa García, *Alejandro Lerroux and the Failure of Spanish Republican Democracy: A Political Biography (1864–1949).*

* Published in association with the Cañada Blanch Centre for Contemporary Spanish Studies and the Catalan Observatory, London School of Economics.

A full list of titles in the series is available on the Press website.

Alejandro Lerroux and the Failure of Spanish Republican Democracy

A Political Biography (1864–1949)

ROBERTO VILLA GARCÍA

Translated by Julius Ruiz

sussex
ACADEMIC
PRESS
Brighton • Chicago • Toronto

Copyright © Roberto Villa García, 2021.

The right of Roberto Villa García to be identified as Author, and Julius Ruiz as Translator, of this work has been asserted in accordance with the Copyright, Designs and Patents Act 1988.

2 4 6 8 10 9 7 5 3 1

First published in Great Britain in 2021 by
SUSSEX ACADEMIC PRESS
PO Box 139, Eastbourne BN24 9BP

Distributed in North America by
SUSSEX ACADEMIC PRESS
Independent Publishers Group
814 N. Franklin Street
Chicago, IL 60610

All rights reserved. Except for the quotation of short passages for the purposes of criticism and review, no part of this publication may be reproduced, stored in a retrieval system, or transmitted, in any form or by any means, electronic, mechanical, photocopying, recording or otherwise, without the prior permission of the publisher.

This research was supported by the Spanish National Project with Reference HAR2015-68013 MINECO-FEDER.

British Library Cataloguing in Publication Data
A CIP catalogue record for this book is available from the British Library.

Library of Congress Cataloging-in-Publication Data
To be applied For.

Hardcover ISBN 978-1-78976-048-4
Paperback ISBN 978-1-78976-053-8

Typeset & designed by Sussex Academic Press, Brighton & Eastbourne.
Printed by TJ Books Limited, Padstow, Cornwall.

Contents

Prologue by Stanley G. Payne ... viii
List of Abbreviations ... xii

Introduction ... 1
The Truth Betrayed: Alejandro Lerroux and his Critics

1 The Forging of a Rebel (1864–1899) ... 10
2 Revolutionary Organiser (1899–1909) ... 31
3 The Respectable Republican (1909–1923) ... 52
4 From Sceptical Conspirator to Minister of the Republic (1923–1931) ... 67
5 Leader of the Republican Opposition (1932–1933) ... 98
6 Prime Minister (1933–1934) ... 112
7 A Conservative against Anarchy (1934–1935) ... 132
8 Much Ado About Nothing (1935–1936) ... 147

Epilogue ... 172
Exile and Return (1936–1949)

Notes ... 184
Primary Sources and Bibliography ... 197
Index ... 202

Prologue by Stanley G. Payne

The introduction of Spain's democratic Republic in 1931 was a unique countercurrent event in European politics of the Great Depression, when the general trend was toward more authoritarian government. Yet the Republic was not a mere anomaly in Spanish affairs, for during the nineteenth century Spain had led nearly all the underdeveloped countries of Europe in the introduction of more liberal, advanced and sometimes even radical political and institutional practices. All the more radical forms had failed – the Federal Republic of 1873 had barely survived one convulsive year amid three concurrent civil wars – but that had not been for want of trying.

A standard narrative about the Second Spanish Republic is that it perished almost inevitably at the hands of two irreconcilable extremes, by lacking significant moderating political forces that could enable a democratic system to function. Yet this is a somewhat distorted and simplistic conclusion that ignores the real history of the Republic, and particularly of its governance by the center and by the center-right from 1933 to 1935, when Spain began to recover from the Depression.

A genuinely democratic leadership existed, and for a brief period governed successfully under the prime ministership of Alejandro Lerroux, the subject of this new biography. Lerroux's lengthy political career reflected the adage attributed to Georges Clemenceau, according to which at the age of twenty almost anyone would naturally be on the left else he had no heart, whereas by the age of forty he would have moved more toward the right, or else he had no head. Lerroux was a leader of radical republicanism still at the age of forty, but within a few more years moved with ever more firm decision toward the democratic center.

He began his political life as a rather typical late nineteenth-century radical, fiercely anticlerical and espousing extreme democracy, autonomy and to some extent a vaguely defined socialism. By 1908 he had founded Spain's most important new republican group, the Radical Republican Party, following the nomenclature of France's Radical Socialists. Unlike other extremist republicans, however, he soon moderated his position. Much like his French counterparts, who began to move toward the center, Lerroux eschewed the revolutionary left and political violence, emphasizing patriotic unity and democratic reformism.

This stance was encouraged by the rapidly changing ambience between 1900 and 1930, in which Spain experienced a remarkable generation of accelerated modernization, the most rapid social, cultural and economic development in its long history of more than two millennia. By 1923, Lerroux seemed on the verge of regular cooperation with the reformist liberal parliamentary monarchy that had governed Spain for half a century. At that point, a national military crisis provoked the imposition of a moderate military dictatorship that lasted for nearly seven years and, despite its initial popularity, pushed Lerroux and others back to the left again. The monarchy's compromise with authoritarian government spurred increasing resentment, accompanied by the rise of new and more radical republican groups. By 1930, at nearly seventy years of age, Lerroux was the senior statesman among Spanish republicans, many of whom had now moved much farther to the left.

When the ad hoc Republican coalition replaced the monarchy in 1931 through a peaceful *pronunciamiento*, based on limited elections, Lerroux was relegated to a secondary role. Unlike the majority of the left Republican government, he was convinced that the new regime should avoid radical reforms until democratic elections had been held to reach a consensus that would represent all of Spanish society. To him, the Republic meant liberal democracy, individual freedom and equal rights for all, but to the new extremist Republican left the Republic meant a progressivist project in which radical reforms and extreme anticlericalism were more important than fully democratic elections. For the Republican left, the trouble with democracy was that it might permit their opponents to win, and therefore they preferred to rely on the increasingly revolutionary Socialists in order to exclude Catholics and conservatives from any participation in government.

Not surprisingly, this radical exclusionary version of Republicanism began to break down within little more than two years. The only fully democratic and constitutional elections in Spanish history were conducted in November 1933. A temporary split between the Republic left and the Socialists, combined with the forceful mobilization of liberal democratic and conservative opinion, led to victory by a new Catholic moderate right and by Lerroux's now misnamed Radicals, who occupied the democratic center. The Catholic coalition, the CEDA, respected Republican legal norms, despite two years of partial suppression by a heavy-handed government. What it demanded was reform of the new Constitution, especially to guarantee full rights for Catholics. The left nonetheless refused to abandon its program of an exclusionary and anti-

Catholic Republic, calling the CEDA "fascist." Thus they mimicked the Comintern's tactic of the past decade in labelling more conservative political opponents of diverse stripes various types of "fascists." To placate the left, the Republican president denied the largest parliamentary party opportunity to participate in government, instead appointing a minority coalition of democratic center groups under Lerroux. This administration of 1933-35 was the most evenhanded and democratic in the history of the Republic, though it had to face two violent revolutionary insurrections, the first by the anarchists and the second by the Socialists in October 1934. The latter was a major rebellion against the Republican government in fifteen provinces and required the imposition of martial law. Despite severe challenges, Lerroux struggled with considerable success to maintain the essence of the Republican democratic system.

The second phase of his government began in May 1935, when he was permitted to form a multi-party majority coalition with other liberal democrats and with the CEDA. Conditions generally improved as the economy started to recover from the Great Depression. After less than six months, however, the government was undercut by the venomous rivalry and resentment of the Republic's president, Niceto Alcalá-Zamora, who enjoyed broad powers and hoped to replace Lerroux as leader of the center. Such an ambition impelled him to call new elections, though the existing parliament had proven its effectiveness and had two more years to serve. This was a prime example of the absurd rivalries that gravely compromised Spanish government, since the highest Republican authority would not permit parliamentary rule to proceed normally.

The following elections of February 1936 became polarized between supporters of the revolutionary insurrection of 1934, as championed by the new leftist alliance of the Popular Front, and those voting for a conservative parliamentary government led by the moderate right, to oppose leftist radicalism and insurrectionism. Amid such polarization the democratic center, discredited by minor administrative scandals that had been artificially inflated by the political extremes, rapidly lost ground. Moreover, at the age of 72, Lerroux had lost political ambition and combativeness amid so strident an atmosphere. Left and right were evenly matched in the popular vote, but mass riots quickly forced the transfer of power to a left Republican government even before the ballots had been fully counted. Vote manipulation in eight provinces then transformed a virtual tie into a victory for the Popular Front. This was magnified by further violence and electoral exclusion in the run-off balloting in several provinces the following month, then by direct cancellation and reversal of results for more than thirty seats by the new parliament, and finally by the outcome of highly controlled repeat elections in two provinces in May. In these and in other respects, democratic constitutional government had begun to come to an end as early as February 1936.

The following seven months, during which the left Republicans maintained their uneasy embrace of the revolutionary Socialists and Communists, were increasingly filled with government abuses and revolutionary violence and disorder. This was climaxed by the revolt of part of the armed forces, abandonment of what was left of parliamentary rule by the Republican left, empowerment of full revolutionary civil war and the formation of a revolutionary Republican government in September 1936. Even before the revolutionary Republic of 1936 to 1939 had fully emerged, such extreme polarization had ended the long political trajectory of Alejandro Lerroux. He had no place in the violent, revolutionary and highly authoritarian politics that emerged in 1936.

The author of this new biography, Roberto Villa García, is the most distinguished of the younger historians in the field of contemporary Spanish political history. His *La República en las urnas: El despertar de la democracia en España* (2011), a richly detailed investigation of the elections of 1933, constitutes the best single study of any historic Spanish election. With Manuel Álvarez Tardío, he is co-author of *1936: Fraude y violencia en las elecciones del Frente Popular* (2017), a pathbreaking history that has revolutionized understanding of the final phase of Republican democratic politics. He has also published two other electoral studies as well as further research on the Second Republic. With Álvarez Tardío, he is co-editor of the volume *El precio de la exclusion: La política durante la Segunda República* (2010).

Villa García's new book is the first biographical account of Lerroux in many years, the only thorough and up-to-date treatment, and the only one that covers carefully both his earlier radical period and his later prominence as the leader of centrist Republican democracy. Its grasp of source materials is comprehensive and its treatment widely informed and critically objective. It significantly broadens our perspective on Republican democracy and the reasons for its failure. It also contributes a further dimension to our understanding of the European crisis of the 1930s and is not without its lessons for our own time.

List of Abbreviations

CEDA	Confederación Española de Derechas Autónomas. (Spanish Confederation of Autonomous Right-Wing Groups).
CNT	Confederación Nacional del Trabajo (National Confederation of Labour).
DLR	Derecha Liberal Republicana (Liberal Republican Right).
DNSD	Delegación Nacional de Servicios Documentales (National Delegation of Document Services)
ERC	Esquerra Republicana de Cataluña (Catalan Republican Left).
FAI	Federación Anarquista Ibérica (Iberian Anarchist Federation).
FIRPE	Federación de Izquierdas Republicanas Parlamentarias Españolas (Spanish Left Republican Parliamentary Federation).
PNV	Partido Nacionalista Vasco (Basque Nationalist Party).
PSOE	Partido Socialista Obrero Español (Spanish Socialist Workers Party).
TERMC	Tribunal Especial para la Represión de la Masonería y el Comunismo (Special Tribunal for the Repression of Masonry and Communism).
UFNR	Unión Federal Nacionalista Republicana (Republican National Federal Union).
UGT	Unión General de Trabajadores (General Workers Union).
UP	Unión Patriótica (Patriotic Union).

Alejandro Lerroux and the Failure of Spanish Republican Democracy

A Political Biography (1864–1949)

Introduction
The Truth Betrayed
Alejandro Lerroux and his Critics

Many years ago, I became familiar with the political life of Alejandro Lerroux as an undergraduate studying modern Spanish history. He was such a puzzle. Historians wrote of him as both a youthful republican firebrand who called for churches to be burned during the 'Tragic Week' in Barcelona in 1909 and the wizened leader of moderate republicanism who entered government with Catholics in 1934, putting down an insurrection led by those leftists who had proclaimed the Second Republic alongside him barely three years earlier. This remarkable political journey from revolution to counter-revolution was not explained in terms of changing ideas during the tumultuous years of monarchy, dictatorship and democracy, but rather as the all too predictable actions of an unscrupulous opportunist who sought power only for the material benefits it could provide. The fact that Lerroux's career ended in scandal seemed to be the fitting end to a lifetime of political immorality and wickedness.

This caricature remains influential in the historiography of twentieth-century Spain. It helps to explain why Alejandro Lerroux remains the least studied and understood of all the major figures of the Second Republic, despite being the leader of its most important republican party. This is the first complete political biography of a man who held the premiership on six occasions. The only other scholarly account, written by José Álvarez Junco in 1990 and published in English in 2004 as *The Emergence of Mass Politics in Spain*, ends in 1910 when Lerroux had only just established a national reputation. This is not to say that we lack studies that deal with aspects of his career. Joaquín Romero Maura's magisterial 1989 account on the emerging labour movement in early twentieth-century Barcelona placed the young Lerroux's political activities in a wider socio-economic context,[1] while Octavio Ruiz Manjón's pioneering 1976 examination of his Radical Republican Party offered a stimulating discussion of his charismatic leadership, despite an over-reliance on Manuel Azaña's partisan opinions of his most significant republican rival.[2]

A more recent study of the party – the first available in English – was Nigel Townson's innovative 2000 monograph that incorporated sources unavailable to Ruiz Manjón to depict a moderate and centrist leader.[3] Ruiz Manjón argued that continued involvement in dubious political practises reflected an opportunism that would finally lead to the party being consumed by the political right. In this sad story Lerroux was fundamental, as he managed to prevent progressives led by Diego Martínez Barrio from renovating the party. Within the exiguous historiography of centrist politics, only Andrés de Blas offered a dissenting view in 1983, acquitting Lerroux of opportunism and avarice, arguing that he offered a genuine liberal and moderate vision of the Republic.[4]

Irrespective of their undoubted merits, these historians of the 1970s and 1980s have failed to shift the negative paradigm on Lerroux. This is less of a surprise if one recalls the loathing that he provoked among his adversaries of whatever political stripe. The Catholic right never forgave him for his incendiary anticlerical propaganda, while Catalan nationalists despised his stubborn defence of Spanish unity. Left republicans, socialists and communists regarded Lerroux with a mixture of jealousy and hatred. On the one hand, his popularity among the 'people' eclipsed that of his rivals, for example Pablo Iglesias, the founder of the PSOE. On the other, Lerroux was condemned as a traitor to the leftist cause after April 1931. His argument for a broadly based moderate Republic led him to oppose Azaña's left republican-socialist coalition government, and after his victory over his one-time allies in the 1933 general election, he became the advocate for constitutional reform as the means to integrate Catholic rightists within the Republic. Any prospect of reconciliation with the left vanished in October 1934 with the suppression of a rebellion intended to coerce president Niceto Alcalá-Zamora into ejecting the elected centre-right government from power. For the defeated revolutionaries, Lerroux's decision to support the Nationalist cause in 1936 only confirmed his perfidy; it mattered little to them that the Radical leader had nothing to do with the military conspiracy.

Ultimately, the left was defeated in 1939, but Lerroux was not one of the victors. His support base of moderate republicans and liberal monarchists perished in the civil war. It did not return with the death of Franco in November 1975. The Radical Party seemed to offer little inspiration to former Francoists turned democrats, while the left remained dominated by the same socialist, communist and catalanist parties that had risen against Lerroux in October 1934. But while makes it easier to understand why the historical reputation of the Radicals remains so low, it does not follow that historians should reassess the party at the expense of its leader. Created by Lerroux in 1908 as an instrument for his charismatic leadership, it had no other *jefe* throughout its almost thirty-year existence. Therefore, to speak of the Radical Party as a centrist and liberal force is to speak of the man who without doubt embodied those values during the Second Republic: Alejandro Lerroux.

With the significant exception of Townson, the myths and distortions around Lerroux's career remain especially resilient in British historiography. To read Paul Preston's newly published *A People Betrayed: A History of Corruption, Political Incompetence and Social Division in Modern Spain* is to read the charge sheet drawn up by his contemporary political enemies.[5] For Preston, the Radical leader is the epitome of the 'corruption' and 'political incompetence' of the book's title, while his rivals on the left appear as virtuous servants of the 'people'. In taking this approach, the historian ignores the sins of left republicans and socialists, who practised *enchufismo* – the concession and accumulation of public posts and salaries to political friends and allies – on an industrial scale during the Azaña governments of 1931 to 1933. Among the most egregious offenders were the Basque socialist leader Indalecio Prieto, denounced in parliament for the favouritism he displayed towards friendly businessmen such as Horacio Echevarrieta in the allocation of state contracts, and the left republican Marcelino Domingo, found to have committed irregularities in wheat imports before opening schools lacking heating despite money being allocated for boilers; these new institutions had to be closed for safety reasons by the 'corrupt' Lerroux government in the winter of 1933–34. Preston even overlooks the leftist theft of arms from state factories to supply Portuguese revolutionaries and the rebels of October 1934, and chooses to forget the robbery committed by socialists of fourteen million pesetas deposited in the Bank of Spain in Oviedo during the insurrection itself. As the police discovered during their investigations between November 1934 and December 1935, this heist was only the most spectacular example of the larceny carried out in the name of antifascism.

If Prieto and Domingo are for Preston laudable defenders of Republican democracy, then Lerroux is dismissed on countless occasions as 'congenitally corrupt' or a practitioner of 'shameless corruption'. The British historian repeatedly accuses Lerroux of being a paid 'puppet' of the millionaire Juan March, dedicated to the protection of the latter's shady activities such as tobacco smuggling, but fails to provide any evidence of a long and mutually advantageous relationship. Characteristically, Preston ignores the fact that March worked with politicians of all ideological backgrounds, and provided favours and even gifts to the PSOE, including a magnificent 'House of the People' [*Casa del Pueblo*] in Palma de Mallorca.

In order to demonstrate his innate malevolence, *A People Betrayed* also provides a highly distorted view of the Radical leader's early career. For example, the appearance of Lerroux in Barcelona in time for the 1901 elections is depicted as the arrival of a 'virtuoso carpetbagger' paid by Madrid monarchists to combat Catalan nationalists. As we shall see, the reality could not be more different: the then young chief editor of *El País*, famous throughout Spain for his campaign against the government for the alleged torture of anarchists in Montjuich Castle, was invited to the Catalan capital by a faction-ridden republican movement to reverse years of decline. For Preston, his success in winning a parliamentary seat was only about making money; his republicanism was nothing more than 'a cynical bid for working-class support'. Remarkably, *A People Betrayed* asserts that Lerroux invented the 'anti-clerical demagogy' that would lead to Tragic Week in 1909, as if violent anticlericalism were not a well-established feature of Spanish populist republicanism that aspired to entice urban workers away from an emerging anarchist movement. According to Preston, Lerroux's most significant contribution was the introduction of 'near-pornographic techniques' to anticlerical discourse, although he does not provide any examples. In fact, anyone familiar with Lerroux's speeches knows that his 'demagogy' could provoke various reactions, but to call as 'near-pornographic' perorations that have no sexual references is comical.

Less amusing are Preston's attempts to associate Lerroux with the anarchist terrorism of the early twentieth century. He claims that in 1908 the young republican fled Spain 'to avoid imprisonment for his involvement in an assassination attempt on Alfonso XIII'. In reality, Lerroux was escaping from a two-year prison sentence imposed for various crimes of defamation committed as a journalist since 1899. No evidence has been unearthed to implicate the young republican with anarchist violence; the only certainty is his connections with Francisco Ferrer Guardia, a former political ally who later converted to anarchism. Yet as the second chapter shows, their friendship reflected the ambiguous and problematical relationship between republicanism and anarchism during this period; there was co-operation born out of necessity, but ultimately they remained rivals as both were fishing in the same barrel of urban workers.

Preston's fixation with corruption as the only explanation for Lerroux's career leads him to make more elemental mistakes. Due to his supposed 'venality', the radical republican made a profitable shift towards constitutional liberalism on the basis of a newly found 'anti-Catalanism' and 'pro-militarism'. This ignores the fact that these positions were the only ones that did *not* change through Lerroux's political life. The leftist scourge of the monarchy was also a passionate defender of Spanish unity and the military, an institution in which his father had served as a veterinarian. Before entering politics, Lerroux had even dreamed of an army career and only the lack of money impeded his entry into the Toledo Military Academy.

Similarly, Preston attributes the wealth that the Radical leader originally acquired in Argentina in 1908 and later augmented in Spain to 'the corruption of party members with positions in local administration'. However, apart from Barcelona, the Radical Party did not have a significant presence in Spain's municipalities. On this flawed premise, Preston argues Radicals were by definition immoral, as 'many were in politics to derive profit from access to the levers of power'. This, of course, was only a reflection of the pragmatic and liberal drift of their leader, who 'accumulated possessions; cars, jewellery and an estate in San Rafael', located in the Guadarrama mountains north of Madrid. No wonder then, the Briton claims, that Lerroux supported the Entente during the First World War as he depended on 'the exports by his companies, particularly of meat, to the French Republic'. In fact, and as we shall see, the Radical leader supported the Allied cause from the outset and therefore well before the great export boom that began in 1915. But for Preston such was Lerroux's greed that he had no compunction about serving the Dictatorship of the 1920s, writing that he was 'suspected of being on Primo [de Rivera]'s payroll'; this explains why conspiracies against the regime were 'easily dismantled by the authorities'. Again, no evidence is provided to support these serious accusations, and *A People Betrayed* is silent on the fact that Lerroux's unremitting hostility to Primo de Rivera from 1925 earned him two spells in prison that almost cost him his life on the second occasion. Such is Preston's disposition against the future Republican prime minister that he remarks that the latter co-operated with Berenguer's monarchist government of 1930–31 as 'no arrest warrant had been issued for Lerroux'. But an arrest warrant *had* been issued by the police, and the politician was forced into hiding for five months until the very day of the proclamation of the Second Republic itself on 14 April 1931, meaning that that he could not take part in the historic municipal election held two days earlier. It may be true that he was not arrested, but neither were five other members of the republican Revolutionary Committee, who would all become members of the Provisional Government following the departure of Alfonso XIII. Among them was Manuel Azaña, and no one has accused the left republican prime minister and president of being a monarchist spy.

In Preston's morality tale, Lerroux's actions during the Second Republic were shaped by his unquenchable desire for money. If he received the marginal and unsuitable post of foreign minister in April 1931, it was not due to internal power struggles within the new government but because the portfolio 'gave him the fewest opportunities for embezzlement'. In any case, while the actions of Lerroux's more left-wing ministerial colleagues were praiseworthy, his tenure of the foreign ministry was 'a disaster', as 'at the League of Nations at Geneva, he would cut a ridiculous figure'. Chapter 4 will demonstrate that this is far from the truth, as Lerroux was the most popular figure within the government both at home and abroad; the June 1931 general election would prove to be the greatest personal triumph of his career. The same chapter will also show that president Niceto Alcalá-Zamora's decision to pass over the foreign minister for the premiership following the bitter constitutional debates around religion that October was not due to 'Lerroux's known corruption'. Far from being 'outraged' by the appointment of Azaña, Lerroux actually proposed him for the job, since he had no wish to lead what he thought would be an ephemeral government that would end after the proclamation of the Constitution in December. In a similar vein, despite the claim that only corruption can explain 'the determination of the Socialists not to collaborate in a cabinet with Lerroux', it is clear that hostility between the PSOE and the republican dated from at least the turn of the century. For Preston, Lerroux would stop at nothing to prevent the reforms of the Azaña governments, accepting uncritically the unfounded allegations of the Radical leader's political adversaries concerning involvement with general Sanjurjo's *pronunciamiento* of August 1932; Lerroux is even named as one of its principal sponsors alongside Juan March and Benito Mussolini.

Yet Preston saves his most bitter invective for Lerroux's premierships of 1933 to 1935. These allegedly stripped the Republic of its virginal purity. The Radical leader 'had always hankered after a life of luxury' and constantly bombarded 'other ministers with requests for official positions for his relatives and cronies'. The British historian is apparently unaware that Lerroux's family was small and any requests for favours generally came from others who were not always those associated with the Radical Party. Chapter 8 will show that while the Radical prime minister was very receptive to clientelist practises, these did not begin with him or his party. In this sense, it is ironic that Preston regurgitates Niceto Alcalá-Zamora's long-standing criticisms of the Radicals. *A People Betrayed* portrays the former monarchist as a paragon of virtue, noting that the president 'lamented that his [Lerroux's] criteria for such [ministerial] appointments were the candidates' need for money and their personal likeability', which provoked 'real alarm ... when it was a question of senior positions in banks'. Preston's sympathy for the president's predicament is very surprising, as few, if any, specialists on modern Spanish political history would deny that Alcalá-Zamora was the perfect example of a political boss in Cordoba before 1923, who maintained and extended his patronage network after April 1931. Such empathy is not extended to Lerroux or his followers, as it is simply assumed that the mere presence of Radicals on the management boards of financial institutions is enough to guarantee malfeasance. Preston argues that everyone was worried by the presence of 'Lerroux and his gang of thieves' in government, an expression taken from the memoirs of Felix Gordón Ordás, a radical-socialist deputy who nevertheless had worked closely with the Radical leader, advocating anti-socialist pact between their two parties between 1931 and 1933. Since the British historian had long since passed sentence on Lerroux, it is logical that he found it unnecessary to investigate the *estraperlo* and Tayá-Nombela scandals that finally brought Lerroux and his party down in 1935. What is the point if both were intrinsically corrupt? This is symptomatic of a book that does not provide any analysis of political influence and clientelism during the Second Republic, and therefore does not recognise the limited impact of the spoils system within a permanent civil service that had been professionalised by reforms introduced by Antonio Maura in 1918.

Preston's interpretation of Lerroux ends with a dismal account of his final years during and after the civil war. Typically, Lerroux is presented as writing from Lisbon 'sycophantic letters to Franco in the vain hope of being allowed to return to Spain', and reduces his memoirs –written during and not after the war despite the claims of the book – to a mere apologia of the 'military coup'. In sum, the thief and traitor Lerroux fittingly ended his days as a propagandist for a brutal dictator.

Given Preston's objective of making the Radical leader the personification of Spanish corruption and incompetence, it is no wonder that sympathetic reviewers have focused on Lerroux. For Dominic Sandbrook of the *Sunday Times*, he was 'the Radical demagogue' and 'outstandingly corrupt';[6] Isambard Wilkinson in the *Times* is more emphatic in his use of adverbs, labelling Lerroux 'outrageously corrupt'.[7] Perhaps the most worrying consequence of Preston's distorted view of Lerroux is the life that it breathes into the dormant clichés of Spanish exceptionalism. As the enthusiastic Sandbrook writes, many 'Spaniards are understandably irritated by the enduring "Black Legend" of a land of "fanaticism, cruelty and uncontrolled emotion", epitomised by the opera Carmen and the travel books of writers such as Gerald Brenan. But as Preston's tremendously rich and learned history shows, the legend only endures because it has more than a grain of truth'.[8]

Lerroux remains the most derided Spanish democratic politician in English-language historiography. This alone justifies the publication of this political biography. Nonetheless, over seventy years after his death, it combines the fruits of the latest Spanish research into the man and his Radical Party with original material that sheds new light on one of modern Spain's most significant statesmen. To understand Lerroux is to understand the evolution of Spanish republicanism from the late nineteenth century to its collapse in the Second Republic. Although others like Azaña and Alcalá-Zamora have attracted more attention from historians, Lerroux was the dominant figure within the republican movement until the outbreak of war in 1936. Despite his modest talents as a journalist, he was a born communicator and successful advocate of the republican creed. His famous campaigns against the monarchy revived a movement still coming to terms with the chaotic collapse of the First Republic in 1874. As a vigorous deputy for Barcelona from 1901, he created a modern party machine capable of attracting liberal critics of Catalan nationalism and weaning workers away from anarchist apoliticism. This was the key to his great electoral victories between 1901 and 1911.

Success at the ballot box mellowed Lerroux's fiery spirit. After 1903, his appeals to overthrow the monarchy were purely rhetorical; he was not prepared to risk everything on a repeat of the farcical republican uprisings of his youth. No firm evidence has yet been produced of his participation in the Tragic Week of 1909, and his lack of enthusiasm for the republican conspiracies of 1917 and 1930 provoked criticism among the plotters. By then, the experienced Lerroux was an unambiguous advocate of liberal democracy. He was prepared to work with monarchist Liberals and was even willing after the republican failures of 1917–1918 and the Bolshevik Revolution in Russia to accept the monarchy as the price for a democratic new deal for Spain.

If Lerroux was more liberal than republican by 1931, this did not imply that he did not welcome the proclamation of the Second Republic. He would become the leader of the republican opposition before holding the premiership on more occasions than anyone else from September 1933. If Azaña symbolises the first two leftist years of the Republic, Lerroux embodies the subsequent centre-right period of September 1933 to February 1936. When the Republic came courtesy of Primo de Rivera's disastrous military coup of September 1923 that discredited the monarchy, Lerroux envisioned the 'beautiful girl' as a liberal and tolerant entity that would continue the democratising processes disrupted by the Dictatorship. For the Radical leader, the Republic could not be identified with any particular party programme; to survive it had to be inclusive and accept governments of the right as well as of the left. His project was met with incomprehension from his old allies on the republican left and the PSOE. When they rose in arms against his centre-right government of October 1934, Lerroux did not hesitate to defend constitutional democracy; his horror of revolution led him to support the Nationalists in the civil war. Yet the fratricidal conflict only came after his political fall from grace in the much-exaggerated scandals of *estraperlo* and Tayá-Nombela.

Lerroux's political demise was much more than a personal tragedy. It led to the dissolution of the centre-right dominated parliament before Lerroux had time to pass the constitutional amendments needed to consolidate the Republic. With the Radical leader's forced departure, a golden opportunity to forge a liberal democratic Republic was lost. We will never know whether this would have been enough to avoid its collapse. What we do know is that the continued conflation of the Republic with left republicans and socialists brought disaster.

1

The Forging of a Rebel (1864–1899)

The famous Spanish novelist Pío Baroja knew Alejandro Lerroux well in the early years of the twentieth century. In 1914, the politician had offered the writer the opportunity to work on *El Radical*, his party's national daily, as well as a place on the Radicals' slate for the forthcoming Madrid city council elections. Like others of the 'Generation of '98', Baroja was fascinated by the charismatic republican tribune of the 'people' [*pueblo*], and accepted the invitation, although in the end he was defeated. While the novelist's dalliance with the party was to be brief, his pen has provided us with the best contemporary description of Lerroux. Writing in his memoirs over thirty years later, Baroja remarked bluntly that as a man of thought, Lerroux was 'mediocre'. Rather, he was a politician who placed improvisation and opportunism above ideology. To illustrate this, the novelist recounted a meeting that both Spaniards had in Paris with Jean Jaurès, the Frenchman widely admired as the embodiment of republican and socialist ideals, shortly before the latter's assassination in July 1914. When Baroja asked Jaurès what he thought of Lerroux, the French socialist leader quipped that he 'is not a political man, he is a politician' [*c'est n est pas un homme politique, c'est un politicien*]. In other words, a professional politician who subordinated all ideological considerations to narrow party interests.

Despite the pejorative tone of the remark, Jaurès captured perfectly Lerroux's penchant for pragmatic politics. While it is the case that he had internalised the gamut of values and heroic myths of nineteenth-century Spanish republicanism, his genuine concern for the 'social question' gave him creditability with organised workers in turn-of-the-century Barcelona. Nevertheless, his rejection of ideological dogmatism gave critics on both the left and right the opportunity to dismiss him as the archetypical political hack. Lerroux would prove them wrong in the 1930s. The Second Republic marked the end of a journey begun twenty years earlier that would see him move from the republican left to liberal positions. Both his political discourse and action demonstrate that it was the Radical leader who best understood the ways in which a Republic could be consolidated in Spain. Rather than revolutionary change, he wanted to build a solid foundation rooted in the constitutional experience of the Restoration period. In his later years, Lerroux did not conceive the Republic as more than representative democracy, whose principal mission lay in suppressing the exclusivist and insurrectional dynamic reopened with the Primo de Rivera Dictatorship of 1923–30. It is no coincidence, then, that the stature of this *politicien* grew between 1930 and 1935.

Lerroux's scepticism towards doctrinal conflict was also due to his membership of that generation of republicans weary of the divisive disputes of the *vedettes* of the First Republic, especially those led by former presidents Pi y Margall, Salmerón and Castelar. The debates surrounding their responsibility for the disasters of 1873 only intensified the factionalisation of the movement and rendered it incapable of seriously challenging the liberal monarchy. Lerroux's appetite for organisation is also explained by the failure of the so-called 'heroic' generation of republican leaders to create powerful parties capable of reassembling the social and electoral forces of the revolutionary years of 1868–74. Only the Radical Party would provide the structure necessary to mobilise the rank-and-file, restoring the popular urban quality that Spanish republicanism had enjoyed during its glory years.

If Baroja was unimpressed by Lerroux's intellectualism, he did not hesitate to praise his gift of making things happen. The novelist was struck by his ability to forge a political career from modest circumstances. The future prime minister overcame a lack of formal education and professional or family connections by the strength of his personality. Lerroux, he wrote, had resolve, a capacity for work, an ability to evaluate circumstances effectively and above all a special talent to inspire loyalty among others. He became a populist tribune with resonant and convincing oratory that was neither abstract nor flowery but vivid and easily understood by very different audiences. He was equally affable at a personal level, and became famous for his gregariousness. He quickly made close friends, and his generosity bordered on naivety. For Baroja, Lerroux was 'a good person', a 'good-natured man' always 'capable of doing a favour for his friends'. Was this largesse a blemish of character or perhaps a way to create and reinforce clientelist ties that were essential to grease the wheels of a political organisation? Probably both. Lerroux's personality evoked that other 'maker' of political parties, the conservative Francisco Romero Robledo, who was equally known for his open wallet. If one adds to these talents a capacity to temper his ambition with the tenacity of an idealist or a believer in the cause, one can understand why he was able to attract the support of more experienced and educated figures who supposedly were better suited to lead a party.

Although Lerroux penned countless press articles throughout his life, his talents were better suited to politics and not journalism. Despite being a fluent writer, a reading of his somewhat wearisome articles reveals archaic and leaden prose. While his memoirs are better written, the tone of his vibrant oratory is best conveyed in his political manifestos. Baroja was not wrong when he stressed that Lerroux was an 'unremarkable' journalist, but he was also brilliant in using the press to popularise his party's political agenda. When the novelist criticised the failures of Lerroux as the proprietor and editor of *El Radical*, he failed to understand that for over a decade journalism was secondary to his purely political work.[1]

Ultimately, Lerroux's political career was characterised by success. A parliamentary deputy with scarcely a break between 1901 and 1936, he was the leader of the most dynamic republican party before the civil war. The most prominent exponent of Spanish republicanism following the disappearance of the First Republic generation, he was essential to the proclamation of the Second Republic in April 1931, taking ministerial office for the first time. Yet this was not to be the apex of his political life; prime minister on six occasions between 1933 and 1935, he successfully overcame the most serious challenge to face the Second Republic to that point: the Socialist-led revolutionary insurrection of October 1934. Nevertheless, *sic transit gloria mundi*, his fall from grace would be remarkably swift in the aftermath of the Strauss and Nombela scandals a year later. His political life came to an end with electoral defeat in February 1936; the civil war and Franco's unconditional victory in 1939 were but a bitter epilogue to an extraordinary journey.

The Early Years

The family background of this *politicien* gave little indication of a future distinguished public career. Alejandro Lerroux y García, baptised Alejandro Casimiro in honour of his saint's day, was born on 4 March 1864 in the Cordoban village of La Rambla. This place had little impact upon him, as scarcely forty days later the baby went to Cordoba, and as a youngster he lived in an unusually large number of towns and cities: Pamplona, Vitoria, Seville, Ciudad Real, Vicálvaro (Madrid province), Madrid, Villaveza del Agua (Zamora), Cadiz, and Alcalá de Henares (Madrid). Such was the price to pay for those children of military officers and policemen consistently posted around Spain due to promotion or the necessities of service. Both factors explain Lerroux's itinerant early life as his father Alejandro Lerroux y Rodríguez, an officer in the veterinary corps, progressed through the ranks while fighting the carlists between 1872 and 1876.

If the young Lerroux identified with any place it was Madrid, where his paternal family had its roots. His French-sounding surname did not signify a foreign background or wealth; his father was from a humble background. Quickly orphaned, Lerroux y Rodríguez became an apprentice blacksmith before using his savings to study at veterinary school; after the completion of his course, he joined the army's newly formed veterinary corps that provided some stability. Lerroux y Rodríguez's experiences were similar to other social climbers who took advantage of the opening of middle and upper ranks within the army during the nineteenth century. He did not fit the romantic image of a nineteenth-century Spanish soldier. He neither romanticised warfare nor involved himself in political adventure. His motivation was strictly vocational. Without any other training than that acquired before he joined the army, his diligence marked him for rapid promotion and he was already a captain when Lerroux was born in 1864. His decision to study medicine and the frequent postings outside his beloved Madrid is evidence of the sacrifices that Lerroux y Rodríguez made to advance his career, with the consequent financial and personal cost that included long periods separated from his family.

Lerroux's mother, Paula García y González, was part of his father's social circle as the daughter of a retired military doctor in Benavente (Zamora). There they married and brought up their first four children: Arturo, Alfredo, Alberto and Armando. Tragically, only Arturo, the eldest brother who was eight years older than Lerroux, survived infancy. Fortunately, four of Lerroux's subsequent five siblings – Adriana, Armando, Aurelio, Amalia and Amador – reached adulthood. The future Radical leader later attributed their father's fondness for Christian names beginning with the letter "A" to his passion for literary romanticism.

Apart from the vicissitudes that marked his childhood, Lerroux's upbringing was conventional. It is certain that the consecutive loss of three children had a significant emotional impact on his mother, who was less affectionate towards Alejandro than one would expect. Paula's strained relationship with her young son would only worsen due to the latter's proclivity for mischief prompted by a struggle for her attention with his eldest (and similarly rebellious) brother and their younger siblings. Lerroux would receive even less love from a father immersed in his career and money problems. Pay rises were not enough to support an ever-growing household and the constant changes of address only drained their finances further. Yet the family's poverty was representative of many reliant on state incomes.

At home, and despite the impression that he later wanted to convey in his writings, Lerroux was a restless and serious child, extremely sensitive to the lack of parental love. As an adolescent, Alejandro would become even more unsettled as he sought to emulate his older brother. With a somewhat intimidating personality, the ill-tempered actions of Arturo brought him constantly to the attention of his mother and earned the jealous admiration of the teenage Lerroux. To some extent, the latter satisfied his need for affection with his younger siblings, for whom he always felt responsible. In 1894, with his parents absent and Arturo refusing to provide any assistance, Alejandro took care of them until they could support themselves. He had a particular bond with his brother Aurelio, who despite being six years younger died young leaving a widow and children. Lerroux would later adopt one of his nephews (also called Aurelio), who became his only direct descendent.

Despite economic penury, Lerroux y Rodríguez was determined to give his children an education. He hoped that his sons would enter those professions best suited for social climbing: law and medicine. He failed with Arturo, who ran off and joined the carlists after becoming fed up with his father's implacable opposition to his favoured life of soldering. After deserting and serving as a cadet in the Spanish army, Arturo began a military career that would end with death in 1909 as a major. Lerroux's eldest brother well reflected the mentality of many sons of officers who had high ambitions despite a lack of interest in study.[2]

Lerroux y Rodríguez therefore placed his hopes in his second son. Yet for Lerroux, school scarcely made up for the lack of a warm family environment. He later recalled the 'dark and wretched premises with inadequate and obsolete teaching materials' as well as 'unimaginative teachers without enthusiasm or love for the profession' who exercised 'despotism rather than moral authority'. He particularly remembered the 'cane and corporal punishment that denigrated . . . memory fostered at the expense of intelligence . . . We sang our prayers. We learned Arithmetic and Grammar singing. The rhythm [of learning] was one of insufferable monotony and helplessness'. Nevertheless, in 1875 Lerroux passed the secondary school entrance exam and entered as a non-fee paying student in the Noviciado secondary school in Madrid. By that point his father held the rank of major and was teaching in the military veterinary school in Alcalá de Henares (Madrid); he also published articles in specialist journals. The family continued to live in the capital, renting a flat in the Paseo de Areneros (later calle de Alberto Aguilera).

It would be there that Lerroux would pass his childhood avoiding schoolwork, playing war games with stones and chasing Victoria, an adolescent four years older than him. Given what had happened with Arturo, his parents and uncle, a priest called Manuel García y González, kept Lerroux under close supervision, and when the latter was in the capital, he helped his nephew to prepare for his entrance exam. His parents also tried to support their son's education by using him to write their everyday correspondence. With Arturo absent, Alejandro had to work to earn extra money, learning to repair and then make the family's footwear.[3]

Between 1876 and 1878, Lerroux went to live with his uncle and priest in the latter's parish of Villaveza del Agua (Zamora). With a large family and a husband again absent from Madrid, his mother could not cope with Alejandro's tomfoolery. It was decided that the boy would enter a seminary under the patronage of Manuel in order to alleviate the family's desperate economic situation. Although Alejandro remembered his uncle as a sullen and curt man, he always felt gratitude towards him, perhaps because he was the adult who showed most interest in him; under the priest's guidance, Lerroux returned to the monotonous humming of Latin, Geography and History lessons while helping his uncle as a sacristan and working in the fields.

The adolescent quickly began to show an interest in religion. Prayers and a re-reading of the Bible took up much of his time. Yet a religious life was not for him. More mundane attractions, particularly a village girl called Marcela, occupied his mind, and the rigidity of Manuel 'inspired more fear [in Lerroux] than pity or love' until he learnt to appreciate 'the spiritual and symbolic values of the cross, that proud and austere sign with all of its simplicity'. Ultimately, close observation of religious rites and the priest's less than sophisticated methods of teaching the supernatural fatally undermined his faith. Alejandro soon realised that he could touch the chalice without burning his hands and that even the chapel's most sacred wooden sculptures could be substituted in times of need. One particular event left a lasting impression, when a damaged statue of the Virgin was replaced by a Saint Anthony of Padua dressed as a woman during a procession: 'One can believe what we cannot see', wrote Lerroux with impeccable logic, but it was impossible to believe 'in that we can see, touch, and feel'. After his second year of study, the fourteen-year-old returned to Madrid.[4]

His uncle's education did help Lerroux to pass two consecutive classes in secondary school in 1878. But this academic promise was curtailed by a return to foolery, failed courses, conflicts with his mother, billiards, and flirtation with his neighbour Blanca. The teenager was soon packed off to Cadiz to be with his father, and this change of scene proved to be a success: Lerroux's grades improved, and he combined study with private tutoring and participation in a youthful literary circle that produced a fortnightly journal entitled *La Edad Moderna*. In 1881, Lerroux won a prize in Rhetoric and Poetry in a competition organised by his school to commemorate the bicentenary of the death of the celebrated Golden Age playwright Pedro Calderón de la Barca; his entry, an essay entitled *El carro triunfal* [The Triumphal Carriage], demonstrated his command of language and some literary talent. It appeared that Lerroux would fulfil the dream of his father: a place at university to study Law.

By this time, the teenage Alejandro exhibited some of the character traits that would later be associated with him during his long political career. His recollections of youth make clear that with greater attention from his father and others, Lerroux had turned into a disciplined and responsible individual. At this point, he did not seem to be a born leader; unlike his brother Arturo, he appeared shy and introverted. He cried easily – 'an unrestrainable weakness of my physiology' – at a time when tears were seen as a weakness of character. He sought affection in friendships, and his effusiveness often produced disappointment. He later wrote wistfully, that 'when I have been someone's friend I did not do it half-heartedly; I put all my heart into it [and] that's where hearts are broken, albeit not all the time'. Loyal and generous, he was gallant if impulsive, and expected others to respond in the same way. He pestered girls with romantic verse, and his elevated sense of honour (accentuated by his family's military background), gave off a quixotic impression that would dissipate but not disappear as he grew older. It is these traits, and not the natural charisma that Lerroux claimed in his writings, that help explain his future popularity.[5]

Much to the consternation of his father, Alejandro was at this time much more interested in the army than university or politics. He did not conceive military service as the easiest way to secure an easy and secure income. Rather its appeal reflected an idealization of army life combined with a sincere admiration for his father. The frequent changes of address, the close relationships with other military families and the experiences of living in barracks made Lerroux feel as if he were already a soldier, and he would forever identify with the military values of patriotism, discipline and loyalty. Nevertheless, his father never believed that he was suitable for the army and tried without success to dissuade him from joining up. After a failed attempt to enlist at the age of sixteen, Lerroux left home to put pressure on his parents. It was only the perennial lack of money and above all the premature death of his mother that forced Lerroux y Rodríguez to give way to his determined son. Under his father's wing, Lerroux completed his military service, and after promotion to the rank of corporal sent him to Seville to prepare for the selection examination for the newly created Toledo General Military Academy. This demanded that cadets pay for their equipment and accommodation costs, and Alejandro turned to his brother Arturo, now a lieutenant in Oviedo and married 'with a respectable Asturian bourgeois lady', for financial assistance. After receiving the essential promise of help, Lerroux passed the examination in Toledo, but did not get a high enough grade to obtain a place. He then returned to his unit in Seville in the hope that an opening would come up in the academy. By this time, his father had returned to the cavalry school in Alcalá de Henares (Madrid) as a lieutenant colonel and moved into a modern flat in the newly built Paseo de La Habana in Madrid. Nevertheless, after being forced to take early retirement, Lerroux y Rodríguez suffered a hemiplegic attack and died in 1894.[6]

By then Lerroux's military career had long since ended. In 1883, he was posted to the North African enclave of Melilla to work in the fortification works of Cabrerizas Altas, built to frustrate incursions by Rifian tribesmen. There he received the long awaited offer of a place in the Toledo military academy. Without money or news of Arturo's promised loan, he managed to reach Spain's old imperial capital by hitching a lift in a Civil Guard coach from Malaga. The vehicle was carrying a prisoner from Manuel Ruiz Zorrilla's Republican Progressive Party who gave Lerroux some money on the condition that he posted some letters. At that time, police surveillance of republicans had intensified following the recent failed risings in Badajoz, Santo Domingo de la Calzada (Logroño) and Seo de Urgel (Lerida). Led by the Republican Military Group, the armed wing of the movement, the conspirators included an important number of generals in the reserve as well as the clandestine assistance of various active officers and commanders. But Lerroux was not interested in republican politics. His objective remained an army commission. On arrival in Toledo, he reported to its director (a colonel), who allowed him to remain while he awaited Arturo's money.

When Lerroux realised that this would never arrive, he resolved to see his brother in Oviedo rather than turn to his parents. There he found that Arturo, an innate gambler, had gone through his salary and his wife's private income. Seeing his hopes of being a cadet dashed, Lerroux decided to remain with his brother. Declared a deserter, Alejandro went into hiding and changed his name to that of his uncle Manuel, the Villaveza del Agua priest. It was only the amnesty promulgated following the birth of Alfonso XIII in 1886, and the direct intervention of his father with the head of the Toledo academy, that the crime was expunged in return for Lerroux's permanent exclusion from the army. Later he would attribute the sad end of his dream to an inability to adjust to military discipline, although the more prosaic reason of a lack of cash was more significant.[7]

Lerroux's financial problems also meant that he could not stay with his brother. Arturo found him a post as a tax collector in Lugo, but Alejandro soon returned to live with his uncle in Villaveza del Agua. Returning to Madrid in May 1886, he slept in the same room as his brother Armando, who worked in a pharmacy. Directionless, without a mentor and often without a meal, Lerroux walked the streets or went to the National Library to consult the job advertisements. While Lerroux began work as a life insurance salesman alongside two professional dealers, the lack of demand in the sector meant that he only received a miserably low wage. He had equally little success in other minor administrative roles that included being a packaging company representative and a clerk for a minor businessman in agricultural insurance. He also found time to audit courses in the Law Faculty of Madrid University, but could not matriculate as he lacked the school-leaving certificate. Returning to the paternal home on Sundays to eat a hot meal, Lerroux would later remember this period as the most difficult of his life.[8]

The Republican Movement

There is little to suggest up to this point any political direction in Lerroux's life, let alone any commitment to republicanism. He belonged to a generation born in the last years of the reign of Isabel II. Lerroux was only four-years-old when the 1868 Revolution overthrew the monarch, and was not even nine at the time of the proclamation of the First Republic in 1873. His political apprenticeship therefore took place completely after the constitutional monarchy was restored under Alfonso XII in 1874–75.

The end of the First Republic did not mean the end of Spanish republicanism. At the end of the nineteenth century, it was a heterogeneous populist and cross-class movement that promised the redemption of the 'people'. Based on the premise on the innate goodness of man and his 'natural' tendency to construct a harmonious society, the Republic embodied the rule of the 'popular will' that would facilitate the free development of mankind. By contrast, republicans saw the monarchy as the basis and the apex of a social order legitimated by irrational principles such as tradition and inheritance; its aim was nothing less than the maintenance of oligarchical privilege. They argued that the relentless 'decline' of Spain, which included the loss of medieval liberties following the revolt of the Comuneros in the 1520s, was indisputable evidence of the incompatibility between the interests of the Crown and the freedoms of the nation. Republicans asserted that only the abolition of the former would release the energies of the 'people' and put the country on a modern, 'European' course.

Such was the diagnosis and the solution offered by republicans of all types. But quite apart from the common belief in the general redemptive qualities of the Republic, each faction had its own idea of the new political order. Consensus did exist about some of the fundamental characteristics of a Republic based on the 'popular will'. There was agreement about the desirability of universal manhood suffrage and the creation of a social democracy based on the abolition of all legal privilege. Nineteenth-century republicans placed faith in the ability of popular militias to defend freedom, or (at the very least), favoured substitution of the old system of conscription by compulsory military service that would lead to a reduction in the size of the professional armed forces. Apart from the followers of Emilio Castelar, one of the five presidents of the First Republic of 1873-74, republicans supported the abolition of all legal restrictions to the exercise of freedoms. Yet this did not signify unfettered liberal individualism. The exercise of these freedoms, like the vote itself, could not jeopardise the irrevocable march of 'progress', the new lay and civil moral code that legitimised the Republic, the ultimate incarnation of Reason and the popular will.

Republicans were confident that once the new regime was constituted, they could utilise the state as an active instrument of social transformation; it would sweep away all obstacles towards 'progress'. They advocated a sweeping secularisation of society, seeing the Catholic Church as the root of the old order that legitimised itself generation after generation by means of anti-natural beliefs and superstitions that were quite different from the Gospel. Ultimately, the new faiths of rationalism and science would replace Catholicism under the Republic. Nevertheless, the extent of change, and in particular the nature of the new relationship with the Church, caused internal strife. Moderate republicans tended to be gradualists who preferred the secularisation of the state, while radicals demanded the complete elimination of any public expression of worship, as well as the secularisation of cemeteries, the subordination of the Church to the state, the proscription of religious orders and the nationalisation of their assets.

Republicanism was also traditionally a cross-class creed that envisaged harmony within the 'nation'. But in the late nineteenth century those who argued that this noble aspiration could be achieved simply through the creation a political order based on the 'popular will' lost ground to those who maintained that a certain degree of economic equality and redistribution of wealth were also necessary. The followers of Ruiz Zorrilla and Francisco Pi y Margall (the latter another former president of the First Republic), stressed the need to attract the support of workers. The means by which they could do this varied tremendously and depended on the individualist or collectivist outlook of the leaders, as the former advocated philanthropy and cooperativism and the latter the subordination of private property rights to the utilitarian priorities of the state. While all accepted free association for workers, the left-wing went further, calling for the replacement of highly unpopular indirect consumption taxes for a wealth tax, land redistribution, and state recognition of a 'right to work'. Yet there were no detailed programmes as to how these objectives would be realised, or a rational analysis of their new society. It was therefore easy to characterise republicans as doctrinaire dreamers, especially given their disastrous first experience of government in 1873.

In any case, how could a Republic be born from an unjust social order that only served the interests of the few? All republicans believed that the old society would not disappear of its own accord. As the progeny of the liberal revolutionary tradition, they were convinced that only a radical rupture with the past could provide the suitable context for social change. Given the insurrectional practices of nineteenth-century Spain, the spark would be a civic-military rebellion that would combine a rising by army units with the creation of revolutionary juntas and guerrilla bands. Wedded to a repeat performance of the 'Glorious Revolution' of 1868, it is not a surprise that republicans did not disown their devotion to conspiratorial politics. The debate only began over the issue of the relationship between insurrectional (or clandestine) and constitutional (or legal) activities. While no one dismissed the advantages of engaging in the latter to disseminate republican ideas, attract followers and undermine the monarchy, the question of participating in parliamentary elections was another matter. Some claimed that it was simply another oppositional tactic, but others worried that it would dilute the revolutionary spirit and facilitate a tacit understanding with the Restoration regime.[9]

Doctrinal disputes reflected a broader crisis in the weak republican movement during the years of Lerroux's youth. Not even the recruitment of Manuel Ruiz Zorrilla, the old leader of the dynastic left under Amadeo of Savoy in the early 1870s, served to bring together the fractious leadership. Nevertheless, at least his Republican Progressive Party managed to attract more support than any other faction, particularly in the army. Ruiz Zorrilla espoused the strategy of boycotting elections in favour of military insurrection from 1875. Exiled in Paris, he took advantage of his many contacts within the French republican elite to organise a logistical network north of the Pyrenees that would replace the officers and money expended in failed conspiracies and risings. An undoubted threat in the immediate aftermath of the restoration of Alfonso XII, its effectiveness would decline to the point that its plots rarely left the coffee house. Failure would prompt Cristino Martos, Eugenio Montero Ríos and others to leave the party and join Práxedes Mateo Sagasta's dynastic Liberal Party in 1881 in an attempt to break their self-imposed isolation. The later collapse of the almost farcical *pronunciamiento* led by brigadier Villacampa in Madrid in 1887 marked the end of any realistic prospect of overthrowing the monarchy by force, and produced another split with the departure of former president Nicolás Salmerón. Equally feeble was the Republican Progressive Party's main rival within the movement, Pi y Margall's Federal Party, which argued that the revolt should be led by civilians rather than soldiers but lacked the popular support to turn this theory into reality.

Given traumatic memories of the cantonalist revolts of 1873, Pi y Margall was also the only significant republican who defended a federal reorganization of Spain. Indeed, in 1890 Salmerón would create a Centralist Party out of his supporters and those followers of Castelar who opposed the rapprochement of their old boss with the Restoration system. The former president of the Republic weakened the movement even further in 1894 when he merged the remnants of his party with the Liberals. Republican hopes that the introduction of universal manhood suffrage in 1890 would revive the cause therefore proved to be rash. Joint electoral platforms in 1891 and 1893 produced reasonable, if ultimately disappointing, results. Republican unity was a chimera; by 1900, the movement had withdrawn from elections and returned to the factionalism of the past. When Lerroux began his political career, the constitutional monarchy seemed more secure than ever.[10]

A Republican Journalist

Three people help explain why Lerroux was attracted to republicanism: his father, his eldest brother, and Adolfo Moreno Espinosa, his secondary school History teacher in Cadiz. The first, Lerroux y Rodríguez, always considered himself a leftist liberal. An admirer of Ruiz Zorrilla during the revolutionary years of 1868–74, he also subscribed to Eduardo Gasset y Artime's progressive daily *El Imparcial*. But this was hardly uncommon among officers in this period, and he had no real interest in politics. Concerned for his career, he was reluctant to speak about current affairs with his colleagues and after 1875 kept well away from republican conspiracies. 'He was not . . . a Voltarian', his son Alejandro remembered, 'he went to mass on Sundays' and 'was a good Christian'. In his family, religion provided general moral guidance rather than militant commitment or fervour. Lerroux y Rodríguez kept a respectful distance from the clergy, only spending time with his regimental chaplain and his own brother-in-law, Manuel. As we have seen, García y González also acted as Lerroux's mentor when the adolescent boy went to live with him in Zamora province in the mid-1870s. This role would be taken up by Moreno when Lerroux studied History in Cadiz. The most significant disciple of Castelar in the Andalusian port, Moreno inculcated into his pupil a slanted interpretation of recent Spanish history which included the heroic myths of republicanism; Lerroux worked with him to produce a bibliographical calendar [*Año biográfico*] of lay republican 'saints'.

Yet the decisive influence upon Lerroux was his brother. Arturo sparked his interest in the conspiratorial republicanism of Zorrilla as well as Freemasonry. When Lerroux lived in Oviedo, both frequented the progressive club (a half-social, half-political centre), where Arturo spent most of his time. On his return to Madrid, Alejandro's predilection for radical clubs was satiated by visits to the *zorrillista* centre in calle de Esparteros, opposite the Plaza de Pontejos. He spent afternoons and evenings in the library reading the provincial press, and became acquainted with its director, Santos Lahoz, who used Lerroux as a contact with officers involved in the abortive 1887 coup. Alejandro also wrote various articles for his brother Arturo that were published under the pseudonym "Fagina" in a progressive Asturian journal. Lerroux also joined the 'Torch' masonic lodge in the capital because the Masons still attracted those of 'exalted imagination and revolutionary temperament' and hoped to find 'an organization of friends, of common ideals, who . . . would help each other as brothers', as well as 'a captivating ideal for those thrown into life by an adventurous spirit'. Disillusion came quickly. By then, Spanish Freemasonry had lost its revolutionary pretensions and even its ability to keep secrets. The brothers whom he met were 'workshy, mere conmen, dunces, or scoundrels who exploited others'. He did not return after a few meetings. While his name appears on membership rolls of various lodges in Madrid and Barcelona throughout his life, he paid his dues irregularly; unlike other republicans never played an active role in the Craft. Ultimately, his involvement was more to do with a desire to make contacts and protect his reputation at a time when republicanism and Freemasonry were seen as synonymous.[11]

In any case, Lerroux's work for Arturo and the reading of the republican press sparked an interest in political journalism. His brother created a job opportunity. During a stay in Madrid, Arturo put him in contact with Antonio Catena, the proprietor of the recently founded *zorrillista* daily *El País* and two casinos that helped finance the party. Arturo was also good friends with its chief editor Rafael Ginard de la Rosa, Ruiz Zorrilla's former secretary and loyal substitute in some of the duels sparked by calumnies printed in the party press. In 1888, Lerroux got a post with a modest salary on the 'Provinces' desk. He soon realised the possibilities open to him, as despite its reputation as the leading republican paper in Madrid, the quality of the journalism in *El País* left much to be desired. It was published as a propaganda arm of the Republican Progressive Party rather than as a profit-making exercise; its chief editor had a place on the party's central committee. Consequently, *El País*'s journalists were poor party hacks without much passion for the job. In that context of mediocrity, the young Alejandro soon became known for his dynamism and eloquent prose, and Ginard quickly allowed him to publish his own news stories and opinion pieces.

By 1890, Lerroux was a full-time journalist with a regular, if small, income. At the age of 26, he covered national politics, and had a press pass for the Spanish parliament. His rising star prompted Catena to appoint him the newspaper's 'official' chief editor – a front man who took legal responsibility for anonymous articles – after the death of the incumbent. While continuing to write articles, Lerroux took advantage of this somewhat dangerous position to burnish his reputation. Following a controversial op-ed on one of the many quarrels that rocked the republican movement, Julio Burell, the chief editor of *El Nuevo Heraldo*, demanded a duel with Ginard. When the latter refused, Lerroux stepped in and emerged victorious. Catena gave him effective control of *El País* as a reward, although he did not relieve Lerroux of the legal responsibilities of the job, or the perilous duels.

The ambitious Alejandro, using the same flair he possessed for duelling, took this opportunity to reduce the influence of his predecessor Ginard on the paper. He announced that he would not take responsibility for the articles of others, and secured oversight of the proofs as a result. This is not to imply that *El País*'s belligerent attitude towards political institutions, the royal family or the leaders of the dynastic parties diminished. Its coarse style, much favoured by its republican readership, delegitimised targets without the need for expert knowledge in political or governmental affairs. Lacking intellectual depth, *El País* switched between merciless invective with uncritical admiration for its own programme and above all devotion to the leadership of Ruiz

Zorrilla. Such crude extremism was the inevitable consequence of factional proselytism. Lerroux quickly realised the price to pay was a growing number of complaints and writs. But he remained unfazed. The courts, with a well-known lax attitude towards the press law, rarely instituted proceedings.[12]

A Man in a Hurry

Where Lerroux stood out from other republican editors was his readiness to embrace sensationalist gossip journalism. *El País* abandoned boring accounts of factional infighting and club activities for highly personalised denunciations of administrative abuses and labour exploitation to undermine the legitimacy of the existing political order as well as to attract all those opposed to it. It mattered little if the accusations printed in the newspaper were true; only the republican cause was important. *El País* therefore became an exemplar for yellow journalism that was as criticised as much as it was read. If it were not for the fact that Lerroux was a politician who used the broadsheet for party political propaganda, his style could be compared to the populism of the late nineteenth century British newspaper the *Daily Mail* or the 'muckrakers' of the United States.

The blunt if fallacious condemnation of the *status quo* attracted young freethinking intellectuals to the paper like José Martínez Ruiz ("Azorín"), Ramón de Maeztu and Ramón de Valle-Inclán; *El País* began to make money as it became the third most read party newspaper in the whole of Spain. A gratified Catena raised salaries and improved working conditions for the staff. Lerroux was able to leave his digs and move into a rented flat on calle de Monteleón. This coincided with his marriage to Teresa López García de Selalinde in 1894. She came from such a modest background that Lerroux felt obligated to take care of his in-laws at a time when he also took responsibility for his younger siblings on the death of his father. Marriage ended Lerroux's bohemian lifestyle and familial stability helped him overcome the gambling addiction that had earlier consumed his brother Arturo.

Despite his meteoric rise within *El País*, Lerroux's journalistic career could not cover the needs of an ever-growing family. Fortunately, he soon had access to other sources of income. In the 1890s, his name appeared on the list of journalists who received under-the-table payments from the infamous 'reptile fund' [*fondo de reptiles*] of the interior ministry. This subsidised the pro-government press as well as hostile newspapers in the hope that the slush money would moderate their criticism. This was nothing unusual in this: influential journalists took the cash to top up their meagre salaries. What is interesting is that a resolute opponent of the monarchy like Lerroux was willing to accept illicit payments. He began to be paid as a parliamentary correspondent after striking up an unlikely friendship with Eduardo Dato, a leading interior ministry official in Antonio Cánovas's government and future liberal conservative leader, participating regularly in his *tertulia* or social gatherings. Although Lerroux would stress his close relationship with the Liberal leader Segismundo Moret in his memoirs, it is evident that Dato receives the more positive treatment. The latter's generous kindness and a common background as sons of military officers produced a friendship that although never intimate was warm. Lerroux would never forget the favours that Dato arranged for his favourite brother Aurelio.[13]

This is not to imply that Lerroux had been 'domesticated' by the monarchy. These relationships did not go further than *ad hoc* personal political contacts that in the case of the press entailed a more prudent treatment of the political opponent in the heated debates of the time. Connections with the opposing side were seen as useful to open lines of communication between the leaders of the various political parties in order to obtain favours or defend the interests of those, like Lerroux, who belonged to organizations without any realistic hope of taking power. They were also an easy way to facilitate interaction between ideologically very different politicians who would normally only clash in public. Therefore, in benefitting from the 'reptile fund', Lerroux acted like other republicans and carlists in a period where it appeared that a healthy distinction between the political adversary and a personal enemy had emerged. Moreover, and unlike many of his colleagues, Lerroux remained loyal to the republican cause despite receiving payments from its enemies.

Naturally, these cross-party relationships also enabled Lerroux to elude the ever-growing pile of accusations and suits directed against him as chief editor of *El País*. He even admitted that he enjoyed and abused this great freedom: he could write about anything and everything. That atmosphere of tolerance towards those who defended anti-system principles and methods explains why in a very short period Lerroux was able to take advantage of his notoriety as a journalist to launch a political career.

Lerroux was a man in a hurry. His ambition went beyond *El País*. At a time when progressive politics was weak, his political standing grew rapidly. From 1894, he took part in public meetings and party organizational work. His press campaigns gave him a place on platforms that he used to speak about the same issues that he raised in *El País*. Naturally shy, Lerroux was not a great speaker and was intimidated by his more illustrious colleagues. His first tour of 1896 – one of many on the recurrent theme of republican unity – took him from Segovia to Gijon. His fame would only increase following his coverage later that year of the Montjuich trials against anarchists accused of a bomb attack on a Corpus Christi procession in Barcelona. The impact of his written criticisms of the mistreatment of the prisoners and the severity of the sentences forced him to up his game as an orator. Like his articles, Lerroux's speeches lacked intellectual depth, but he quickly became known for his proselytizing zeal and his ability to maintain the attention of the audience. Compared to the long-winded expositions of veteran republicans, Lerroux could discern what really preoccupied his listeners, and his orations soon made him a very popular figure. Audiences in Madrid and Barcelona certainly believed that the emotive and vibrant tone in which Lerroux delivered his words better conveyed the suffering of the prisoners than the boring circumspection of his co-speaker Pablo Iglesias, the socialist leader.

A reading of Lerroux's speeches makes clear that he was a demagogic figure. The republicans were an irresponsible opposition. Since their main aim was to attract left-wing critics of the constitutional monarchy, their ideas were barely more than simple slogans designed to entice working-class movements to the cause. Faced with this type of people, Lerroux discovered that reason did 'not move the crowds'. Of course, there was no shortage of demagogues at the turn of the century, but what separated Lerroux from the rest was his ability to match his words to his audience. When he addressed workers in Madrid or Barcelona, they always believed that he was one of them, someone who talked about their issues with their language. His tone and form of argument gave him a credibility that others could not attain, yet ultimately it came from deeply held convictions. His choice of direct language shook the lethargy of the crowd, but also served to establish the limits that differentiated the just and redemptive revolution from a simple incitement to riot.

The revolution that Lerroux yearned for was that led by his hero Ruiz Zorrilla in 1868. *El País*'s chief editor fulfilled his dream when he finally met the great leader following an introduction by Francisco Ferrer Guardia, who later became a friend. Thanks to José María Esquerdo, a doctor and Zorrilla's right-hand man, Lerroux would work alongside his idol until the latter's death in 1895. This event sparked a civil war among progressives about the future. Most of the party, including Lerroux who joined its central committee, supported Esquerdo's policy of electoral abstention and a turn to the left to attract working-class militants. This prompted the departure of the right-wing who merged with those republicans who advocated the legal route to power. Among them was Catena, who detached *El País* from the party, and Lerroux gave up his control of the paper.[14]

Lerroux and the Non-Republican Left

Lerroux's departure from *El País* was only a minor setback in its career. By October 1897, he had become the chief editor of a new pro-Esquerdo newspaper entitled *El Progreso*. Financed initially by party supporters, after a slow start it attracted many of *El País*'s columnists including anti-clerical intellectuals such as Leopoldo Alas "Clarín" and Luis Bonafoux. The growing number of subscribers sustained its chief editor and a staff who identified politically and personally with their boss. Lerroux took care to improve their working conditions, partly as a way to demonstrate his identification with the working class. Embracing an even more polemical and vulgar tone than *El País*, *El Progreso* opened its pages to federalist and anarchist writers who did not hesitate to condemn 'industrialism' and 'big business' for 'the implacable exploitation of man by man' that weakened the spirit of human fraternity so beloved by republicans and the working-class left. Yet the appearance of anarchist and syndicalist articles, and the constant demand to revise the sentences of the Montjuich prisoners, did not signify that Lerroux was sympathetic to 'direct action' terrorism or 'propaganda by the deed'. From his days on the payroll of *El País*, he condemned these methods as inhumane and counter-productive for the republican cause, and throughout his life remained deaf to those who advocated the redemptive qualities of political violence.

Lerroux also attempted to use *El Progreso* as a path towards cooperation with the socialists. But the Socialist Party (PSOE) and its trade union organization, the General Workers' Union (UGT), remained anchored in a 'class' strategy that isolated themselves from 'bourgeois' republicans. Not even cooperation between Lerroux with Pablo Iglesias in the Montjuich campaign of 1896 prompted the socialists to reassess their attitude towards a rival movement. Characteristically, Pablo Iglesias saw *El Progreso*'s chief editor through the lens of Marxist sectarianism, dismissing Lerroux as one of those petit bourgeois demagogues who delayed the onset of class-consciousness. Antipathy turned into outright enmity from 1899 when the socialists attempted to undermine Lerroux with accusations of corruption. The trigger was a subscription opened by the progressive newspaper for the strikers at the Altos Hornos ironworks in Bilbao. Lerroux announced that he would transfer the strike funds to the UGT, but then retracted his promise and donated the money to strikers in the Jerez wine trade instead. The socialists repeatedly accused Lerroux of keeping the money for himself, and in the face of socialist hostility, the growth of progressivism among the workers of Bilbao stalled. This was not the only occasion where the PSOE made allegations of malfeasance against Lerroux: they claimed that he had appropriated cash raised by another subscription intended to establish a mining cooperative in Andújar (Jaen). With *El Progreso* in financial crisis, the firm's profits were always going to be used to keep the paper in business, but promises were made to contribute to strike funds. In the end, there was only enough capital to open the mine, although some money did end up in *El Progreso*'s coffers. This confirmed socialist accusations of Lerroux as a corrupt demagogue in the pay of the monarchy, and a bitter mutual antagonism would last almost without interruption until the civil war; for the PSOE, the republican leader was a duplicitous servant of capitalism and a serious impediment to the revolutionary emancipation of the working class.[15]

Still, it is worth recalling that at the turn of the century the socialists only represented a minority within the workers' movement. There was also an anti-Marxist and pro-republican wing sympathetic towards Lerroux that offered assistance during his brushes with authority in 1896. The most serious of these concerned the harassment of Arsenio Martínez Campos on his return from the Cuban war. This general was the *bête noire* of republicans for his instrumental role in the restoration of the Bourbon monarchy in 1874–75. A progressive campaign against Martínez Campos sparked clashes with police in Madrid and forced Lerroux to flee to France to avoid jail. This sojourn abroad only lasted two months, but Alejandro took the opportunity to visit Biarritz and Paris, the centres of republican exile activity in France. On his return, he resumed his journalistic career and took part in the campaign to revise the sentences of the Montjuich prisoners in 1897; for good measure, he also accused the Civil Guard of torture in Barcelona. With the assistance of anarchist propagandists, Lerroux sought to turn this scandal into one akin to the Dreyfus Affair that was then agitating politics in Spain's northern neighbour. He gathered around his campaign prominent figures from all parts of the Spanish left, sharing a platform in Madrid in 1899 with dynastic Liberals such as Segismundo Moret, José Canalejas and Álvaro de Figueroa, the First Count of Romanones, republicans like Salmerón, Melquíades Álvarez, and the socialist leader Pablo Iglesias. At this *dreyfusard* type gathering, the chief editor of *El Progreso* explained that a struggle between 'freedom' and 'reaction' was taking place, with the villains being members of the Silvela-Polavieja government. 'Freedom' eventually prevailed when the new Sagasta government pardoned the prisoners in 1901 in exchange for their departure from Spain.[16]

It is likely that beatings were used to extract confessions and secure the unjust conviction of innocent anarchists, although the allegations were never wholly proven. Lerroux happily admitted that the campaign began before any firm evidence of torture materialised and that the truth was twisted for partisan purposes. Humanitarian and political interests became intertwined, as the fate of imprisoned anarchists was only as important as the exposure of the innate malevolence of the 'bourgeois state'. Similarly, Lerroux saw the campaign as a way to attract anarchists to the republican camp. He used all his talents to raise the political temperature and construct a myth that at the same time would discredit the constitutional monarchy and unite republicans and proletarians. The results were encouraging. The Barcelona anarcho-collectivist Trade Union Federation announced *El Progreso* to be its newspaper, and its relations with its chief editor became even closer once Lerroux promised to organise subscriptions for the families of the convicted prisoners.

The accommodating attitude of *El Progreso* prompted anarchist theorists like Federico Urales, Ricardo Mella and Fernando Tarrida to believe that Lerroux could join their struggle. After all, other republicans had abandoned the cause, including his old friend Ferrer, who frustrated with the insufficiently revolutionary stance of Esquerdo leadership, had converted to anarchism. This was a delusion. In the midst of the conflict against the United States and the suspension of constitutional guarantees in 1898, Lerroux began to combine his Montjuich crusade with another against the Crown and the Liberal government of Sagasta. Republicans on the left and carlists on the right hoped to take advantage of the crisis to rise against the constitutional monarchy. Like others loyal to the insurrectionary tradition of Ruiz Zorrilla, Lerroux did not hesitate to praise general Valeriano Weyler, in the hope that the recalled governor of Cuba would repeat Prim's *pronunciamento* of September 1868. Somewhat predictably, his typically fiery invectives led not to revolution but to an eight-month prison sentence following the Santiago de Cuba naval defeat in July 1898. As a political prisoner, Lerroux was placed in a comfortable cell, and under a 'very benign and tolerant' regime continued to 'spew bullets' from the pages of his newspaper. He was released in February 1899 after the intervention of Castelar secured him a special pardon from Sagasta.[17]

By then, the combined pressures of the prosecutor's office, fines, confiscations of copies and the lack of income had turned *El Progreso* into a weekly publication. Lerroux still controlled the editorial line, if only because he produced all its articles with the occasional assistance of his brother Aurelio and unpaid anarchist writers. When an attempt to relaunch the title as a publishing concern failed, *El Progreso* entered the twentieth century as little more than a serious drain on Lerroux's personal finances.[18]

So Lerroux's political star was on the wane when he received an unexpected invitation from Barcelona to extend the joint republican-syndicalist Montjuich campaign to the whole of Catalonia. Working closely with the Catalan section of the progressive movement, he rapidly discerned its enormous popularity. At a meeting in the Catalan capital, his incendiary denunciation of the actions of the military authorities in the Montjuich trial provoked extraordinary scenes as cheering crowds carried Lerroux to his hotel before attacking the police sent to dissolve them. Barcelona prepared itself to receive the 'Emperor of the Paralelo'.[19]

2

Revolutionary Organiser (1899–1909)

In 1901, the sweltering summer heat in Madrid did not deter the arrival of the parliamentary deputies elected the previous May. They came to take formally their positions and discuss disputed counts. Those of Barcelona were especially controversial, as the votes of barely 137 out of the 241 electoral districts were deemed sufficient to make a declaration. Among the victors were four catalanists of the Lliga, the elderly federalist Pi y Margall and a certain 37-year-old republican from Madrid, Alejandro Lerroux. Of average height and erect posture, the former journalist stood out from the other deputies by virtue of his youth and strength. Lerroux, with his fair complexion and open and expressive face, had a black moustache like a musketeer and rippled curling hair and magnetic defiant eyes. This gave him the appearance of an *enfant terrible* determined to bring down the whole edifice of that monarchist parliament. His dress sense also betrayed his rebelliousness, as Lerroux preferred a lounge suit to a frock coat and a red to a white collar. Soon parliamentary debates would include his impassioned speeches delivered by a booming voice. With the passage of time, that young deputy would become yet another party leader with greying hair, elegant spectacles, made-to-measure suits and a relaxed expression. While he would gain in authority what he lost in sparkle, he always maintained a sense of gallant dignity that when caught off guard would produce a warm and welcoming gesture that made him such an attractive personality to political friends and foes alike.

Lerroux expressed relief when the Sagasta government chose not to question the validity of his election. On the instructions of the prime minister, the Liberal majority accepted the Barcelona results. Not so Romero Robledo, the experienced Conservative leader, who claimed that the Lliga's success was fraudulent. In an energetic and pointed speech, he accused Moret, the interior minister, of abandoning the monarchist electoral slate, the supposed real winner of the elections in the Catalan capital. For Romero Robledo, the significance of events in Barcelona went beyond a disputed count; really at stake was nothing less than 'the integrity of the Patria' as 'national unity in Catalonia' would henceforth have 'no other defenders than the republicans'. He did not understand why the government, flouting the 'democratic spirit', should want to 'flatter the ravings of Catalanism' at the 'expense of the law'. 'Fortunately for the Patria', Romero went on, 'Catalanism, that cursed seed, has not fallen or taken root among the working masses, [or] fallen or taken root in the democratic masses, because it is a reactionary seed that only flourishes in reactionary, clerical and carlist centres'.[1]

With his characteristic perceptiveness, Romero identified the factors that would make Lerroux the leader of the left in Barcelona: class and patriotism. His renewal of the republican movement created a significant obstacle to the political hegemony of the Lliga in Barcelona. In 1900, this appeared inevitable due to the disastrous electoral policies of the dynastic Conservatives and Liberals under Silvela and Sagasta, which ended their once undisputed dominance in the Catalan capital. Not that their traditional opponents, the old republicans and federalists, were in much better shape. In the 1901 election, republican grandees like Salmerón, Sol y Ortega organised a unity slate that failed to obtain a single seat; Pi y Margall, the Federal leader, was more successful, but he still polled less votes than Lerroux. Therefore, at the dawn of the twentieth century, the former sacristan from Villaveza del Agua seemed the best bulwark of 'Spain' in Barcelona; Lerroux was soon to demonstrate that the electoral victory in 1901 was no one-off.

An Election Winner

The triumph of 1901 only came after defeat two years earlier. For the 1899 elections, trade unions linked with the Federals offered the republican journalist a place on the party slate in Barcelona. As a persecuted figure who had fervently defended the cause of the Montjuich prisoners, offering his newspaper to those who denounced labour exploitation, Lerroux was a vote winner in working-class areas. The one-time fierce advocate of electoral abstention was delighted with the proposal. Disenchanted with the leadership of Esquerdo, Ruiz Zorrilla's one-time disciple was now open to the opportunity of participating within the monarchist political system. For Lerroux, the progressive cause had long ceased to be a revolutionary vehicle and its anti-electoral stance doomed it to irrelevance. He was keen to take advantage of his popularity among republican and working-class voters. Far from converting him to the revolutionary class struggle, Lerroux saw his contacts with anarchist circles as a means to harvest votes. If elections gave him the opportunity to make a political breakthrough, so much the better. Therefore, he supported the campaign of José Mir y Miró, the Catalan progressive leader. Yet he soon discovered that those workers' associations that originally proposed him were not prepared to work for his candidature; moreover, the Federal Party went into the 1899 elections without securing a pact with Salmerón's Republican Unity. As a result, the progressives only secured a few hundred votes; the republicans suffered their customary defeat to the monarchist slate.[2]

Lerroux did not have to wait long to try again in better conditions. In 1901, he was briefly imprisoned for his violent campaign against the marriage of princess María de las Mercedes, the eldest sister of King Alonso XIII, with the Count of Caserta, a Bourbon cousin with a carlist descendant; the marriage placed him in the line of succession. With the aureola of a victim, Lerroux moved to Barcelona and became the candidate of the broader-based local progressive committee. He also soon became the chief editor of *La Publicidad*, the most influential republican paper in the city, and with his customary zeal turned it into a powerful advocate of republican unity in Barcelona. Since Lerroux assumed that this happy outcome required his leadership, he sought a parliamentary seat.[3]

In the cities, electoral success required organisation. That was not easily achieved in Barcelona where the progressive movement suffered from the curse of factionalism. Republican clubs, those social spaces where leisure was preferred to politics, could potentially become an effective tool of electoral mobilisation, but they were riven by ideological and personal disputes. Despite the existence of freedom of association and manhood suffrage, republicanism remained a minority credo in the city. The commemoration of the proclamation of the 1873 Republic every eleventh of February only marginally rallied the faithful more than elections. The relations that progressives and federalists had with the trade unions, as well as the interest generated among skilled workers by the establishment of cultural centres, cheap canteens and mutual societies, did not bring much success from 1893. The popularity of republicanism in the Catalan countryside, though greater than other regions, was similarly weak.

Lerroux swiftly understood that his inclusion on the electoral slate suggested the waning appeal of once admired figures like Pi y Margall or Salmerón and the ineptitude of those responsible for the republican organisation in Barcelona: Eusebio Corominas and José María Vallés y Ribot. It is true that Emilio Junoy, a close friend of Lerroux from 1901 until the Catalan Solidarity crisis of 1906–7, had attempted to establish closer relations with the trade unions, but his Republican Unity faction, on the right of the movement, held little attraction for workers. Moreover, others like the disillusioned Sol y Ortega, were tempted to work with dynastic parties and indeed made electoral agreements with them. There is no doubt that this made them unpopular among diehard republicans fearful that any deal with monarchists reduced the chances of a change of regime, but it meant that Sol became the only republican elected for Barcelona in 1899.[4]

After a spell as a parliamentary correspondent, Lerroux was familiar with the ins and outs of parliament and the obvious failings of the old republican leadership dispelled any qualms about standing for election. As someone of 'modest cultural background', who had failed to complete a secondary school education, he had thought that he would not even be considered for a seat, let alone obtain the respectability necessary to stand out in parliament. He overcame these doubts with the same determination and spirit that he displayed in other matters. With time, Lerroux not only obtained the relevant professional certificates but also gained a knowledge of government and legislation greater than that of the average republican leader in the early twentieth century. Above all, he learnt that to become a deputy it was necessary to 'belong to a party, to establish roots in a parliamentary constituency, to secure the support of the local authorities and *caciques* who control the electoral census, and most importantly not just having enough money to spend during the campaign but also obtaining the protection or the tolerance of the Government'. As an antimonarchist candidate without access to the normal patronage networks, he had to prioritise organisation rather than rely on cash or influence.

This was precisely what Lerroux did in his 1901 election campaign, surprising his more languid colleagues on the slate. He made up for the lack of finance by effectively mobilising his base, as well as overseeing the efficient distribution of pamphlets, agents and representatives to the polling stations. He personally intervened to prevent the all too common attempts at fraud and corruption, although only when the republicans were the victims. He also took advantage of his opponents' lack of zeal to dispute an electoral register riddled with dead or missing voters. As the republicans' most effective campaigner, he took part in an unusually large number of meetings held despite a violent anarchist-orchestrated boycott. We have already seen the result of all this energy: despite the undeniable if normal irregularities, Lerroux won with 5,446 votes. This was followed up with an excellent performance in the municipal elections of November 1901, as a Lerroux-inspired campaign secured 13,000 votes for the republicans, preventing the Lliga from obtaining a majority of councillors in the city.⁵

Fighting the Clericals and the Catalanists

By then Lerroux has fully aware of the limitations of sectarian politics. He was longer interested in defending declining progressivism. Electoral success and his control of *La Publicidad* gave him sufficient authority to launch a political project that would rise above the old divides, shake the republican rank-and-file out of their apathy and establish firm ties with trade unions immobilised politically by the anti-electoral line of the anarchists. To achieve these aims, Lerroux understood that a radical discourse that linked the republican vision with an uncompromising rejection of the status quo was essential to take advantage of the desire for change that had emerged following the 'Disaster' of 1898. This required the formulation of an inter-class programme that eschewed anti-statist rhetoric: only a Republic that protected freedom and order would defend the workers' moral and material interests. This reworking of the trite theory of social harmony was based on the idea that all trade union demands that did not conflict with republican principles were legitimate. Lerroux wanted a French-style 'socialist Republic' that would actively intervene in the 'social question'.⁶ This made sense in turn-of-the-century Barcelona reeling from the loss of the colonial market. The economic crisis, with its business failures, rising unemployment and falling wages, stimulated the growth of trade unionism, and the republicans were not blind to the political advantages of increased labour militancy.

Neither were they oblivious to the uses of anticlericalism as a means to bring workers over to their side. Lerroux was particularly vocal in his opposition to the Church. For republicans, this institution was a powerful obstacle to the urgent restructuring of Spain after the 'Disaster' of 1898. To the horror of anticlericals, the Church's influence had grown after 1875 in a benevolent political climate that brought civil liberties and official protection. The most visible manifestation of this was the growth of the clergy and religious communities and their pastoral, educational and charity work had a noticeable impact in towns and cities. Under the constitutional monarchy, the Church not only regained ground in its struggle to be the moral guardian of the nation, but also had become more active in politics by 1900 as both a proponent and a beneficiary of the conservative programme of regeneration undertaken by the Silvela government, the 'Christian general' Polavieja, and the regionalists. This included the extremely controversial decision by the development minister, the Marquis of Pidal, to establish the hitherto voluntary subject of religion as compulsory at secondary school level. Furthermore, the carlists, an extreme right-wing confessional movement with support of part of the clergy, had organised guerrilla groups that posed such a threat in Catalonia that the government felt obliged to suspend constitutional guarantees. It was in that context that Count of Caserta, who had fought with the carlists in the 1870s war, entered the royal family, even if by that time he has a soldier who unconditionally supported King Alonso XIII. All this served as convenient pretexts for the Liberal Party, already irritated by the support of the Church hierarchy for the Silvela government, to associate with an anticlerical campaign that focussed on the religious orders, a campaign that had as its most enduring cultural legacy Benito Pérez Galdós's play *Electra* of 1901.

For the dynastic left, the bone of contention was the Church's identification with the Conservative government. The Liberals argued that as a legally protected institution with representatives in the Senate, the Church should not identify with any party. The struggle was more ideological for republicans. It was nothing less than a transcendental conflict between 'freedom' and 'reaction', with the Church as the nefarious bulwark of the monarchy. Lerroux dismissed those who argued that the secularisation of the state was enough to construct a 'free' society. He even rejected attempts by republican intellectuals to depict the battle as a clash of values, with Catholicism eventually being supplanted by a kind of lay morality. Lerroux resembled a latter-day Savonarola in his speeches, lashing the Church for its corruption that ignored the humble and protected the powerful with all their inequities, depravations and unjustified wealth. For the republican leader, the Church's superstitious nonsense and unbending moral hypocrisy enabled respect and submission to a social order of which it was both the foundation and beneficiary. Lerroux stressed that the constitutional monarchy had not ended the old alliance of Throne and Altar. Just like in centuries past, greedy bishops remained in the pockets of the King. The Church, in sum, was by its very nature anti-republican and anti-revolutionary. The struggle against it, and in particular the elimination of the increasingly common religious orders, was the struggle for the Republic, for the emancipation of all Spaniards and the precondition for a lay paradise based on human fraternity. However, Lerroux did distinguish between the institution and its servants; he condemned 'crude' anticlericalism that turned revenge against the clergy or their brethren into a political issue. Catholics had to be emancipated, not persecuted. Lerroux also tried to differentiate – albeit artificially – between religious brothers and sisters and the parish clergy. Perhaps thinking of his uncle in Villaveza del Agua, he argued that the educational activities of priests, particularly in the countryside, remained essential.[7]

This way of thinking is not strange if one recalls Lerroux's own education. His anticlericalism lacked an alternative worldview to Christianity. It was a simplistic but effective denunciation of the falsification of the message of the Gospels, similar to those believers who rejected any intermediate institution between God and the individual. Even the phrase that he habitually used to prevent his incendiary rhetoric from leading to violence – 'hate the crime, not the criminal'[8] – was a re-working of the old proverb about sin and the sinner. It had nothing in common with a modern sense of citizenhood based on the responsible exercise of individual rights and recognition of responsibilities towards the conservation of civil society and the rule of law. As a 'civic religion', Spanish republicanism remained antiliberal. Its lay saints fought the same moral ground with the Church, harping on about sacrifice and virtue. Lerroux, like others in the movement, was determined to strip priests of the Christian values of fraternity, piety, generosity, loyalty, forgiveness and equality. His lay paradise sounded suspiciously like the biblical one with its emphasis on redemption and social harmony. Reflecting his education, Lerroux's speeches and articles contained countless implicit and explicit references to the message of Christ and other sacred texts. Given the circumstances of time, this secular egalitarian re-reading of Christianity initially found favour among his half-catechised voters. Within a decade, Lerroux would abandon anticlericalism when he found that it dragged him into the dangerous waters that produced the Tragic Week of 1909. Nevertheless, anticlericalism would remain a salient issue among his supporters until 1931 and beyond.

Perhaps the most original feature of Lerroux's anticlericalism was its refusal to admit the association between Catholicism and Spanish patriotism, pointing to the links of the Lliga with the Church. Although these were not uncontested within the Catalan clergy and laity, the diocese of Barcelona was headed by José Morgades and Salvador Casañas y Pagés between 1899 and 1908, and these clerics sympathised with Catalan nationalism, favouring among other things religious instruction in Catalan. This would be more significant than anticlerical discourse in the decision by many in the region, particularly those who spoke Spanish, to abandon the Catholic Church.

It is worth noting here that despite the claims of his opponents, Lerroux was no agent of a Jacobin-style centralist conspiracy to destroy catalanism. Rather, he was imbued with old progressive ideas about strong municipalities being a guarantee against tyranny. This was why, he claimed, the Habsburg and Bourbon monarchs had abolished them.

Strikingly, he also praised the doctrines of Pi y Margall, arguing that the municipality, the province (or region), and the nation should be endowed with its own specific powers: 'The Nation [is] divided in regions already delineated by Nature and History. The region [is] divided in municipalities. The three entities [are] autonomous. The *patria* [is] intangible and one'.[9] The lack of connection between these various entities, a perennial problem for the liberal state that in times of crisis produced a proliferation of juntas or cantons, meant less to Lerroux than a territorial redistribution of power that would protect freedoms and permit the direct participation of citizens in public affairs.

But one should not go as far as to describe Lerroux as a federalist. His proverbial ambiguity was based in the indistinct use of the term 'autonomy' as a synonym for both federation and decentralisation, although he never believed in a Spanish federation of states. On the contrary, as a good progressive he prioritised individual freedoms and local autonomy, but insisted that these should apply to the whole of Spain. He despaired of Pi y Margall's flirtation with the Lliga in the final years of his life, as for him the main rationale for autonomy was to prevent special rights being conceded to particular regions.[10]

Of course, any territorial reorganisation could not question the Spanish Nation as both a sovereign body and the sole legitimate basis of civic loyalty. Indeed, the Republic was consubstantial with Spain in that it represented the resumption of the sovereignty of the nation. Since Lerroux saw Spain as an entity both earlier and superior to any form of government, it was the non-negotiable basis of the republican project. So even during his radical years in Barcelona, Lerroux did not hesitate to make common cause with monarchists against separatism, even if catalanists were minded to support a Republic. He could not resist the urge to defend national symbols, including those associated with the constitutional monarchy, when he felt them insulted by catalanists. Lerroux was particularly vexed by whistles against 'the national flag and national anthem'. His classic liberal sense of patriotism, reinforced by pride of being the son of a military officer, would give him a distinctive profile within the republican movement when it considered issues related with the military and the Moroccan question.

Lerroux's hostility towards the Lliga was not that of a rabid nationalist against an illusory separatist enemy. Thanks to Enric Prat de la Riba, another tireless and efficient organiser, catalanism had been transformed from a folkloric movement to an unmistakably nationalist party that hid its desire to recreate the Austro-Hungarian conundrum behind autonomist circumlocutions and vague imperial ambitions. Lerroux well understood the nature of the party by taking what it said seriously. The

Lliga rejected the political and quasi-juridical unity of liberal Spain, invoking the spectre of the famous ninth-century Count of Barcelona Wilfred the Hairy and exhuming the Usatges, medieval Catalan laws, to legitimise the creation within Catalonia of a nucleus of a new state under its own exclusive control. For that reason, Lerroux did not hesitate to define catalanism as a 'reactionary, impossible and absurd ideal' as well as 'selfish separatism'. It was the 'clumsy outgrowth' of a 'mediocre' intellectualism intent on mimicking the Cuban rebels by using 'economic and administrative discontent' caused by the 'Disaster' of 1898 to shatter national unity. For him the only true believers in autonomy were the republicans.[11]

The Lliga's leaders were not slow to respond to Lerroux's rhetorical salvoes. Surprised that an 'outsider' could revive republicanism in Barcelona, they disparaged both the man and his voters, calling the latter 'scum' and the former the 'Emperor of the Paralelo', a sarcastic reference to one of the seedier districts of the Catalan capital. The party also created the myth that Lerroux was a government agent, 'disguised as a republican' with the well-paid mission to fight catalanism.[12] Such insults help explain the failure of the Lliga to capture the working-class vote, and show the extent to which nationalism entailed a backward-looking reinterpretation of the idea of representation. For the catalanists, Barcelona deputies were no longer representatives of the entire Spanish nation, but rather mere *ancien régime* type delegates of an ethereal Catalan *Volksgeist*.

In theory, there was ample political space for Lerroux's liberal patriotic discourse as the relationship between Spanish nationalism, Catholicism and conservatism formed the basis of Polavieja, Maura, and Silvela's opposition to catalanism, while the Lliga had a close relationship with carlism, the traditionalist movement that had supplied a significant proportion of its activists. Yet Lerroux was not a good position to capitalise on a liberal 'Spanish' reaction to the Lliga or lead an anti-catalanist campaign that would unite monarchists and republicans. As someone on the extreme left of the republican movement, he wanted to bring over to the cause working-class militants fed up with the economic crisis and fired by anarchist propaganda to express 'mortal... and rebellious hatred towards political authority'. He could hardly make deals with the Liberals, let alone Manuel Planas, the Conservatives' once powerful political boss in the region. Against the revolutionary rhetoric of Lerroux, the Lliga's gradualist and pragmatic public position, focused in the first instance on greater decentralisation, put catalanism in a much better position to win over a monarchist electorate; the dynastic parties were willing to accept the Lliga as a strategic ally as long as they did not pose a serious challenge to the *status quo*.

Lerroux knew it and although he never gave up on using patriotism as a means to attract the liberal left vote, he favoured an unequivocally populist anticlerical discourse that associated the Lliga with capitalist exploiters and reactionary clergymen. He was not alone in this, as some former federalists and even republicans who had flirted with catalanism like Valentín Almirall struck a similar note. This lawyer and journalist, the most significant theorist of early Catalan nationalism, ended his days renouncing these 'ridiculous theories' in favour of the 'grand ideals' common to all men of 'freedom and democracy'.[13]

The Party Machine

Lerroux's dynamic campaigns for workers against Catalan nationalists and clericals turned him into a hero among young republicans weary of the old leadership. Having identified his voters, the people's tribune set about the task of organising them. The electoral committees of 1901 and the newspaper *La Publicidad* became the nucleus of a permanent organisation that would soon secure Lerroux's control of republicanism in Barcelona. Apart from arranging activities that would keep his troops active during non-election years, he set about creating a patronage network that would provide him with a permanent and professional bureaucracy. He intended to recreate the Valencian model, where republicans had successfully mobilised their electorate to give the novelist Vicente Blasco-Ibáñez control of the city.[14]

To do this, Lerroux did not intend to make the same mistake of other republican leaders of ignoring provincial and municipal elections. He knew that the control of city councils would not only create an opportunity to showcase the potential benefits of the Republic, but also would provide the structure and resources necessary for a dedicated party organisation. Local subsidies and public employment were better able to support the network of republican clubs and activist groups than the irregular subscriptions of better-off members. Moreover, the exercise of power in provincial and town councils provided republicans with much needed experience. Instead of 'living with the platonic hope of the coming Republic', Lerroux argued, activists had to 'do a little bit of revolution', by organising 'democracy'. Republican control of the cities, he noted plausibly, made a change of political regime more credible in the eyes of the public.[15]

It had dawned on the one-time conspirator that planning insurrections was a waste of time when one could win elections. After 1901, Lerroux acted on the assumption that legal political activity was the most effective means of implementing the republican policies while undermining the constitutional monarchy from within. He merged the various election committees into a single organisation, the Barcelona section of the Republican Federation, which soon opened new branches thanks to *ad hoc* donations. By 1903, Lerroux's powerbase had the most support in the city, and the coming together of the diverse factions of the Republican Union effectively handed control of the movement in Barcelona to the ex-journalist from Madrid. This created a virtuous circle for Lerroux, as undisputed leadership facilitated access to new resources that reinforced his clientelist networks. In other words, Republican councillors in the city administration depended on his electoral machine to win, and success at the ballot box enabled Lerroux to get his hands on municipal funds. Therefore, in 1903 victory in the local elections for Lerroux's candidates provided public money that enabled their leader to coordinate and discipline Republican Union cadres, as well as developing his recruitment network by patronage. Similar tactics were employed in nearby industrial districts, widening Lerroux's influence further.

Yet electoral activism does not entirely explain why Lerroux's organisation was able to dominate the republican movement, as this was apparent even before it took control of the city council. If the Republican Federation was able to raise funds to open district branches it was because it was able to transcend the old club model, creating around 500 new 'Republican Fraternities' or civic centres that served as meeting places for trade unionists as well as republicans. In a similar vein, Lerroux also established republican women and youth groups. These public places of sociability, designed to capture the working-class vote, were a hive of activity; on the premises were schools, libraries, discussion groups, cafes, consumer co-operatives, legal and medical drop-in centres, mutual societies, and even theatre troupes and choirs. This network had as its hub a grand *Casa del Pueblo* built in 1906 in imitation of the *Maison du Peuple* in Brussels. This was the focal point for all republicans in Barcelona and offered a greater range of services than those available in the Fraternities. These were the 'food for the body' to complement the 'food for the soul' of the republican message, or put more simply, concrete benefits for the working-class voter, which were the best 'propaganda of the deed' for the future Republic.

Moreover, Lerroux inspired the creation of a republican calendar full of meetings, festivals and commemorations designed to keep progressives busy between the languid celebrations of the proclamation of the First Republic on 11 February. Apart from its mobilising function, these events were designed to strengthen ties between members and encourage the emergence of a common identity that would eventually conquer the streets. The traditional banquet was transformed into mass 'republican picnics' where eating coexisted with sporting events and curious ceremonies like the planting of 'the liberty tree'. At these jamborees, Lerroux eschewed formalities in favour of rolling up his sleeves and serving drinks or eating a sandwich while chatting to his voters.

Lerroux's charisma therefore shaped the Republican Union in Barcelona. His leadership was its most valuable electoral and organisational asset. Although it was formally part of a national party, Lerroux did not hesitate to set the Catalan section's agenda, define its social base and control its structure through his close political friends. He also oversaw the distribution of incentives and took all the key political and organisational decisions. Lerroux resisted with success any attempt at administrative rationalisation that would reduce his power. He was given free rein by the movement's old guard, delighted with the revival of cause and the young leader's respectful attitude towards them. Although Lerroux's unquestioned control of the Barcelona section was not yet formalised in its statutes, there was no doubt that it was *his* party. As we shall see, during the Catalan Solidarity crisis Lerroux was able to overturn traditional hierarchies and eliminate any sense of deference towards the movement's historic leaders. His organisation became the nucleus of the future Radical Republican Party that would contain on a greater scale all the characteristics of a party based on charismatic leadership.

During these years, the more that Lerroux worked to build a powerful political force, the more reluctant he became to risk it all on the old revolutionary dream. The reaffirmation of his leadership and doctrinal ambivalence were the most efficient barriers to a return of past ideological and factional quarrels. Similarly, Lerroux's electoral strategy rejected the temptations of anarchist apoliticism. He was the first to attempt the organisation through legal channels of a hitherto dispersed trade unionism that was receptive to calls for direct action, as well as being the most serious obstacle to the growth of Catalan nationalism. It was no accident that significant monarchist politicians at the time such as Dato, Moret and Montero Ríos saw Lerroux as a stabilising factor in the convulsed world of Catalan politics. With the end of dynastic party control of Barcelona, they saw the existence of a strong and disciplined republican movement as a way to 'civilise' the political debate. They believed it would increase the chances of an elite pact that would mitigate partisan animosities and safeguard public order.[16] This monarchist idea of Lerroux as a dam against the rising waters of catalanism would not outlast the arrival in power of the Conservative leader Antonio Maura in 1907. His unbending hostility to Lerroux and his movement – supported by Catalan Solidarity – gave the Lliga the keys of local power and created an assumption that this political dominance would be permanent. With his proposed Local Administration Law, which promoted regionalism and the corporative vote, Maura unwittingly helped to create the conditions that produced the Tragic Week of 1909.

If one recalls events earlier in the decade, it is important to remember that even after winning a parliamentary seat, Lerroux's ambitions were not limited to Barcelona. His success in the Catalan capital was only one part of a national project of a renewed Republican Federation. Founded in 1902, its objective was to unite organisations not identified with any faction. Lerroux drafted its founding manifesto and formed a directorate that also included Blasco-Ibáñez, the Castellón deputy Fernando Gasset, and his friend Emilio Junoy.[17] Furthermore, Lerroux travelled around Spain to establish local committees that would, like the sections attached to Blasco-Ibáñez and Gasset, publicly declare for Lerroux. The initiative was so successful that the Federation formed the basis of the Republican Union, a party that included all the old factions of the movement. Nicolás Salmerón, the only surviving president of 1873, became its leader, the thirtysomething Lerroux represented the future; he headed the list of public declarations of support to the veteran at the party's founding congress of March 1903.

More significantly, Salmerón chose to run on Lerroux's Barcelona slate in the general election held a month later. Thanks to the republicans, a trade unionist, Juan Anglés, entered parliament for the first time in Spanish history. Lerroux's electoral machine ran like clockwork and the Republican Union obtained 35,000 votes, tripling those of its bitterest rival the Lliga. This success was soon replicated at the municipal elections, where pro-Lerroux candidates seized control of Barcelona city council. Significantly, these victories were repeated in the more tranquil political climate of 1905 due to efficient organisation; the unpredictable isolated waves of republican enthusiasm had finally been replaced by a mechanism able to mobilise supporters and deliver votes.[18]

Salmerón's honeymoon as party leader ended in the 1905 general election. Despite victory in Barcelona, he had presided over a decline in the national republican vote and Lerroux blamed it to the old president's inability to take advantage of the new electoral politics of the twentieth century. Even so, he was well aware that Salmerón enjoyed the continued support of the 1870s generation and did not want to challenge for the leadership for fear of splitting the party. He therefore decided to concentrate on building up the Barcelona section, and await an opportunity that did not take long in coming.

Lerroux and the Revolution

As well as street politics in Barcelona, Lerroux established a reputation as a parliamentarian. He intended to use all his skills as an orator to become a nationally recognised politician. This entailed effectively defending the interests of his voters in the Cortes by working with the monarchist state without renouncing his republicanism. Although initially intimidated by his new place of work, Lerroux was determined not to remain silent and made his maiden speech in July 1901 on government policy towards labour disputes. While this used the same 'tropes'[19] deployed at mass meetings, it was good enough for fellow republicans to notice that they had within their ranks a 'bona fide deputy', and Lerroux received an ecstatic welcome on his return to Barcelona. Thus encouraged, his early speeches caused a furore in the chamber for their radical tone, but the ambitious young politician moderated his language after his re-election in 1903 to stress his statesmanlike qualities. Soon, the force of his criticism of Catalan nationalism, reinforced by his knowledge of the subject and his electoral successes in the Catalan capital, prompted favourable comments from more than one monarchist deputy.

This did not signify that Lerroux had abandoned the 'people'. He wanted to become the parliamentary voice of the trade unions. His maiden speech was one of many that condemned poor working conditions or the flouting of labour legislation. He was particularly successful voicing the grievances of workers in the publicly owned mines of Almadén (Ciudad Real). Due to his pressure, the government ordered various inspections that raised health and safety standards, founded a school for apprentices and mining engineers, and established a range of benefits for miners that included grants of common land. Delighted with this outcome, Almadén's trade union became one of Lerroux's most fervent supporters outside Catalonia. This proved not to be an isolated event as the republican made similar speeches on conditions in the Riotinto, Linares and Cartagena mines, leading to socialist fears that Lerroux's popularity among Catalan workers would spread outside the region. Yet the republican deputy only secured short-term electoral success for his pro-labour stance. Attempts to create a trade union linked to the Republican Union failed even in Barcelona. Nonetheless, his achievements only served to reinforce his penchant for legalist tactics as Lerroux acknowledged the 'effectiveness' of the monarchist parliament when 'aroused or worried public opinion made it interested in just causes.'[20]

Yet it would be an exaggeration to say that by this time Lerroux had explicitly repudiated the revolution. His words remained those of an insurrectionary. Despite the victories in Catalonia, he continued to believe that 'elections were rigged' at national level and that a change of regime was impossible 'as a result of natural and peaceful progressive change'. The republicans still believed that they had the right to rebel because most voters remained estranged from the system and did not actively support the dynastic parties. Curiously, Lerroux did not apply his correct analysis for the previous failures of republicanism in Barcelona – the lack of political mobilisation – to explain election results in the rest of Spain. Rather, the republicans' entrenched belief that they could never win through the ballot box justified the continued attachment 'to force' despite participation in legal political activities. Lerroux did not abandon the conspiratorial world as he sought to develop a secret network of contacts within the military. His long-standing identification with the insurrectionary doctrine of Zorrilla set strict limits to his parliamentary reformism; convinced that only an armed rising could overthrow the constitutional monarchy, he pressured Salmerón to redouble his subversive efforts to demonstrate that the republican movement had not abandoned its revolutionary spirit.

Therefore, Lerroux's constant tours around Spain were not just about laying the foundations of electoral success; his new local organisations had to contribute towards any future revolt. This would be different from past *pronunciamientos*. Republican generals were now old and without postings. Their waning influence within the military could not be compensated by the few junior army officers still interested in overthrowing the monarchy. Making a virtue out of necessity, Lerroux put forward an alternative insurrectionary model. While still believing – correctly – that the military remained essentially liberal, he suggested that others lead the revolution. The republicans should organise 'a civilian based popular movement' or 'a national uprising composed of [different] social groups' that would be supported by those military officers who believed in the cause. In reality, this federalist vision of rebellion was purely theoretical. Since the republicans did not have the funds, weapons or men to undertake the 'national uprising', Lerroux was never tempted to reprise the farcical insurrections of Zorrilla. He preferred to await events and prepare for an institutional crisis that would facilitate the growth of the republicanism and sap the confidence of monarchists. He was determined that the movement would not be caught napping as he believed it had in 1898.[21]

So it was not just for electoral reasons that Lerroux sought to continue his relationship with the anarchists. But the intimacy forged in the Montjuich campaign had dissipated as the revolutionaries regarded him as simply another politician. Lerroux himself dispelled any ambiguity on the matter as he openly declared himself to be a 'radical republican' not tainted by association with anarchism or those intent on implementing its ideas 'in a criminal and mistaken way'. Rather than cooperating with his one-time comrades, he wanted to curb their influence on trade unions for his own benefit. In this he was generally successful, and he also managed to convince well-known anarchists to join his 'Republican Fraternities' and vote for the party. Nevertheless, some common ground remained. While the anarchists were aware that Lerroux would never back sustained strike action for fear of risking his organisation by directly confronting the government, they knew that he would continue to offer them material and moral support, publicise any arbitrary arrests, arrange pardons and assist them in court. It was a marriage of convenience that exchanged favours for votes and kept the lines of contact open between two organisations opposed to the *status quo*.[22]

Not all anarchists were prepared to do deals with Lerroux. Militants accused him, correctly, of injecting the virus of politics into the working-class movement and killing its revolutionary pretensions by satisfying grievances through legal means. Only 'the former *zorrillista*' Ferrer, who embraced anarchism 'with all the faith, ardour and enthusiasm of the convert', saw Lerroux as the possible leader for a revolution. Not the real revolution of course, but one that would create an unstable Republic doomed to be replaced by libertarian communism. Ferrer openly told his friend that international anarchist movement intended to assassinate the young Alfonso XIII and leading monarchist politicians. In these circumstances, he went on to explain, the republicans should 'give evolution a push and hasten the journey on the road of political progress'. As a coffee house revolutionary, Ferrer imagined that the confusion caused by the magnicide would allow previously organised revolutionary juntas led by Lerroux to seize control of state organs and proclaim the Republic.[23]

Such plans appalled Lerroux. As chief editor of *El País*, he regularly denounced 'direct action' terrorist tactics in France and Spain. Although like other republicans he saw revolution as the midwife of history, his model remained that of 1868, when a bloodless *pronunciamiento* occurred on the orders of a military leader. However much some sympathisers defended anarchist terrorism as a desperate act of protest against an unjust order, Lerroux condemned it as a particularly odious form of violence 'whose target of hatred' was not oppression but 'the life of the human individual'.[24] But Ferrer's revelations created a serious political problem for the republican leader. Any refusal to take advantage of a monarchical crisis would enable the anarchists to expose Lerroux as a revolutionary charlatan, a hypocritical bourgeois dilettante incapable of forcing a change of regime. He therefore remained ambivalent when the anarchists acted. Warned of their plans against Alfonso XIII in his visit to Paris in 1905, and then at his wedding in 1906, Lerroux ordered his supporters to remain vigilant, await orders, and . . . then do nothing.

Catalan Solidarity

By this time, Lerroux's attention was consumed by crisis within the Republican Union. This was sparked by Nicolás Salmerón's decision to campaign with carlists and the Lliga against the proclamation of the Jurisdictions Law of 1906. This gave military tribunals the power to punish any insult made by civilians against Spain and the army, especially those made in the anti-monarchist press. Moreover, Salmerón argued for the creation of a 'Catalan Solidarity' slate for the 1907 elections, which would demand autonomy without receiving any in return from the Lliga. This decision marginalised Lerroux within the party. As a newspaper editor himself, he hardly approved of a law that threatened to throttle the republican press, still less when it was prompted by an assault on the premises of the satirical magazine *Cu-Cut* by officers of the Barcelona garrison. Following the general antimilitarist attitude of the catalanist movement, this publication poked fun at the army week after week, and it was no surprise that officers in the rest of the country gave their unqualified backing to their colleagues in the Catalan capital. This unanimity prompted the Liberal prime minister Eugenio Montero Ríos to appease the army by giving it the legal right to defend itself against criticism. But if Lerroux did not condone assaults on newspapers, he nevertheless considered the indignation of the army officers to be justified and chronicled the constant attacks by catalanist press organs on national symbols and the Barcelona garrison. He blamed the civil authorities for not putting an end to them, especially as they insulted an institution that could not easily answer back. The catalanist movement, Lerroux stressed to his followers, should not get away with using the *Cu-Cut* episode to present itself as a victim. Ignoring the line taken by Salmerón, Lerroux told republicans to support the military and confront those who offended the flag or the national anthem. He soon became famous for his walks down Barcelona's famous Ramblas in the midst of the Lliga's campaign wearing a hat displaying the Spanish colours of red and yellow.[25]

The breach between Salmerón and Lerroux was obvious. The young apprentice refused to back down and work with his adversaries. The idea that republicans should advocate Catalan autonomy with those considered particularist reactionaries was repulsive to Lerroux given 'that memories of cantonalism were not so remote . . . that we should not be alarmed' by the stirring of a 'sentiment that undermined national unity'. He was not whistling in the wind. Republicans in other provinces were disgusted when Salmerón put aside party interest to accept the leadership of Catalan Solidarity. They were astonished that this was not simply a protest against the Jurisdictions Law but also a denunciation 'against centralism' and 'the oppressive administration of the Spanish state'. While the Republican Union leader regarded these Catalan Solidarity slogans as attacks on the constitutional monarchy, a wiser Lerroux interpreted them as 'fermenting separatism'. In any case, their monarchist opponents used republican connivance with catalanism as a useful political weapon during the 1907 general election.[26]

Catalan Solidarity brought republican disunity. Lerroux dismissed Salmerón's calls for discipline, accusing him of exceeding his powers by agreeing to an electoral coalition. The party assembly of June 1907 formalised the split, with Salmerón retaining control of the national bureaucracy. Lerroux's defiance cost him the editorship of *La Publicidad*, as owner Eusebio Corominas placed the newspaper at the disposition of the former president. But he ruthlessly demonstrated who controlled the Republican Union in Barcelona by removing Corominas from its presidency. The party split meant that while Catalan Solidarity took control of Barcelona city council, the majority of republican councillors remained loyal to Lerroux.

The 'Emperor of the Paralelo' faced the 1907 election with a weakened organisation and a powerful opposing coalition made up of republicans, catalanists, and carlists. Even worse, Catalan Solidarity enjoyed the benevolence of the Maura government, which withdrew the Conservative slate in Barcelona. Moreover, since Lerroux was the leading anti-Solidarity figure throughout Spain, he had to expend much energy and resources outside his own constituency. He founded *El Progreso*, a new daily that served effectively as his mouthpiece during a bitter election campaign that began with the murder of one of his supporters and witnessed assaults on Salmerón, Cambó and Lerroux himself. Catalan Solidarity may have finally won a clear victory, unseating their chief antagonist, but Lerroux's 22,000 votes indicated that he retained the loyalty of most republican voters. Following declarations of support from other provinces, he resolved to create his own party, and characteristically toured Spain to publicise his decision. On 6 January 1908, the Radical Republican Party was born at a meeting in Santander. Lerroux remained committed to it for the rest of his political life. Although its name invoked Zorrilla, its programme reflected the priorities of its leader. Like Georges Clemenceau's French Radicals, it would be a party that was secular, autonomist and socialist.

The construction of Spain's most successful republican organisation had begun. But in the short-term, Lerroux faced the unremitting hostility of Antonio Maura. The Conservative prime minister saw him as more dangerous to the constitutional monarchy than Catalan Solidarity, and was determined to prevent his new party from spreading to other parts of Spain. Taking advantage of Lerroux's loss of parliamentary immunity following the election, the government pressured prosecutors to charge him for supposedly slanderous press articles. Despite the intervention of his friend Eduardo Dato, Lerroux was sentenced to two years four months jail, and barred from holding any public post. When he eluded prison by going into exile, Lerroux's enemies believed that his now leaderless movement would collapse or re-join Salmerón's pro-Solidarity faction. They did not realise that for any anti-system party, persecution and an exiled leader were perfect bedfellows, and the Radical Party survived the loss of public subsidies and the desertion of 'moderate' or pro-Salmerón republican donors. In December 1908, by-elections between pro-Solidarity catalanists and the Radicals saw the victory of those who stood as 'liberals and Spaniards'. Lerroux was among them, and his election was celebrated in the Catalan capital and the Cortes itself with acclamations to the Radical leader, Spain and Spanish Barcelona rather than the habitual 'vivas' to the Republic.[27]

Until this unexpected turn of events, Lerroux had struggled to live with his family in exile in Paris. In October 1908, he accepted an invitation from Spanish republicans in Argentina to visit Buenos Aires. The visit showed his great popularity among the well-to-do Spaniards in the Argentine capital. Apart from organising meetings and lectures, they donated large sums of money that allowed Lerroux to put himself and the party on a more secure financial footing. In exchange, the Radical Party offered to represent their interests in the Cortes. Lerroux was dazzled by the sheer wealth of Argentina, its pro-business attitude, and the prosperity of his fellow countrymen in this once Spanish colony. He became interested in investing in electricity companies and amusement parks and sought to place his family and friends within these successful enterprises in order to provide economic security. But Lerroux remained a professional politician, and he was determined to return home to take possession of his seat. Maura thought otherwise and used his Conservative parliamentary majority to bar the republican leader on the basis that his criminal conviction for slander was still in place. The prime minister maintained his veto despite a Radical victory in Barcelona's municipal elections of May 1909, and Lerroux realised that he would have to remain in exile until Maura fell from power. His allies in the

Cortes intensified their efforts, joining a Leftist Bloc under Segismundo Moret, the leader of the Liberal Party.[28]

That summer, Lerroux left Buenos Aires to tour various European capitals. The motive was economic rather than political, as he looked to purchase rides for a part-owned Argentine amusement park. His political friends in Spain had assured him that he could disembark safely in Santa Cruz de Tenerife, where his family would be waiting for him. On the long journey from Rio de Janeiro to the Canaries, Lerroux received confused reports of a revolution in Barcelona. His fears intensified when told that the spark was the embarkation of reservists for Melilla. He considered it impossible that the Radicals would have dared take part in an anti-militarist movement 'with little republican overtones', especially when his party had little objection to the idea of reducing the threat of Riffian tribesmen to the Spanish enclave in North Africa. In this, he was not mistaken; the initiative came from a strike committee composed of anarchists, socialists, and members of Workers' Solidarity, a new trade union that would eliminate Radical influence within the labour movement in Barcelona. But while leftist catalanists took the opportunity to give free rein to their militant anti-militarism, Radicals in the city also protested against the colonial war and the embarkation of reservists, although they refused to take up the strike committee's invitation to declare the Republic. They struggled to make contact with their leader, as Lerroux did not land in Tenerife because the government had suspended constitutional guarantees.[29]

Diverted to London, the exiled republican was in the British capital when he received all the details of what became known as the 'Tragic Week' in Barcelona. Lerroux read with disbelief that his own party members had taken part in building barricades and firing convents. Some of his supporters then fled to France, but most were arrested, including various councillors and district committee chairmen accused of aiding the rebels. His old friend Ferrer was among those anarchists arrested and one of the five condemned to death for the crime of rebellion. Lerroux discovered that he had arrived in Barcelona after the disturbances had begun, and despite visiting various Radical Party centres to drum up support for the revolt, had not personally taken part in the violence. Concluding that the death sentence had more to do with Ferrer's previous verbal backing for terrorism, Lerroux joined the international campaign for clemency, but after the execution rapidly dropped the subject, failing to take part a demonstration against the Spanish Embassy in Paris, despite being in the French capital at the time. This attitude hardened when the foreign pro-Ferrer campaign degenerated into a boycott of Spanish goods. He increasingly felt uncomfortable in appearing in public with anarchists and was not prepared to risk the survival of his party in the repression following the end of Tragic Week.[30]

Lerroux returned to Spain on 31 October 1909 after the Liberal leader Moret replaced Maura as prime minister. Following the usual celebrations for the re-appearance of a persecuted leader, he set out to reconstruct the party organisation in Barcelona and consolidate the Radicals nationally. The local elections of December 1909 sealed Lerroux's revenge against Maura and his civil governor in Barcelona, Angel Ossorio y Gallardo, but he declined to launch a Montjuich-style campaign for Tragic Week prisoners, preferring to co-operate with the forces of law and order. By now, Lerroux had no interest in being the 'redeemer' of the false 'tormented ones', preferring not to risk his respectable reputation for four anarchist visionaries. He told his supporters that the triumph of 'freedom' over 'reaction' was inevitable as he had seen it in Argentina and France, and therefore the Radical Party's task was to accelerate this outcome by becoming the bulwark of freedoms, peace, order and work. Lerroux's leadership and his turn to the right reversed the decline in the party's fortunes in Barcelona, reinforcing its control over the city council.[31]

The participation of rank-and-file Radicals in Tragic Week proved to be a watershed moment for Lerroux. Many of his followers regarded the disorders as the revolution that their leader had promised, and indeed the Radical Party would commemorate it as a 'glorious' act, boasting that the destruction of customs posts and convents did not produce any victims, even if some clerics and officials had been killed.[32] Yet Lerroux condemned this apologia of popular violence. His insurrectionary past would ensure that he kept the dream of winning the military over to the Republic, but he would not lift a finger while the constitutional monarchy was not on the brink of collapse. If he once thought that the republicans should prepare themselves for the revolution, he now advocated that the conspiracy should await the revolutionary moment. This meant that the Radicals were now a 'normal' party, dedicated to participating in elections to win power at a local and national level. It also meant that the party was more likely to co-operate with the dynastic parties.

In this way, Lerroux resolved the dilemma that he had faced since 1900. He did not suspect that reinforcing his leadership and protecting his party would postpone *sine die* the revolution, leading to a permanent accommodation with the monarchical system. Indeed, while Lerroux may have believed that his talents and successes earned him the right to regain control of the republican movement, his increasing readiness to adopt liberal values and methods as well as the warm relationships that he cultivated with monarchist politicians made this much less likely.

3

The Respectable Republican (1909–1923)

On 9 October 1922, the press reported a conversation between Alfonso XIII and Federico Anaya, the Radical Party mayor of Salamanca. In the lunch organised by the town council, the King praised a statesmanlike speech that Lerroux had made the previous month in Tenerife which demonstrated a firm understanding of 'international questions'. The monarch concluded that Lerroux 'had all the qualities of a lawmaker', noting that 'he only needs to take one further step [accepting the monarchy] that would not harm his reputation' since 'we agree on one basic thing: love of Spain...what can possibly divide us [in the common endeavour] of making the *Patria* great? For that cause Lerroux has made undoubted sacrifices and his words are always worthy of his talents'.[1]

What had prompted the King to praise one of the greatest adversaries of the monarchy, a man who a few years previously had been a mere journalist with no experience of government? These were not polite words to one of Lerroux's political friends, but rather a significant overture: Alfonso XIII wanted the Radical leader to strengthen the dynastic left enfeebled by the recent implosion of the Liberal Party. This was not just about neutralising a threat during a difficult period for the monarchy. Although Lerroux had not abandoned republicanism, he had for some time not considered a change of regime a major priority. To the dismay of his supporters, Lerroux referred in the aforementioned September 1922 speech that the 'revolutionary romanticism' which previously impelled him to demand 'a change of institutions', had waned. The Great War had transformed everything, 'shaking the foundations of society and altering the configuration of peoples'. For that reason, while he did not wish to serve the King, the sheer 'magnitude of the problems' facing Spain demanded that 'partisanship' between monarchists and republicans 'be buried'. The priority was to tackle illiteracy, fight separatist movements in Catalonia and the Basque Country, and confront the economic crisis. 'Despite what my friends feel', he went on, 'I say to you that the future of

Spain lies in Africa, a work of redemption that should be carried out for our sons, grandsons, and future generations'. Spain therefore had to fulfil her international obligations, win the protracted Moroccan war and establish the protectorate. Lerroux also warned his audience that the principle of authority needed to be upheld in the face of social indiscipline and revolutionary threats; irrespective of whether Spain was a republic, a successful democracy could only be built on the elimination of a 'fanaticism that pitched some classes and parties against others' and which saw an 'adversary' as an 'enemy'.[2]

It very much appeared as though Lerroux was flirting with the same kind of arguments that had taken reformists like Melquíades Álvarez to the brink of constitutional monarchism. His continued protestations of republicanism sounded increasingly formulaic as he preferred to concentrate on the serious problems facing the postwar world. In Tenerife, Lerroux dismissed the idea of revolution as republican democracy needed to build 'a barrier, a wall against the extreme left'; 'the archaic practises of the gun and barricade', his once favoured methods of political action, were now condemned as they would bring 'disgrace to the country and submerge [Spain] in horrors not seen since the Middle Ages'. Pleading that the Radical Party should be open to those workers who sought equality and cooperation rather than the class struggle, he argued that it was 'pointless to seek the root of all evil in only person [Alfonso XIII]'. Given this, Lerroux announced that he would not shy away from 'personally contributing to good of the country' and proclaimed his support for those on the monarchist left who 'had a democratic programme'. It was a win-win situation; if they failed, the Republic would arrive 'amid cheers' and not by violence. Not surprisingly, Lerroux's increasing proximity to the constitutional monarchy provoked scorn from republican rivals. Manuel Azaña ironically granted him the titles of 'His Majesty's republican' and 'First revolutionary of the King s Court with title and servants'.[3]

Lerroux's conversion to moderate republicanism between 1909 and 1923 can be seen in various ways. It was evident after Tragic Week when he repudiated illegal action to focus on bringing electoral success to his party. Conscious that the deaths of Salmerón in 1908 and Costa in 1911 made him the most prominent republican within the movement, Lerroux was determined to reinforce his leadership at national level. To this end, he resisted the temptation to play the revolutionary in 1917 and ensured that most Radicals stayed aloof from conflict with Eduardo Dato's Conservative government. Moreover, since he continued to attract anarchist votes, Lerroux did not immediately repudiate his claim that the Radicals represented the interests of the unions. Even so, he shunned any contact with the CNT after 1919 when it embraced terrorism and the revolutionary general strike. He also accentuated his anti-separatist language following the creation of the Catalan Mancomunidad in 1914 and the intensification of the Lliga's nationalist campaigns.[4]

Pursuing Respectability

During this period, Lerroux's personal circumstances also changed substantially. After his foreign adventures, he was financially comfortable and could look forward to a life without money worries. As leader of a national political party, he returned to Madrid permanently, buying a house with a garden at 9 calle O'Donnell in November 1911. This was an expensive new build property that only increased in value with the improvements that the Radical leader carried out over the following years. Enjoying the use of a car and driver courtesy of a well-off supporter, he discovered the delights of the village of San Rafael in the mountain pass of Alto del León during an excursion to the Guadarrama mountains north of the capital. Like his mother and eldest brother, Lerroux's adoptive son Aurelio suffered from respiratory problems and his need for fresh air prompted the purchase of a modest chalet with adjoining land near the village's railway station. When he could afford it, he extended the building and brought the neighbouring three small cottages with the aim of creating a family estate with extensive gardens and a small farm. Lerroux would spend every Thursday and Sunday at San Rafael until the approach of the civil war. He would also pass long parts of the summer there in the company of family relatives. Yet the mountain retreat was only one of his property investments. With the aid of wealthy Argentine political supporters like Rafael Calzada and Toribio Sánchez, Lerroux leased and renovated the spa resort of Baños de Montemayor in Cáceres province until 1936, building a hotel that he frequented regularly.

Property ownership helped to provide political respectability. But it was not enough. Any aspiring statesman also needed to be educated, and Lerroux sought to obtain the usual qualifications of a Spanish political leader. In 1905, he finally obtained his secondary school leaving certificate in Figueras with the assistance of an examination board dominated by republicans. A law degree was the logical next step, but the daily demands of party politics long impeded study. With the assistance of Dámaso Vélez, a Radical lawyer who wanted to use Lerroux's popularity to build up his own law firm, the latter nominally took a revised degree in the Canary Islands that was finally granted by the University of La

Laguna in September 1922. Not coincidentally, his Radical colleague Rafael Guerra del Río used his contacts to arrange the examination board.[5]

Yet Lerroux's extensive network of contacts did not always bring him success. The Radical Party in Madrid was unable to replicate the electoral machine that had brought it victory in Barcelona, and Lerroux felt it necessary to locate its headquarters in his own home at 9 calle O'Donnell. He also published the party newspaper, *El Radical*, with money donated by political friends in Spain and abroad. Lerroux believed that subscriptions and printing contracts from Radical-controlled town councils would provide *El Radical* with enough income to survive financially, but this proved not to be the case as the cost of maintaining a large and well-paid workforce produced a deficit of 100,000 pesetas. Lerroux personally sustained the paper for political reasons, but it finally closed in 1917 leaving him only with the money obtained from the sale of the old printing presses to show for his investment. This bitter experience would mark the last time that Lerroux would ever be a newspaper proprietor, as he swore that 'never, ever, to return to being an employer of workers and intellectuals'.[6] From this time, he became regular contributor to pro-Radical national and international newspapers like the Barcelona daily *El Progreso*.

The main reason why *El Radical* failed was that Lerroux was unable to devote his time to its activities, appointing his former *El País* colleague Ricardo Fuente as its chief editor. As the leader of a party dominated by his own charismatic personality, Lerroux divided his time between parliament and public meetings throughout Spain. His appearances in the provinces acted as a catalyst for the emergence of rudimentary local party organisations. Lerroux was conscious that outside the big cities of Madrid, Barcelona and Valencia, and some regions like Aragon, western Andalusia, Extremadura and the Canary Islands, the Radical Party looked too much like the old and largely irrelevant republican movement of the late nineteenth century. In no way could it be called a truly national party, although it certainly was the most dynamic part of republican movement following the disappearance of the Republican Union after the death of Salmerón and the failure of Melquíades Álvarez's Reformist Party to attract support beyond its Asturian stronghold. But the point remained that the Radicals had deepened rather than eliminated factionalism within Spanish republicanism. This was apparent even within the party. Lerroux later reflected on the difficulties involved in leading a charisma-based party, writing in his memoirs that there 'is nothing more difficult than leading and disciplining a mass political . . . and democratic organisation. Every step forward is a difficulty overcome, and every difficulty means opposition and every triumph [means] a struggle and every struggle [means] winners and losers.'[7] In a populist party, these losers had no other option than to submit or leave.

Since Lerroux's own home became the Radical Party's headquarters, he was obliged to provide offices to accommodate the archive and its permanent staff. With a mixture of humour and scorn, Lerroux's senior colleagues soon called it the 'customs house' [*aduana*], although it rapidly became evident that it was incapable of processing anything competently. Typically, Lerroux selected staff on the basis of friendship rather than ability, later ruing that 'no-one was able to prepare press cuttings, files or information for parliamentary debates for me'. The 'customs house' turned out to be merely a 'whispering backroom' and 'political club' that arrogated to itself access to the leader. In this sense, its last boss, Antonio Sánchez Fuster, wholly deserved the epithet of 'head of customs', although at least he did try to create some order out of the chaos by employing professionals rather than relying on old cronies to do multiple tasks. The latter included men like Antonio Aguirre, Lerroux's private secretary before September 1923, who also managed *El Radical* and his leader's wine and cattle export interests during the First World War.[8]

The Emperor Flees Paralelo

We should resist the temptation to ascribe Lerroux's political moderation to greater personal wealth. After all, he was reasonably well off before being forced into exile in 1908, and yet still led the radical wing of the republican movement from Barcelona. Moreover, he would demonstrate his leftist credentials again when the Radicals agreed a common slate with other republicans and socialists for the 1910 general election. The Republican-Socialist Alliance was essentially an antimonarchist copy of the previous year's leftist bloc that had brought republicans together with Moret's Liberals, and the results confirmed Lerroux's domination of the left in Barcelona. Nationally, the election also gave the republicans approximately the same number of seats as the Republican Union in 1903 and the Socialists their first ever parliamentary deputy.

Internal divisions made the Alliance a much less successful parliamentary force. Salmerón's former associates could not forgive Lerroux for the split of 1907, and the socialist leader Pablo Iglesias regarded the Radicals as his most dangerous enemy for their efforts to attract working-class support. Ultimately, the Alliance had been forged solely on opposition to another government under Maura. Such was the mutual hatred between supporters and enemies of the Conservative leader that the 1910 election campaign degenerated into violence, and both Lerroux and Maura narrowly survived assassination attempts.[9]

The fragile unity of the Alliance finally collapsed following corruption allegations made against various Radical councillors in Barcelona. Lliga deputies accused the latter of enriching themselves when awarding a water supply contract and managing a local tax on construction materials. Unexpectedly for Lerroux, the parliamentary debate –which soon widened into a broader denunciation of the Radicals' record in local government – was led by Pedro Corominas, the leader of the Republican Nationalist Federal Union (UFNR), a left catalanist party that had absorbed Salmerón's remaining supporters in the region. The Radical leader vehemently denied the accusations and walked out of the Alliance with six other deputies after witnessing that the latter's leader, Gumersindo Azcárate, and Pablo Iglesias backed the UFNR's stance.[10]

Lerroux's protestations of innocence were not convincing. He knew that Radical councillors used public funds to support the party. He even knew that some of them, including his close associate Emiliano Iglesias, used their public positions to obtain commissions and business opportunities. Yet dealing with miscreants was politically difficult. Lerroux recognised that he should expel them from the party, but feared that such an action would destroy a political organisation 'that had provided protection to so many legitimate interests'. He was not making excuses. On this occasion, Lerroux eventually took action that led in the short-term to splits within the party and the loss of its majority on Barcelona city council, even if the Radicals were able to cling onto power. Lerroux subsequently preferred to tolerate a certain level of corruption in the expectation of eliminating the offenders from later elections. This less painful solution for the party nevertheless damaged its reputation, but Lerroux remained obdurate, arguing that while 'probity is one of the qualities that most elevates man in life, but it is not the principal [quality] in politics and can even sometimes act as a cloak that covers and disguises the failures of some [politicians]'.[11]

This pragmatic attitude reflected the evident reality that clientelist practises were necessary to provide organisational cohesion and electoral success. Throughout its existence, enemies of the Radical Party such as catalanists, socialists, mauristas, and even some republicans railed against its corruption. Yet none of Lerroux's opponents had a spotless record in government. Scandals involving the Lliga in the Mancomunidad, and later the Esquerra in the Generalidad were well known, even if they ultimately did not tarnish the reputation of catalanism. A corruption allegation was the favoured political weapon of the partisan press against an administration. Ironically, the young Lerroux in his muckraking days did much to stimulate public outbursts of anguished virtue, although the Barcelona city council scandal recalled the 'moral campaigns' against a recently elected Conservative administration in Madrid city council almost two decades earlier in 1895. In the face of a demonstration by so-called 'honourable men' organised by the opposition, the then prime minister Cánovas quipped that he was delighted to see in Madrid so many 'honourable men' among politicians, journalists and businessmen.[12]

The mutual hostility between the Radicals and its former Alliance partners only intensified when Lerroux decided to support the new Liberal government of José Canalejas in February 1910 over the issue of Morocco. The prime minister had decided to occupy coastal positions on the north Moroccan coast to prevent the French or the Germans from getting a foothold in the Straits of Gibraltar. For the Radical leader, any suggestion that Spain should relinquish its treaty rights in the region would be an admission of weakness to the Great Powers and undermine Spanish security. He supported the creation of an internationally recognised *cordon sanitaire* around the Straits of Gibraltar, the Gulf of Cadiz and the Alboran Sea similar to that established for the Canary Islands by the occupation of Río de Oro and Ifni in Western Sahara. At this point, Lerroux was principally concerned with coastal towns such as Ceuta and Melilla and did not advocate the complete occupation of northern Morocco, but as we shall see, this would change in 1921.[13]

Radical rapprochement with the Liberals can also be seen in other areas such as the registration of unlicensed religious orders. Lerroux's constructive relationship with Canalejas, which also included co-operation over numerous pardon petitions, contrasted with the uncompromising opposition of other republicans and the PSOE. The two leaders only differed on the question of the creation of a Catalan Mancomunidad, when Canalejas disregarded Lerroux's fears about possible catalanist control of the institution to support the Lliga's demands for self-government. Nevertheless, this issue did not curb the Radical leader's admiration of the prime minister, and he reacted to news of Canalejas' murder by an anarchist in 1912 with shock and dismay.[14] At least Lerroux consoled himself with the thought that the assassination did not bring the return of his bitter Conservative adversary Maura to government. The Radical publicly praised Alfonso XIII's decision to prolong the Liberals' occupation of power by giving Romanones the premiership, even if he was not as effusive as reformists like Melquíades Álvarez and Gumersindo de Azcárate.

The King's choice of Romanones had more to do with Maura's refusal to serve under him than any particular desire to keep the Conservatives out of power. Yet Maura's withdrawal from front-line politics opened the door for Lerroux's great friend Eduardo Dato to take office in October 1913. Somewhat ironically, therefore, the return of the Conservatives proved to be a great boon for the Radical Party. In elections held the following year, the political fallout of the Barcelona city council scandal tarnished a credible performance elsewhere in Spain and placed Lerroux's continued presence in the Cortes in jeopardy. Although he reluctantly made a pact with his UFNR rivals to stave off the threat of the Lliga, it appeared that the so-called 'San Gervasio' Pact would not be enough to save his seat. So Lerroux entered negotiations with the government to obtain the Cordoban constituency of Posadas which contained his home village of La Rambla. In other words, he became an 'official' candidate and his presence in the district was celebrated by fireworks and music, a far cry from the Radical leader's previous experience a decade earlier when he was faced a hail of stones.

While the Radical leader was fated by local notables and enthusiastic crowds listened to his speeches from the balconies of village councils, he only beat his Liberal opponent by a narrow margin. Yet the Lliga's victory in Barcelona confirmed that Lerroux's decision to leave the city was ultimately a wise one, although the temptation to relocate permanently to Posadas was banished by the continued strength of monarchist parties in the area and the heavy blow to his political creditability. Antonio Maura taunted him in parliament, expressing surprise that a so-called anticlerical was elected on the votes of priests. Similarly, Niceto Alcalá-Zamora, a young Liberal deputy from Cordoba, joked that Lerroux had 'lost his empire in Paralelo' and had gone to Posadas to take refuge in the inns [*posadas*] of Cordoba' under the patronage of Dato.[15] Although it was common for opponents to strike political deals, Lerroux's compact with the Conservatives made him a much ridiculed figure by the summer of 1914.

The Impact of the War in Europe

The outbreak of the First World War provided Lerroux with the opportunity to reaffirm his republican credentials, though it was not without risk. As a fervent Francophile, he supported the Triple Entente from the beginning of the conflict in numerous public meetings and press articles, and quickly called for Spain to abandon her neutrality.[16] This was not a popular position in a divided Spain where neither the political elite nor public opinion wanted to enter the war. Most republicans were content with a policy of benevolent neutrality towards France, while socialists and anarchists denounced the militarist overtones of the Radical leader's position and expressed their sympathies for the workers and peasants who formed the cannon fodder of the belligerent armies. Lerroux, on the other hand, argued that a declaration of war against the Central Powers would increase Spain's international prestige, claiming that her geographical position would ensure that the financial and human contribution to the Allied war effort would not be as great as those of her French neighbour. Yet for all the talk of the conflict, Lerroux's stance was ultimately shaped by domestic considerations. He hoped to attract Francophile intellectuals and military officers to the republican cause and saw belligerency as the means to accelerate the end of the monarchy.

Characteristically, Lerroux's opponents refused to believe that principle was behind his actions, later accusing him of profiting personally from his advocacy of the Triple Entente by receiving large subsidies for *El Radical.* Such claims are overblown. As we have seen, his newspaper did not survive the war, while his support for the Allies was immediate and unequivocal. He even drove to France in August 1914 to visit the front and assure president Raymond Poincaré and his prime minister René Viviani that the bulk of public opinion – including the King – favoured the Allies. Clarity brought personal danger. On his return to the Spanish border town of Irun that September, he was attacked in his hotel, an experience later repeated in San Sebastian and Andalusia.[17]

Despite Lerroux's efforts, Alfonso XIII and his governments skilfully managed to preserve Spanish neutrality. Nonetheless, the inevitable economic problems caused by the protracted war raised hopes among republicans and socialists that the ensuing rise in social conflict would have significant political consequences. Particularly serious was high inflation caused by the shortage of goods and foodstuffs. In a society used to stable prices and wages, trade unions used the threat of strikes to obtain pay rises from employers fearful of disruption to production. The advantages of collective action did not go unnoticed among state employees who saw their fixed salaries being consumed by inflation. This was particularly true for army officers who illegally created Defence Councils [*Juntas de Defensa*]. These professional unions rapidly took on a political character under the leadership of such figures as colonel Benito Márquez. He issued a vaguely regenerationist programme and intimidated governments with veiled threats. Despite the opposition of generals, these Defence Councils took hold in garrisons, dividing the army and undermining its discipline and professionalism. This was the beginning of the 'military question' that would cause so much trouble for governments before Primo de Rivera imposed his answer in the coup of September 1923.

Recalcitrant army officers were not the only threat to the constitutional monarchy. When Dato's Conservatives replaced the fractured Liberal Romanones government in June 1917, the customary dissolution of the Liberal dominated parliament provoked a rebellion by catalanist and anti-monarchist deputies determined to obtain greater autonomy for Catalonia and constitutional reform. They demanded a 'Parliamentary Assembly' that would replace the Dato administration with a 'national government' before calling elections for a constituent assembly. Lerroux was part of this insurrectionary movement, and the Radicals entered a Leftist Alliance with Melquíades Álvarez's Reformists and the PSOE that June. Consequently, he attended the first session of the Parliamentary Assembly held in Barcelona's Ciudadela Park. When the government peacefully closed its proceedings, the republicans proceeded to assist the revolutionary general strike led by the UGT and the CNT in August. The future republican minister Marcelino Domingo, one of the leaders of the Catalan Republican Party that had displaced the UFNR as the main force on the Catalan left, had pledges of military support via his high-level contacts with the Defence Councils, but the plan required Radical support for a daring armed operation in Barcelona to release rebel officers. Lerroux, who had previously expressed sympathy with the aims of the movement without receiving anything in return, preferred to distance his party from a risky revolutionary enterprise not under his control. Therefore, although he verbally backed the rebels to save face within the republican movement, the party bureaucracy remained aloof. This did not prevent orders for his arrest for the crime of inciting sedition in September, as the military authorities suspected some Radical involvement in the most violent leftist rising so far that century, but Lerroux went into hiding. As in 1909, when the Radical leader finally re-emerged, he discovered that his much-vaunted party organisation was in ruins.[18]

Lerroux's *annus horribilis* climaxed with the closure of the second and last session of the Parliamentary Assembly in Madrid's Athenaeum by the police. Afterwards, Alfonso XIII replaced Dato with a national government under Manuel García Prieto, the leader of the Democratic Party. Since the new administration included catalanist ministers, it supported the principle of Catalan autonomy, although its main task was to organise an 'honest' election in 1918. This experience at the polls gave Lerroux a political lesson that he would not forget in the 1930s. The PSOE fought on the issues of the revolution and amnesty for political prisoners and obtained six seats, while the Radicals lost all but one of their deputies. The vanquished did not exclude its leader, as Lerroux lost his Barcelona seat. Not only was he no longer an icon for the working-class left, but increasing political polarisation also deprived him of the moderate vote. The result was a crushing blow for the Radical Party.

Much like during the Second Republic, political polarisation did not lead to the creation of two monolithic blocs. On the contrary, the newly elected parliament was a myriad of minority groupings that made the creation of majoritarian governments difficult. The collapse of the *turno* – the consensual transfer of power – made patent the crisis of effective government that had existed under the constitutional monarchy from 1909. As Luis Arranz has perceptively suggested, there was a 'legitimacy block' within and between the two dynastic parties, a failure to construct a common reforming project that would safeguard the constitutional system by transforming it into a modern liberal democracy. In the 1930s, Lerroux himself would feel the frustration that led Alfonso XIII in 1921 to despair publicly about governmental instability and impotence. Yet when the King felt obliged to play a more active role in ministerial appointments, his critics accused him of 'encouraging... hopes of a total assumption of [personal] power'.[19]

Such criticism was also borne out of frustration. The Restoration system may have been on the ropes, but there was no obvious alternative. There was certainly little prospect of a Second Republic. By the summer of 1918, Lerroux could look back at a series of recent disasters that included a failed alternative parliament, electoral catastrophe, García Prieto's replacement by a Defence Council backed Maura government, and an increasingly militant CNT intent on direct action. A complete change of approach was necessary. For Lerroux, the solution to the crisis lay in the holy grail of republican unity, and he created a refashioned Republican Federation in November 1918. To placate his Catalan Republican Party allies, he expressed sympathy towards Catalan autonomy, and even tried to enlist the Lliga, as their mutual enmity had diminished following a joint campaign in 1915 to get free trade status for Barcelona.

The Federation proved to be the perfect springboard for Radical recovery. Lerroux regained his Barcelona seat in the 1919 elections and he would not suffer defeat again before September 1923. During that period, the party also regained control of the Catalan capital's city council. In November 1920, Lerroux's comeback was crowned by the decision to nominate him the official republican leader. In other words, while republicanism remained at the margins of Spanish politics, the Radical Party now dominated the republican movement, taking control of its exiguous parliamentary group after winning a dozen seats in the 1923 elections.[20] But for a politician approaching sixty, this was small beer. His life's ambition was the Republic, but this increasingly seemed an irritating obstacle to entering government with a liberal left that was no longer part of the enemy.

Finding New Friends

The dominance of Lerroux and his centrist Radicals within Spanish republicanism did not silence his internal critics. These 'new republicans', including Marcelino Domingo, used the language of class to express their categorical rejection of the monarchy,[21] and were discomfited by a leader who frequently called for strong action, including the suspension of trial of jury, to be taken against anarchist terrorism. This was just one of a series of fundamental disagreements. They did not share Lerroux's views on the Bolshevik Revolution, which he described as the 'tyranny of the multitudes without thought of quality'. Similarly, the young Turks were baffled by Lerroux's changed attitude to the Defence Councils as he was no longer interested in winning them over for the Republic, lambasting them for undermining military discipline and leading the country 'by the head to a Soviet regime'. If that was not enough, they were also horrified by his support for military operations in Morocco and the decision to break off relations with the PSOE in parliament.[22] Lerroux's moderation stoked fears that he was going over the monarchist side, a not entirely groundless notion as the Radical leader had no shortage of advocates among monarchists, including Santiago Alba, the leader of the Liberal left. Lerroux's attitude made sense: with the republicans' electoral space being eroded by socialists and catalanists, alignment with monarchist reformists like Alba did indeed seem to be the best way to prevent political extinction.

This is not to imply that Lerroux was the suitor in this courtship. The unlikely wooer was Alfonso XIII. With a good track record of taming anti-system forces, the King believed that the defection of Lerroux would strike a terminal blow to the republican movement. He had made a previous attempt in 1918, sending general Lóriga of his military household to exchange views with the Radical leader. The encounter went so well that Lóriga suggested that Lerroux meet Alonso XIII in person. Although barely five years previously the former ridiculed reformist figures like Azcárate and Melquíades Álvarez for speaking with the King, Lerroux now agreed to a conversation on the important condition that it took place in secret. After all, there was 'no ethical or significant reason' why 'two politicians should not converse and discuss important matters of related to their country'. The meeting in the monarch's car that November in El Pardo was a success, and even if the republican did not adjure his faith, he was 'less of an enemy of Alfonso XIII than previously'. To forestall any embarrassing leaks, Lerroux gave an account of the episode to Natalio Rivas, a close associate of Alba, in which he stressed that the King struck him as 'extremely likeable and charming, very intelligent and knowledgeable, even if somewhat superficial'. Rivas was euphoric and predicted that the one-time republican firebrand would eventually serve under Alfonso XIII.[23]

While this did not come to pass, Rivas's optimism was not without foundation. With Bolshevism supposedly lurking in the background, Lerroux rejected any plot that could plunge Spain into chaos. When he got wind of an anarchist conspiracy to murder the King during the ceremony to launch a warship in Bilbao, Lerroux warned Lóriga because 'the Republic cannot and must not come by means of a crime that the Republicans could have prevented'. His information was good: when the police raided an unremarkable property near the dockyard, they found a sailor's suitcase containing bombmaking equipment and documents indicating the location of King's podium.

Lerroux's entente with the constitutional monarchy was not confined to the monarch himself. The Radical leader found that he was conformable in the world of 'gentlemen politics'. Apart from his party pals, Lerroux preferred the company of monarchists to that of republicans, let alone socialists. This bond only became stronger following the murder of Eduardo Dato by three anarchists in 1921. Lerroux described his disgust at the killing of his long-time friend in his memoirs, confessing that his countless past campaigns against the monarchist system had been 'clouded by passion' and had 'exceeded justifiable limits'. This, Lerroux explained, made him blind to the virtues of his Liberal and Conservative opponents which among things included magnanimity and mutual respect. This re-evaluation of his one-time bitter adversaries helps explain the ease with which Lerroux was able to attract the support or cooperation of former monarchists in the 1930s. When he looked back on his long political life, Lerroux thought the politicians of the so-called 'oligarchy' were far superior to those of the Second Republic in terms of training, generosity and commitment to the rule of law.[24]

The End of Liberal Constitutionalism

Lerroux may have been willing to come to terms with a liberalising constitutional monarchy, but he lacked a strategy to convince his followers that the coveted Republic was of less importance than the democratisation of the existing political system. While he could support the reforms of others, he hesitated to take the huge emotional step of actively co-operating with the monarchist left. Changing political circumstances did not help. Spain had resumed its 'pacification' of northern Morocco following the hiatus of the First World War. This brought disaster at Annual in July 1921, when inadequate defensive preparations allowed the Riffian troops of Abd-el-Krim to breach the security perimeter around Melilla and inflect heavy losses on the Spanish. Although later military operations recovered lost territory and brought Abd-el-Krim to the brink of defeat, the disaster produced a political clamour for heads to roll. In bitter debates, the antimonarchist opposition and some Liberals blamed the military and the then Conservative Allendesalazar government of being responsible for the defeat, while the socialist leader Indalecio Prieto implicated the monarch himself in the catastrophe, arguing that Alfonso XIII had used his close relationship with the army command to interfere in operations. Lerroux remained in the background, supporting the Maura government's counteroffensive and stilling republican calls to abandon the protectorate. He told parliament that Morocco was 'internationally valuable' for Spain and that after Annual, the limited strategy of holding coastal areas should be replaced by the complete occupation of the territory.[25]

Lerroux's line became untenable when the 'responsibilities' campaign reached the Cortes in the summer of 1923. The Radical leader refused to serve on the investigation committee until pressure from within his own party forced him to take a more active stance. Irrespective of Lerroux's dalliance with the King, the most effective means of preserving Radical unity remained attacking the monarchy, and in a meeting in Valencia he accused Alfonso XIII of being 'indirectly' responsible for Annual. After stressing that constitutionally the King could not be held to account, Lerroux claimed that the parliamentary campaign was pointless and only the abdication of the monarch could bring an end to the crisis.[26] However, this did not mean that he had changed his views about the rationale of the military campaign itself. Despite the popularity of withdrawal among socialists and republicans, Lerroux insisted that the Radical Party would not join the anti-colonial campaign led by Domingo and Prieto; he therefore played no role in leftist attempts to secure the backing of Miguel Primo de Rivera, a leading general known for his opposition to continued Spanish presence in northern Morocco.

Primo de Rivera was an acquaintance of Lerroux, but the republican knew nothing of his plans to overthrow the Liberal García Prieto government. On 15 September 1923, the Radical leader was in Malaga when his provincial party chief, Gómez Chaix, told him a military coup had just taken place. Although the general would soon become the head of a

Military Directorate, Lerroux did not yet understand that Primo de Rivera's action had destroyed constitutional liberalism. A new chapter in his political life was about to begin.

4

From Sceptical Conspirator to Minister of the Republic (1923–1931)

Despite his many duties as head of the Republican Provisional Government, Niceto Alcalá-Zamora always found time during the early summer months of 1931 to write down his feelings during this most wonderful time of his political career. His belated conversion to republicanism had given him the prize that veterans of the struggle had long worked towards during the dark years of the monarchy. A relatively peaceful revolution had produced the coveted change of regime, and Alcalá-Zamora had climbed to the top of the greasy pole; things would get even better that December, when he was given the presidency of the young Republic.

In his diary, the former monarchist did not hesitate to express his gratitude to Lerroux for the 'extraordinary sacrifices' that he had made during those historic months. The Radical leader was a 'giant' politically speaking, whose stature only grew due to his 'superior attitude and high self-esteem'. Alcalá-Zamora recognised that despite being Spain's most eminent republican, Lerroux had accepted 'a subordinate and at times secondary role in the preparations of the revolution, [and] in the drawing up of agreements and programmes'. Even if the veteran republican had 'naturally been disappointed' with this, he swallowed his pride to ensure victory: 'Doubtless the general atmosphere was more wary of him [Lerroux] than even on other occasions, but he recognised and accepted that reality, showing once more his intelligence as well as his heartfelt commitment to the republican cause'.[1]

In many ways, these friendly words corroborate the bitterness that characterises Lerroux's account of 1931 in his memoirs. Rather than being a crude hatchet job on his ex-ministerial colleagues, his later resentment reflects the fact that the leader of the only significant republican party in 1923 had been pushed aside by others in the Republican-Socialist

Alliance of 1930. It is difficult to think that a man of Alcalá-Zamora's personality and track record would have swallowed such a bitter pill. But Lerroux felt that he had no choice. He could not remain aloof from the only serious movement demanding a Republic, especially when Primo de Rivera had destroyed any prospect of the democratisation of the 1876 constitutional system. Ironically, it was the military dictator's failure to institutionalise his seizure of power that made a Republic a serious possibility. Since deposed monarchist politicians were reluctant to confront the regime for fear that opposition could end up overwhelming the Crown itself, growing resistance to the new regime took the form of a republican tide that, much to the amazement of veteran republican leaders like Lerroux, swept the cities. In this context, the Radical leader could hardly stand aside although the price was high: co-operation with long-standing enemies and rivals like republican Marcelino Domingo, socialists Indalecio Prieto and Francisco Largo Caballero, and maurists and left-wing catalanists.

Lerroux Turns Against the Dictatorship

For Lerroux, the dictatorship had been created with the complicity of a desperate Alfonso XIII intent on eliminating any constitutional obstacle to his powers. Certainly the King did not challenge the military rebellion, but the idea that September 1923 ushered in a period of royal despotism was based more on republican prejudice than a sober analysis of political realities. When Primo de Rivera suspended the Constitution, he also seized control of royal prerogatives; the King never intervened less in matters of state than after 1923. This is not to say that the new dictator had a blueprint for power, as the coup was a desperate move to avoid a dangerous split within the armed forces. Apart from the collusion of Alfonso XIII, Primo de Rivera's gamble succeeded because his fellow generals, including war minister Luis Aizpuru, were not prepared to defend the Constitution. The survival of the dictatorship therefore depended on Primo de Rivera's ability to retain the loyalty of his military colleagues rather than the confidence of the Crown.

Lerroux was on surer ground when he placed the dictatorship in the broader context of the crisis of liberal constitutionalism after the First World War. That conflict had not 'simply been a war' but a 'revolution' and a 'crisis of civilisation' that had provided the perfect breeding ground for 'the extremes' of left and right. The fear of revolution, he argued, enhanced the prospects of counter-revolution, with liberalism seemingly incapable of preventing an ideological war to the death. For Lerroux, the republican movement was essential to avoid this dreadful outcome for Spain. It should reaffirm its commitment to 'the ideals that gave birth to western civilisation' and refuse to co-operate with the dictatorship while at the same time striving to ensure that the fall of Primo de Rivera would not produce the triumph of 'revolutionary socialism'.[2]

This strategy was reinforced by the popular reaction to the end of constitutional government. Lerroux recognised that Primo de Rivera's action was not unpopular among a public tired of conventional politicians, detecting a 'millenarian spirit' among his fellow Spaniards. This did not mean that the new regime would last. In an open letter to fellow republican Blasco-Ibáñez, he predicted that the *pronunciamento* would not signify the 'salvation of the Monarchy' but the opposite: the army, he insisted, had in reality provided 'the coup de grâce' against the Crown, 'in the same way as it restored it [in 1874–75]'. Hence the dictatorship was the transient rule of a 'soldier of fortune' and would inevitably make way for the Republic. Yet Lerroux was adamant that this great event required the participation of the military to prevent its degeneration into revolution. For that reason, he ordered his party to abstain from active opposition against the new regime. Knowing Primo de Rivera well after meeting him in Paris during the First World War, he even agreed to a secret meeting with the dictator after the seizure of power to discuss the situation in Catalonia. When Lerroux later wrote about the dictatorship, he stressed its efficacy rather than its lack of legitimacy, asserting that it did not cause 'any material damage to the country' or 'governed worse than its predecessors'. He went so far as to praise its restoration of public order, noting that for six years Primo de Rivera took advantage of its pacification of the Riffian rebels in Morocco to 'suppress assassinations and put the wind up strike organisers'. Recognising the prosperity that produced a huge increase in public spending, he saw the dictatorship in classical terms as a temporary regime of exception and the dictator as a regenerationist 'Costa like . . . iron surgeon'. Lerroux therefore had no particular animus towards Primo de Rivera as long as the dictator held to his promise not to remain in power indefinitely.[3]

This explains why Lerroux decided to retire temporarily from politics to start his own legal firm. However, his career as a lawyer was a short one. After taking on a few cases courtesy of his friend Dámaso Vélez, the greenhorn found that he preferred political to courtroom dramas. In June 1924, he travelled to Paris to meet the exiled leaders of the Conservative and Liberal Parties, José Sánchez-Guerra and Manuel García Prieto. They all rejected a revolutionary response to the end of the dictatorship, preferring a constituent assembly would decide the thorny issue of the monarchy. Soon afterwards, Lerroux joined the liberal opposition under Romanones. This was in contact with general Cavalcanti, the head of the King's Household, and later with general Aguilera. The latter was involved in the first failed military coup against the dictatorship in June 1926 and Lerroux defended one of the conspirators, Domingo, in the subsequent military trial.[4]

Any chance that Lerroux would come to terms with Primo de Rivera came to an end in November 1926 when the general announced the creation of a new political system. The Radical leader indignantly refused to join the proposed National Assembly, seeing the dictator's new party, the Patriotic Union (UP), as an attempt to cling onto power permanently. Moreover, he was well-aware of the rumours that the dictatorship would deepen its mutually advantageous relationship with the socialist movement by agreeing that the UP would share power with the PSOE.[5] Yet Lerroux's firm opposition to Primo de Rivera did not mean that his scepticism about the viability of any popular insurrection against the dictator had been allayed; on the contrary, he much preferred to align the republican movement with the more congenial politicians of the Restoration era.

The Republican Alliance

On 11 February 1926, Lerroux was proclaimed leader of a new Republican Alliance. This was born out of a proposal from Antonio Marsá, a member of both the Radical Party executive and the *Escuela Nueva*, a 'New Generation' republican intellectual group. During the initial negotiations in José Giral's pharmacy, the Radical leader met other *Escuela Nueva* republicans such as Manuel Azaña and Luis Araquistáin for the first time. The Alliance brought together the Radicals, most of the Federal Party, Republican Action – an embryonic party led by Azaña and based on members of the Athenaeum – and provincial republican organisations including the Catalan Republican Party. Lerroux provided its headquarters and met its administrative costs. The purpose of the Republican Alliance was to re-energise the republican movement and make it the principal focus of opposition to the dictatorship. In this it was a success, as many critics of the regime came to republicanism after reaching the conclusion that Alfonso XIII's fate was irrevocably bound up with that of Primo de Rivera. Thanks to the Republican Alliance, the Radical Party finally became a truly national organisation.

But clandestinity did not eliminate the worst vice of the republican movement: factionalism. Doctrinal and personal quarrels continued to sap energy. In 1929, Marcelino Domingo founded the Radical Socialist

Party with Álvaro de Albornoz, a former Radical. They left the Republican Alliance following Lerroux's insistence that it had to co-operate with monarchists in the restoration of legality and the convocation of a constituent assembly.[6] They were also frustrated by Lerroux's reluctance to organise an insurrection that would overthrow the monarchy. The success of the Republican Alliance only made the Radical leader more reluctant to gamble on an adventure that had little chance of success, and unlike Domingo or Albornoz, Lerroux had a long history of failed conspiracies behind him. Nevertheless, this revolutionary past was not much of interest to Radical Socialists, who accused Lerroux of wanting to restore the *status quo ante*.

While extremists within the Republican movement may not have liked Lerroux's connections with monarchists, they could not question his commitment to the overthrow of the dictatorship. His contacts with dissident military officers and trade unionists led to a brief time in prison in November 1926 with Giral and a longer stay in 1928, in which the now veteran politician contracted furunculosis that was serious enough to require an emergency operation and two months convalesce at home. On bail and under police surveillance, Lerroux fled to Paris in 1929 and through Santiago Alba offered to become involved in José Sánchez-Guerra's planned rising against Primo de Rivera, but as the former Conservative prime minister did not want republican involvement, he turned Lerroux down. The result, as the more experienced conspirator later wrote, was an 'almost infantile adventure' that January in Valencia, where 'heroic and gentlemanly sacrifice' did not even secure the support of the general designated leader of the revolt. This disappointment did not discourage Lerroux. Almost a year later, he instructed Diego Martínez Barrio, the Radical leader in Andalusia, to assist a more serious military plot that general Goded had been organising in the region's military garrisons. It was only called off after the resignation of Primo de Rivera and the appointment of a conservative transitory government under general Berenguer.[7]

The End of the Monarchy

The departure of Primo de Rivera transformed Spanish politics. Although some former Conservatives and Liberals still harbored hopes that the monarchy could be saved, the republicans were intent on toppling Alfonso XIII. To achieve this historic goal Lerroux concentrated his efforts on securing republican unity, and this did not just signify bringing the Radical Socialists back into the camp but also reaching agreement with the new republican right led by monarchist deserters like Niceto Alcalá-Zamora and Miguel Maura, the son of the Conservative statesman. This was realised with the so-called San Sebastian Pact of August 1930, which included left-wing catalanists after obtaining a pledge of Catalan autonomy. Two months later, Primo de Rivera's one-time socialist allies also signed up to a Republican-Socialist Alliance.

Despite his significant contribution to the San Sebastian Pact, Lerroux received few of its rewards. Not surprisingly, he clashed with the catalanists. While they wanted – and obtained – the right to define the Catalan Statute, Lerroux only supported it on condition that its implementation was reserved to the constituent assembly; the Radical leader remained stubborn in his belief that Catalan autonomy had to be placed within a wider territorial re-organisation of Spain that protected individual and local rights. Similarly, the creation of the Republican-Socialist Alliance did not signify that the socialists' hostility towards their long-time political rival had mellowed. Therefore, when the Alliance created a Revolutionary Committee to prepare a new insurrection against the monarchy, Prieto and the catalanists vetoed Lerroux for the presidency. The Radicals' allies could hardly deny them a place in the Revolutionary Committee – they were the most significant republican organisation within the movement – but they were determined to marginalise them as much as possible. This became all too obvious when the Revolutionary Committee transformed itself into the Provisional Government of the Republic. Without consultation, Lerroux was excluded from the premiership and key ministerial portfolios. After regarding Azaña, the designated war minister, as part of the Radical quota, Alcalá-Zamora proposed nominating Lerroux as foreign minister to keep him away from domestic affairs. The Radical leader responded by demanding the interior ministry, essential to his project of creating a 'Republic of order' that would prepare 'serious and trustworthy' elections, thereby ensuring the 'definitive installation of Republican democracy'. Yet Lerroux was never going to get that job because Alcalá-Zamora and others feared that he would use the state's electoral machinery to manufacture a Radical majority in the constituent assembly. In the end, Lerroux settled for the foreign ministry and a new communications ministry under his Radical colleague Martínez Barrio.[8]

This was a serious political defeat for the Radicals as it was a clear admission that its leader was going to occupy a secondary role in any future Republican government. Under these circumstances, he could have broken the Republican-Socialist Alliance. It is certainly true that he felt more comfortable with reformists like Melquíades Álvarez, Francisco Bergamín and Manuel Burgos y Mazo, and was certainly closer to dynastic Liberals like Romanones and Alba than he was to the socialists. Lerroux's decision to stay reflected a political rule that US president Lyndon Johnson would later apply to FBI director J. Edgar Hoover: the Radical leader preferred to be inside the tent pissing out than outside the tent pissing in. He knew only too well that other party leaders were looking for any pretext to exclude the Radicals from the Alliance; if he had left over a squabble over ministerial chairs, it would have split the republicans and Lerroux would have been blamed by public opinion for dividing the opposition to Alfonso XIII. This could have torn the Radical Party apart as it had turned to the left after 1923 and its leader could therefore no longer rely on the unconditional loyalty of the membership.

In sum, Lerroux preferred to remain inside the Republican-Socialist Alliance to protect his party as much as possible during the uncertain times that lay ahead. Like in 1917, he refused to bet all his chips on the botched insurrection of December 1930, and the Radicals' main contribution to the disaster was Lerroux's signature on the revolutionary manifesto. However, Berenguer snatched defeat from the jaws of victory when he permitted the execution of two rebel captains, Fermín Galán and Ángel García Hernández. The creation of 'martyrs' undermined an already weak transitory government that had called elections in the hope of taking advantage of republican weakness. Lerroux was convinced that without the captains' sacrifice, 'the popular Spanish soul would not have raised its voice of protest and its desire for change in the municipal elections of [April] 1931'.[9]

Nevertheless, republican electoral success did not seem very likely in the last days of 1930. Lerroux was one of six Provisional Government ministers who eluded arrest, the Radical leader taking refuge in the house of Dámaso Vélez. He later hid in a flat in the western Argüelles district of Madrid where he created a false medical clinic in the name of a friend to meet contacts without suspicion. From there he re-established communication with imprisoned ministers who gave him the interim leadership of the movement. Desperate times did not alter the balance of political power within the Republican-Socialist Alliance; Alcalá-Zamora refused to give Lerroux access to its Military Committee. The Radical leader's main task therefore was to restore links with provincial republican organisations and UGT leader Julián Besteiro, as well as providing aid to those who fled to France. At this point, the police had discovered Lerroux's whereabouts, but he left undisturbed and met general Sanjurjo, the head of the Civil Guard from 1928, who was a friend of his from their days drinking and talking together in Madrid's Fornos café. Lerroux tried to secure the general's neutrality in the event of another rising, but the latter was non-committal. Even so, the very fact that a meeting took place was evidence enough of the government's crumbling authority, and by March 1931 all of the Provisional Government's ministers were back on the streets. A change of regime seemed imminent, but Lerroux was painfully aware that if the Republic 'depended on the revolutionary organisation created by the Provisional Government, we would have been left high and dry'.[10]

The Republican-Socialist Alliance therefore reverted to electoral politics. Berenguer had been succeeded by Juan Bautista Aznar, and this admiral decided to replace a general election with a three-stage electoral process that would end with a national poll. The decision to begin with local elections was a curious one as these had traditionally given republicans and socialists their best results, but the date was set for Sunday, 12 April. The prospect of striking a blow against the monarchy in the towns and cities was far too enticing for petty partisanship, and as the best organised party within the Republican-Socialist Alliance, the Radicals provided the most candidates. Lerroux himself concentrated on rebuilding the party in Barcelona to prevent his old enemies of the Lliga from winning as a majority on the city council. Although he was also concerned about the threat posed by left-wing catalanists, their influence was perceived to be on the wane.

Lerroux followed the municipal election results that Sunday night in his bogus clinic, as there was still an order open for his arrest. His joy at the unexpected Republican-Socialist Alliance victory in most of Spain's provincial capitals was marred by the calamitous Radical performance in Barcelona, which lost in its strongholds to the Catalan Republican Left (ERC). Its leader, Francesc Maciá, took advantage of his triumph on 14 April to occupy the provincial council building and unilaterally declare a Catalan Republic. Emiliano Iglesias, the Radical leader in Barcelona, responded by proclaiming the Spanish Republic in the civil government building and pressuring captain general Despujol to disperse the catalanists. This was a complete failure, as Despujol was replaced by general López Ochoa who placed the garrison under the orders of Maciá. Radical Party impotence in Catalonia was then confirmed by the Provisional Government's *de facto* acceptance of the new situation in the region.[11]

Lerroux's role in the proclamation of the Republic in Madrid was almost as inconsequential. He could not see how the Republic could come from local election results. Although the scale of republican and socialist victories in Spain's towns was unprecedented, any seasoned political observer could see which way the electoral wind was blowing in urban areas even before 1923. Moreover, monarchist candidates had still won a majority of councils, and therefore it seemed that there was still all to play for in the upcoming provincial and national elections. But critically the Republican-Socialist Alliance's conquest of the towns dissuaded many army officers from actively defending the monarchy. In other words, the Republic was not the inevitable consequence of election results but rather the result of a revolutionary rupture occasioned by the occupation of state institutions by antimonarchists cheered on by mass crowds. With the military looking on and the Civil Guard being placed at the disposition of the Revolutionary Committee by Sanjurjo under the watchful eye of Radicals Dámaso Vélez and Ubaldo Azpiazu, the monarchical regime imploded. The departure of Alonso XIII on 14 April ensured the bloodless arrival of the Republic.[12]

Minister of the Republic

Although he spent the previous day in the Madrid home of Alcalá-Zamora to keep up with the news, Lerroux was stunned when an emotional Vélez informed him of the King's departure at three in the afternoon of 14 April. This was followed by a summons to join the other members of the Provisional Government. The journey was more easily said than done. The ride to Miguel Maura's flat (where the ministers had gathered), and then to the interior ministry building in the city centre, was anything but straightforward. His car could not escape the crowds singing the French Marseillaise or the republican anthem Himno de Riego. They proudly held aloft the tricolour flag that thanks to the Radicals had previously been popularised as the symbol of the Republic; it would formally become the national flag a fortnight later. Finally, at five o'clock, Lerroux arrived at his final destination in the Puerta del Sol. After the solemn proclamation of the Republic, the one-time outsider took up his first ministerial post the following day. His first speech as foreign minister received a good reaction from civil servants relieved that they would be judged by their actions and not by their political ideas; anyone not prepared to serve the Republic loyally were able to leave without losing their service benefits.[13]

From the outset, Lerroux was prepared to accommodate conservatives and monarchists. This does not imply that his Republic would merely be traditional Spain without a King. The Radical leader was clear that the new regime had to satisfy the wishes of his republican and socialist allies; their expectations of democracy could not be dismissed. For Lerroux, the Republic meant above all civil supremacy and the absence of military interference in politics; the separation of Church and state and the absence of the latter in religious matters; and a federal structure based on individual, municipal and regional freedoms. He also recognised that the Republic would intervene in social affairs in order to protect the weak and powerless; this would be the first step towards a more harmonious society. A more active state would also introduce secular education, improve public health, carry out agrarian reform to create more smallholders, protect workers' rights, and favour direct over indirect taxation. Ultimately, the objective was nothing less than the secularisation of society in which the Church would no longer play a role in education or shape legislation in such areas as marriage and divorce.

This was an ambitious, if hardly novel, programme: in its essentials it reiterated the 1920 manifesto of Republican Democracy. The Radical Party presented this future vision of Spain in its meetings and public events throughout 1930 and 1931 to underline Lerroux's commitment to social justice. More equality, the Radical leader argued, would not only produce a fraternal society free of socio-political conflicts but would also be the bedrock of a new republican patriotism and a barrier against the disorders that could produce the return of an authoritarian regime.

Lerroux entered government in 1931 still imbued with republican ideals. Despite the claims of his critics, he was not a hack politician without a programme or model of society. Yet there were great differences between leftist republicans and the Radical leader, and these would become more evident during the first months of the Republic. As an experienced political figure active in Spanish public life from the late nineteenth century, his analysis of the 'social question' became ever less militant. Adhesion to liberal principles tempered his republicanism. While he believed that the state could be an instrument of social change, he dismissed the idea that government decrees were enough *per se* to fight injustice and facilitate progress. More important, he averred, were individual initiative and pragmatism. Lerroux believed that the implementation of the republican agenda should be gradual, measured and guided by a liberal spirit that prioritised conciliation over confrontation. It certainly should not be begun by a transitory and ideologically heterogeneous Provisional Government. Its only mission, according to Lerroux, was the consolidation of a 'radically conservative' Republic based on public order and private property. Reform should be left to the forthcoming constituent assembly.[14]

If the timing of change was one issue that separated Lerroux from other ministers in the spring of 1931, another more divisive subject concerned the extent to which previous constitutional practice should inform the institutional framework and the political culture of the new regime. Left republicans and socialists maintained that the Constitution should represent a radical departure from the past, and Lerroux did not deny that the constitutional monarchy had many weaknesses. But he also argued that the Restoration system defended liberties and brought stability and suggested that its mechanisms to ensure the peaceful transfer of power between parties be adopted by the Republic. Thus for the Radical leader, 1931 did not mark a year zero but the recuperation of civil liberties and parliamentary government after the dictatorship. This recovery of political rights should not just benefit republicans but all Spaniards; a patriotic and fraternal Republic, he believed, should not be the exclusive property of any group.

Of course, Lerroux did not demur from Azaña's dictum that the Republic should be governed by republicans. At issue was the definition of 'republicans'. Reflecting on the municipal election results, Lerroux thought it an act of madness to institute tests of political purity. The Republican-Socialist Alliance may have obtained a historic result in the towns, and performed creditably in the countryside, but it nevertheless still lost to weak monarchical opponents.[15] Therefore, it did not seem irrational to suppose that these voters would form the basis of a strong future conservative movement. The wily politician certainly understood the electoral advantages for the Radicals if they could capture the monarchist electorate for themselves; in this sense the interests of the party and the Republic were aligned. Since the overwhelming majority of parties and voters outside the Republican-Socialist Alliance were to its right rather than its left, it was political common sense to make overtures in that direction; radical change could not happen until there was a broad consensus in favour of the Republic.

This was not the dominant view within the new government. Lerroux's republicanism had more in common with former monarchists like Alcalá-Zamora or Maura than with Azaña. Unlike other ministers, Lerroux preferred to proselytise among former liberal monarchists than dispatch the routine business of state. This reflected a broader strategy. Once the Constitution was passed and the Provincial Government dissolved, the Radical leader wanted to convert his party into a centre-right alternative to the socialists and left republicans. The Republic would then have its own *turno* system, and political stability would be guaranteed. He also saw Spanish monarchism as a talent pool. Lerroux did not want to govern with junior civil servants, journalists or intellectuals. In his speech to the Madrid Casino Club in May 1931, he pleaded that the former political elite should not hesitate to work with his Republic as this would represent 'national opinion in perfect balance' and prevent any danger of 'the extreme right' or 'left'.[16] Lerroux's aspirations were encapsulated in the pithy phrase "a Republic of all Spaniards". It would bring understanding and reconciliation between long-standing republicans and their traditional adversaries. With the proclamation of the Republic, he declared, the revolution was over. After 14 April, Spain would enjoy the benefits of gradual change within an open and tolerant regime that defended property.

Such a message could not appeal to a socialist movement still wedded to the class struggle. More surprisingly perhaps, left republicans were equally hostile. Colleagues like Azaña rejected the idea that elements of the old political class could widen the social base of the Republic. Lerroux responded to their hostility in kind. He became increasingly dissatisfied with the performance of other ministers, seeing them as a hindrance to his vision of nationalising the Republic. Within in his own ministry he faced fewer obstacles. He placed emphasis on continuity of personnel, spurning the opportunity to place his political friends in embassies and consulates. His deputy was Francisco Agramonte, a professional diplomat who had served the monarchy before April 1931 in the post of director general of Morocco and the Colonies. Given Lerroux's lack of expertise and languages, he relied on the advice of his civil servants when he went to represent the Republic at the League of Nations in Geneva for the first time in May. During disarmament negotiations and debates on agricultural exports he did not depart from the lines established by his monarchist predecessor; as the new foreign minister, Lerroux told his fellow representatives, that he came to continue a 'political task' that was neither 'monarchist nor republican' but 'Spanish and patriotic'. These moderate words were greeted with applause from his audience.[17]

Lerroux's speech to the League of Nations was opportune as it coincided with disorders that culminated in the infamous burning of convents on 10–12 May. In Switzerland Lerroux deplored the pitiful response of his ministerial colleagues, which would be a harbinger of things to come. He did not hesitate to denounce the sorry affair as a plot to create a leftist Republic based on an alleged public demand for radical measures against the Church. As Lerroux warned, the latter had as an institution not been hostile towards the Republic and so 'it was impolitic and unjust and therefore foolish' to provoke a Catholic backlash. Certainly, the recognition of the new regime by the Vatican owed much to the conversations held between the foreign minister and the papal nuncio, monsignor Tedeschini. Lerroux had promised that the separation of Church and State would not take place unilaterally and stressed that it would not presage a period of religious persecution. Similar assurances were made to Spanish bishops.[18]

These comments indicated how far Lerroux had travelled from his youthful anticlericalism. He supported the principle of freedom of worship that recognised the rights of Catholics without discriminating against those of other faiths. Suppressing religious orders and payments to clerics had long disappeared from the programme of the Radical Party. Even secular education and divorce were not immediate priorities if they jeopardised relations with the Church. Lerroux's pragmatism reflected his agenda of consolidating the Republic. By safeguarding the legal status of the Church, worship and its rights of association, Lerroux believed that Catholics would accept the new regime. Unlike his leftist colleagues, he did not consider them inherently reactionary or antirepublican, pointing out that Catholics were politically heterogeneous, and even included those in Alcalá-Zamora's Liberal Republican Right (DLR) who had worked to bring about the end of the monarchy. To alienate them would doom Radical efforts to incorporate the right into the Republic.[19]

Lerroux Inveighs Against the Left

Lerroux's "a Republic of all Spaniards" also had an economic dimension. Any revolutionary change provoked concern among businessmen and investors, and fears of political anarchy were exacerbated by the after-effects of the Wall Street Crash of 1929 which reduced trade and placed international pressure on the peseta. The Provisional Government took power amid the fight of capital, the closure of enterprises and a subsequent rise of unemployment. In this context, the designation of a socialist as finance minister was not helpful, especially a man like Prieto who was ignorant of the markets and prone to verbal gaffes. Lerroux was relieved that his socialist colleague did not embark on any radical economic adventures, although he put this down to circumstances more than to political acumen. For the Radical leader, government policy should concentrate solely on restoring confidence, as a rise in public spending or socialisation measures would only increase production costs and depress demand.

Lerroux's public opposition to the policies of Largo Caballero in the labour ministry was a logical reflection on his views on the economy. It is absurd to claim that this reflected a desire to represent employers against the socialist defence of workers' rights.[20] As we have seen, the Radical Party supported state intervention to address the 'social question', and this included better working conditions and wage increases for peasants and workers. This was all about bringing the classes together. Moreover, and unlike others in the government, Lerroux had some notion of what it was like to run a business. So, while he recognised the legitimate grievances of organised labour, he was a firm champion of private property and free enterprise and argued that socialist remedies for the economic crisis were not just ill-advised but dangerous.

Lerroux was particularly critical about Largo Caballero's efforts to transplant the framework of industrial relations into the countryside. The agrarian economy, he reminded the labour minister, could not be run like a factory or a shop. Of course, he did not fail to realise the politics of these measures. Forced employment, the rural equivalent of the ban of factory lockouts, facilitated the intervention of socialist councils and trade unions in the production process. The obligation to hire labourers within the local district from strict alphabetical lists provided by the unions meant that farmers had no freedom to select their workforce. Even worse, mixed labour boards [*jurados mixtos*], presided over by socialist inspectors appointed by the labour ministry, ordered wage rises and shorter working hours without reference to the agricultural cycle, the real value of the harvest, or the differences in production of each municipality. The inevitable result of this rise in labour costs was unemployment, but socialist mayors transferred the costs to employers by forcing them to provide paid work.

Although Lerroux was committed to improving the lot of underemployed and poorly paid day labourers, he was clear that the Republic was not about ruining the rural economy, especially if this was the price for ensuring socialist domination of the countryside. He was similarly unimpressed by the UGT's determination to increase its influence among urban workers by attempting to control the arbitration panels within industry and commerce. Lerroux suspected rightly that ultimately the UGT wanted to be sole mouthpiece of organised labour. As the socialists themselves made clear, this was a necessary part of the transformation of the 'bourgeois' state. Largo Caballero's decrees, which entailed the influx of his comrades into central and local organs of power, were part of a programme that included collectivisation and secularisation. These would be the levers that would propel Spain towards socialism. In other words, while the PSOE held the reins of political power, a UGT dominated state would own and manage the means of production and exchange.[21]

This march towards a socialist Republic not only threatened employers and property owners, but also the rival anarchosyndicalist movement. The CNT, of course, was never going to be a friend of the Republic. Indeed, it saw the events of April 1931 as the ideal opportunity to kickstart its revolutionary struggle for libertarian communism. But the CNT also entered the 1930s with an enormous appetite for revenge against a socialist movement that had co-operated with Primo de Rivera against it. The swift integration of the UGT within the Republican state ensured the victory of insurrectionist wing of the anarchosyndicalist movement over moderates; henceforth the CNT sought to break socialist hegemony by a series of strikes that would discredit its new arbitration system as well as preparing the ground for an insurrection against the Republican government. Employers quickly found that inter-union warfare was bad news for them. Despite obeying official strictures regarding pay rises and working conditions, industrial conflict continued unabated. This was one of the reasons why Lerroux saw the socialists as a destabilising element in government. Even before the constituent assembly had debated the question of whether the Republic should be liberal or socialist, the PSOE was taking advantage of its presence in the cabinet to appropriate parcels of power within the state and reinforce the position of its trade union partner. For that reason, Lerroux maintained that the socialists should not remain in power after the Constitution had been promulgated, and even before then a republican should occupy the labour ministry.

Yet the Radical leader had his doubts about whether his left republican allies were on the same wavelength. On taking office, he soon received disturbing reports from friendly army officers about the actions of their war minister. Lerroux considered Azaña one of the most dynamic figures of the government: he welcomed the reforms that dealt with the bloated size of the officer corps, since this deprived the army of the resources to modernise its armaments and installations. However, for the foreign minister, this was secondary to the task of converting the military's passivity of April 1931 into real support for the Republic. This was an exceptionally good opportunity, he believed, as most army officers had concluded after the experience of the dictatorship that they should never again get involved in politics. Lerroux regarded as essential not only a liberal Republic that preserved public order, but also a military policy that rewarded the tiny minority of republicans without discriminating against the majority of professional officers who had loyally served the monarchy. Only on this basis, he argued, could recalcitrant monarchists be safely deprived of their commands and the threat of insurrections disappear. So Lerroux deplored the pompous verbosity of Azaña's speeches whose sole purpose was to burnish an image of an energetic and radical leftist republican leader. His offensive language meant that the government's measures concerning officer retirements, postings and the restructuring of ranks were interpreted as politically inspired reprisals against the officer corps. Lerroux continued to develop his already extensive network of contacts within the military, and made contact with those disillusioned with Azaña, promising them directly or via the retired General Staff major and future Radical deputy Tomás Peire that a future Radical government would address their grievances.[22]

The Constitutional Debates

The Radicals' moderation received its political reward in the June 1931 general election. Lerroux was much more successful that Alcalá-Zamora and Maura in attracting not just those republicans who wanted an end to the revolution, but also former liberal monarchists who saw him as a symbol of stability and common sense. While the DLR failed to prosper in a generally leftist atmosphere, Lerroux was the most voted candidate on the electoral slates of both the Republican Alliance and the Republican-Socialist Alliance. He was elected to no less than five parliamentary seats, and received over 100,000 votes in Madrid, an unprecedented figure in Spanish politics. The overall result made the Republican Alliance the largest parliamentary grouping with 120 seats, and 89 of these deputies were Radicals, making Lerroux's party second only to the PSOE in the Cortes. A once marginal political force was now a serious contender for government.[23]

On the other hand, the result of the 1931 general election was hardly a triumph for those who wanted a liberal and moderate Republic. This was a self-inflicted defeat, as its advocates supinely gave the socialists control of the electoral register, allowed the sacking of 3,000 councils elected on 12 April, and agreeing to an electoral system that exaggerated the victory of the winning electoral slate. Since in the main monarchists did not engage with the election, and Lerroux chose to remain within the government, the victory of the governing Republican-Socialist Alliance was assured beforehand. The most important feature of the election therefore was the distribution of places on the governing coalition's electoral slates. In this, the interior minister Miguel Maura inexplicably refused to immerse himself in the negotiations, giving free rein to civil governors and the provincial leaders of the various parties. This led, as Alcalá-Zamora memorably put it, to a 'struggle towards the radical extremes' that 'pronounced the excommunication of moderate republicans'.[24] For every place given to a Radical or a moderate, 2.6 places were allocated to the socialists and left republicans.

Why was this the case? The role of the PSOE was critical. In socialist strongholds, local leaderships preferred to make pacts with left republicans to reduce the representation of those further to the right. This meant that the republican left were the biggest winners of the nomination process, as they were more likely to be included in socialist dominated slates while maintaining their quota within the Radical dominated Republican Alliance.[25] The PSOE's electoral strategy was logical. They wanted to take advantage of muscle provided by the UGT to establish a significant presence in parliament and aid those republicans who would not oppose their constitutional proposals. The marginalisation of Alcalá-Zamora's Liberal Republican Right, although it did not have a direct impact on the number of seats obtained by the Radicals, shifted the balance of power within the governing coalition to the left. Azaña and not Lerroux was now its political centre of gravity. Realising this, Azaña, who had been elected in Valencia and the Balearics due to Radical support, decided to create his own parliamentary group with the socialists as his preferred allies. The real winners of the election were therefore the Radicals' rivals on the left, as Lerroux could not obtain a majority that would enable him to govern.

The Radicals were not wholly comfortable with their unexpected new position on the right of the constituent assembly. Many of the party's deputies still held to traditional republican values and biases, especially after the experience of the dictatorship. On issues like the Church, the majority agreed with the socialists and left republicans, and did not much like the conciliatory discourse of their boss. After all, anticlericalism was one of the original pillars of the party and ditching it would create a great deal of fuss, especially among those Radicals who joined in the late 1920s. Yet ultimately the party was nothing without its charismatic leader. As we shall see, during the Republic Lerroux would encounter internal resistance, and even lose some of his colleagues, but as long as his leadership was the party's most important asset, he was still able to impose his agenda.

The evolution of the Radicals into a centre-right movement was also aided by other factors. These included its changing base as monarchist liberals flocked to the party. Also significant was the changing political context. Socialist demands for greater state control of the economy provoked the unanimous opposition of Radicals, and many were more strident in their criticisms than their leader. Proposals for greater regional autonomy did not muster much enthusiasm either and Lerroux had to use all of his authority to convince his deputies to support what had been agreed in the San Sebastian Pact. Without the religious issue, the Radical Party was indistinguishable from the Liberal Republican Right.

So it was hardly surprising that divisions between Lerroux and his left-wing partners in government deepened after the election. His 'Republic for all Spaniards' faced its most serious challenge in the constitutional debates. The socialists and left republicans advocated a regime that placed secularism and collectivism above civil liberties and representative government. The socialists supported left republican leaders such as Azaña, Domingo and Albornoz when they denounced Lerroux as the last defender of outdated monarchist politics. The Radical leader's own inconsistencies only facilitated the work of his rivals. Lerroux had little confidence in the proposed Constitution but did not want to burn his bridges with a republican left that he would need to govern in future. He really wanted the whole issue to be delayed until the revolutionary passions of April 1931 had subsided. Lerroux warned against Spain becoming 'an experimental guinea pig'. But this was precisely what the opponents of a moderate Republic wanted.

The new foreign minister cut an increasingly isolated figure in the Provisional Government. Much of this was self-inflicted. He distanced himself from many of its most controversial measures in order to elude responsibility and protest against his 'bottling up' within his ministry. He took advantage of his post to spend long periods abroad, especially in September 1931 when he chaired an assembly of the League of Nations. As relations with the Vatican began to deteriorate, Lerroux gave a formulaic defence of government policy, while cordially hinting that a Radical administration would do things differently. His *de facto* abstention from daily politics left his party rudderless during the constitutional debates. Rather than provide a clear and consistent stance that would obtain conservative support, his deputies preferred to pick fights with the socialists on questions that they vainly hoped would bring the left republicans back to them. Lerroux himself, anxious to avoid giving any hostages to fortune, seemed to prefer the public meeting to parliament, and sought to enhance his public image with more right-wing voters by calling his party 'conservative Republican'.[26]

This meant that Lerroux did not take part in the so-called 'responsibilities' debates when republicans demanded that the King and leading members of the dictatorship and the Berenguer government be put on trial. He left the famous Article 26 parliamentary debate on the religious issue early, although only after he gave his deputies a free vote on Azaña's motion which undermined a more moderate decision taken earlier by the government and which provoked the resignation of Alcalá-Zamora. Since Article 26 dissolved the Jesuits, banned religious orders from teaching and economic activities as well as giving parliament the right to dissolve them and confiscate their assets, Lerroux quickly clarified that his party had only voted in favour of the separation of Church and State. The Radicals, he went on, were not committed to the rest of the Article, or indeed the other 'ultra-radical criteria' of the Constitution that denied 'the rights of citizenship to those who did not share our ideas'. He would respect all constitutional clauses while 'not in power' but intimated that when he takes office he would promote 'a policy of consensus, tolerance and respect for the other'.[27]

Lerroux's lack of leadership at this critical juncture in the history of the Republic needs to be placed in the wider context. The convergence of socialists and left republicans gave the Radicals little opportunity to play a more active role as this would have entailed accepting the definition of Spain as a 'Republic of workers of all classes', as well as other leftist shibboleths like regional autonomy and expropriation without compensation, which subordinated property rights to the whims of parliament. The marginalisation of the Radicals also meant that they had little input in the institutional organisation of the new Republic, and their well-founded proposals on bicameralism and the inviolability of a directly elected presidency were consigned to the dustbin of Republican constitutional history. Certainly, one cannot accuse the Radicals of devising a constitutional distribution of powers that were 'confused, anarchic and impractical' and that in Lerroux's opinion problematised 'the exercise of presidential, governmental and parliamentary power'. Ironically, the only issue where the Radicals succeeded in isolating the socialists concerned female suffrage, and on that occasion the party disowned its own deputy Clara Campoamor by opposing votes for women.

The Radicals only supported the Constitution in order to remain within the political system. Lerroux was convinced that it needed to be revised before the ink was dry. During discussions with Cambó in Paris that autumn, the Lliga leader advised him that the Radicals should concentrate their efforts on reducing the obstacles to constitutional reform because 'the Constitution that they are voting on is a centipede that cannot be sustained'. In an interview with *Ahora* weeks before its promulgation, Lerroux warned that it would be difficult to enforce the Constitution because one had to combine loyalty to its clauses with 'indispensable flexibility' towards its 'pernicious precociousness'. The text reflected 'the evolutionary stage' of a people that Spain 'does not yet have'.[28]

Azaña Takes Power

The resignations of Alcalá-Zamora and Maura over Article 26 created a difficult political problem. As there was still no Constitution, the socialist president of the Cortes, Julián Besteiro, provisionally took on the powers of a head of state while a solution emerged from within the Provisional Government. To the surprise of many of his ministerial colleagues, Lerroux provided the answer. Knowing that he was in a minority within the cabinet, Lerroux ruled himself out of the premiership, and proposed Azaña instead. He knew that the left republican leader enjoyed the confidence of the socialists, and given that he provoked the crisis, it seemed obvious that Azaña should be the man to end it.[29]

Lerroux's refusal to fight for the top job was logical. The departure of the Liberal Republican Right from the government and Alcalá-Zamora's evident desire to lead a movement that would revise the Constitution suggested that the Republican-Socialist Alliance of 1930 was broken. Azaña's new government, Lerroux reasoned, would be ephemeral, created only to pass the Constitution and elect the first president. After that, his nominal subordinate within the republican movement would have to resign, as Azaña was not politically strong enough to lead a government needed to pass the subsidiary constitutional legislation or continue the reforms interrupted by the June 1931 election. In the Radical leader's mind, there were three options: the *status quo*, a PSOE or a Radical led government. Lerroux preferred the first, as long as the socialists occupied fewer ministerial posts, with Largo Caballero being one of the casualties. If the socialists refused and left the government, the Radicals were prepared to lead an exclusively republican government that would dispatch a minimum legislative programme before calling fresh elections in the following spring or summer.[30] Lerroux was only too aware that he could not govern with the current parliament as the socialists, radical-socialists, the ERC, and conservatives could come together to vote down his government. The Radical leader was also conscious of the risk that the socialists and left republicans could form a coalition, although he believed that circumstances worked against the formation of such a government. After the bitter constitutional debates, it seemed to him inevitable that the legislative programme needed to be moderate; the downturn in the economy, worsening industrial relations and the deterioration of public order were evidence enough that the socialist presence in government did not contribute to the stabilisation of the Republic.

The Radicals' problem was to convince the left republicans to form a coalition without the socialists. Lerroux did not understand the weak parliamentary position of his party. Irrespective of whether the Radicals joined a PSOE-republican government or not, it could not vigorously oppose its policies, as this would mean criticising the left republicans, their future coalition partners. This, of course, was the basic dilemma during the debates on the Constitution, and only a fresh election could overcome it. Meanwhile, Lerroux was obliged to strike a difficult balance between collaboration and opposition, and in terms of the Constitution this meant not moving beyond vague promises to 'sweeten', 'slow down' or 'make more flexible' its implementation. Unconcerned with the detail, Lerroux attempted simultaneously to reassure the left republicans that the Radicals would not support constitutional revision, while at the same time encouraging moderates to believe that they would be less sectarian than the left republicans. While in the short-term these contradictions excluded the Radical Party from power, Lerroux would benefit from the swing to the right in the 1933 elections.

Therefore, those who thought in the autumn of 1931 that Lerroux would soon be prime minister were being excessively optimistic. This prospect horrified the socialists, and they were prepared to offer the Radical leader the presidency in order to stave it off. Lerroux correctly saw this proposal as an attempt to decapitate the only serious opposition to the PSOE, and suggested Alcalá-Zamora. For the Radical leader, the former prime minister represented the constitutional past and present, and symbolised better than anyone else the end of the revolution. On a more mundane level, the elevation of Alcalá-Zamora also eliminated a rival for the moderate vote. In any case, Lerroux could not think of a better partner to steer the Republic away from the rocks of political extremism, asking rhetorically: 'what other government could better obtain the confidence of the new president than a centrist coalition led by the Radicals?'[31]

Alcalá-Zamora's candidacy also attracted the support of the left republicans mindful of political advantage. For them, his occupation of the presidency would neutralise a significant threat to the new Constitution. Therefore, with the support of all the parties of the Republican-Socialist Alliance, Alcalá-Zamora became the first president of the Republic on 11 December 1931. As expected, Azaña resigned the premiership immediately: he required the confidence of the new head of state to continue. Yet Alcalá-Zamora did not have complete freedom to appoint the prime minister. Following pre-1923 constitutional practise, any Republican government now required the confidence of both the president and a parliament that had met for at least five months in a year. Alcalá-Zamora's responsibility, then, was similar to that of Alfonso XIII: he was expected to arbitrate between the government and the parliament, either choosing a prime minister who was able to secure a majority or giving a prime minister of his confidence the opportunity to obtain a majority by dissolving parliament and holding fresh elections. In the event that the president's favoured head of government failed to win, the head of state had to accept the reality of a hostile new parliament. Unlike Alfonso XIII, however, the president could only dissolve parliament twice; after the second occasion, the Cortes would examine the reasons behind the dissolution and had the power to sack the president if it was deemed unnecessary. This potentially made the president politically responsible for a decision taken with the support of ministers.

This constitutional rule made a mockery of the principle that the head of state should be an honest broker between the parties. It was like giving football managers the opportunity to review a sending-off and dismiss the referee. What made this even worse in December 1931 was the uncertainty surrounding the status of the constituent assembly. Could Alcalá-Zamora dissolve a parliament whose length of term was undefined? The consensus within parliament was that it could only be dissolved once it had completed its work or that it could no longer produce majority governments. Therefore, Alcalá-Zamora had no choice but to work with the existing Cortes. In theory, the new prime minister would have come from the largest parties, which meant the PSOE or the Radicals. But neither wanted to head a government, and both argued for the continuation of the coalition. This would have a legislative agenda, although its extent remained conjectural; as we have seen, the Radicals preferred a minimum programme followed by an election, while the socialists and left republicans spoke of dozens of laws and a prolonged parliament. Alcalá-Zamora's decision to approach Azaña for the premiership was thus a predictable one. This was not the case of asking the leader of barely 26 deputies to form a government, but a representative of the Republican Alliance who enjoyed the support of the socialists.

Lerroux did not object in principle to Azaña's appointment. Yet as he reminded the latter, the Republican Alliance's National Council had agreed that any coalition government should have a reduced socialist presence and a new incumbent in the labour ministry. If this was unacceptable to the PSOE, then an exclusively republican administration should be placed before the president. Azaña ignored these conditions. After consulting the socialists, the left republican leader informed the Radical leader that the PSOE would occupy education and public works portfolios, with Largo Caballero continuing in his post. This meant, as Lerroux realised, that the socialist permeation of all levels of the state would continue unchecked. Even worse, the Radicals were only offered the same ministries that they had held under Alcalá-Zamora: foreign affairs and communications. Azaña alleged that he could not get more: 'the socialists were intransigent, irreducible and threatening'. Nevertheless, he bowed to the PSOE in order to avoid them going into opposition. Lerroux immediately refused to join the new government.[32]

Azaña should have turned down the premiership as the Radicals dominated the Republican Alliance. Indeed, he had previously promised the Radical leader that without his approval he would withdraw his candidacy. To be fair to Azaña, Lerroux wanted it both ways: he did not want to serve with the socialists or be seen as the politician responsible for breaking the Republican-Socialist Alliance. He therefore announced that while there would be no Radical ministers, his party would continue to vote for the government. On that basis, Alcalá-Zamora asked Azaña to form a more narrowly based coalition government. On 17 December, the new prime minister told the Cortes of his wide-ranging but ambiguous programme, and told deputies that there would be no elections until his ambitious agenda had been implemented. This was a disaster for Lerroux; not only were his hopes of an early dissolution dashed, but he was in political no-man's land, both out of power and not in opposition.[33]

1 When the Second Republic was proclaimed in 1931, Lerroux was 67 and towards the end of a long political career.

2 Between 1931 and 1935, Lerroux made the Radical Party the most popular republican party in Spain. The Radical leader is here shown voting in the 1931 elections.

3 Lerroux founded the Radical Party in 1908 and was its only leader. The party leadership, from left to right: Rafael Guerra del Río, Juan José Rocha, Antonio de Lara and Ricardo Samper. Sitting from left to right: Diego Martínez Barrio, Alejandro Lerroux and Santiago Alba.

4 If Lerroux was an unremarkable journalist, he was nevertheless one of the greatest orators in Spain before 1936.

5 On his 69th birthday in March 1933, Lerroux received more than a million cards and letters from well-wishers all over Spain, anticipating his electoral triumph that autumn.

6 Lerroux formed his first government with left republicans in September 1933. It lasted for less than a month, and new elections were held two months later.

7 In October 1934, the President of the Generalidad, Luis Companys (on the left), rebelled against the Lerroux government.

8 In October 1934, Lerroux defended liberal democracy against the Workers' Alliance of socialists and communists, enabling the democratic Republic to last almost two more years. In the photo and its enlargement, Lerroux comes out to greet a demonstration in support of the government.

9 General Domingo Batet (on the left) defeated the catalanist rebellion in Barcelona in October 1934. Lerroux receives Batet to congratulate him.

10 The *estraperlo* scandal was the promotion of a rigged roulette game that involved Lerroux's nephew and other minor Radical officials. In the image, the roulette wheel set up in the San Sebastián casino.

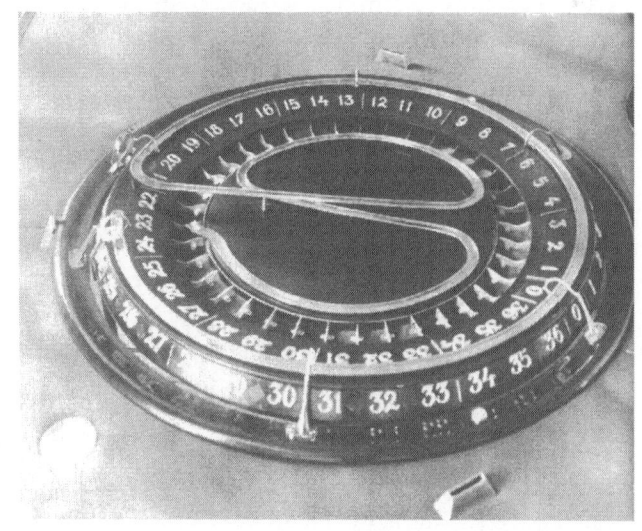

5
Leader of the Republican Opposition (1932–1933)

Azaña's diaries show the extent to which Lerroux's efforts to avoid a break with his fellow republican became hopeless by June 1932. After initially expressing gratitude to the Radical leader for getting the top job, the prime minister increasingly distanced himself from his one-time ally and publicly poured scorn on the suggestion that he should step aside to allow Lerroux to form an all-republican administration. Although his parliamentary group only existed courtesy of the Radicals, Azaña saw the socialists as his strategic partners. The bloated legislative programme of an ongoing constituent assembly reflected the fact that the prime minister saw the passage of the Constitution not as the beginning of the end but rather the end of the beginning of his government. With scarcely 26 deputies – barely 5% of the seats – and a weak extra-parliamentary party, Azaña was determined to lead a coalition that would infuse the still skeletal constitutional body of the Republic with a leftist spirit that was incompatible with the liberal and moderate hopes of Lerroux and which would inexorably lead the Radical leader into opposition. This would signify the failure of the Radicals to separate the left republicans from the socialists, and the death knell of a now meaningless Republican Alliance.

The divorce between Azaña and Lerroux – later described by the famous historian and diplomat Salvador de Madariaga as nothing less than the most significant single cause of the civil war – was rooted in a basic political disagreement. The former passionately believed that the fall of the monarchy gave Spain a golden opportunity to redeem herself with a republican and class-based programme that would integrate the socialist movement. The prime minister considered that Lerroux's efforts to widen the social base of the Republic by incorporating former monarchists repeated the baneful compromise between 'liberal' and 'reactionary' Spain that had characterised the Restoration period.

Indeed, as far as Azaña was concerned, Lerroux was nothing more than another monarchist, interested only in holding power and rewarding his minions with public money. 'The dominance of Lerroux in the Government of the Republic', he wrote in his diary, 'would mean immorality and vacuousness'. His leadership was barely 'average', inspired by a 'narrow, mean and unprincipled spirit'; the Radical leader would never evolve from an 'agitator corrupted' by the monarchy into a 'Republican statesman'. Leftist republicans therefore should have nothing to do with the 'advent of Lerrouxism' that would 'discredit the Republic by committing the cardinal sin of creating a lack of trust in the probity of its politicians'. In any case, a confident Azaña prophesised that the Radicals had already passed their peak, having 'reached a position in Spanish politics that [they] could only swiftly fall from'.[1]

In sum, the rise of Lerroux was regarded as an 'infection', as it placed the new regime in danger of being 'monarchised' or being poisoned by the values or political practises of the Restoration. Leaving aside Azaña's typically pejorative style, the prime minister's analysis was not too far from the truth. It was true that the once fiery young republican leader now happily associated himself with the set of values that emphasised respect, freedoms, compromise and a consensual transfer of power that had characterised constitutional politics before 1923 and which was clearly antithetical to Azaña's project of privileging some Spaniards over others. This, and not the doubts about the moral integrity of the Radicals, was the cause of his split with Lerroux. After all, the republican-socialist coalition was hardly a government of civic virtue as clientelist practises flourished and the politically favoured were given government jobs. It is no accident that the term *enchufismo* (literally being 'plugged in') was popularised during Azaña's premiership to describe how public positions were used to reward political friends.[2]

The only uncertainty is whether Azaña's aversion of Lerroux was merely a pretext to legitimise a refusal to countenance a change of government. It was certainly odd that he stressed the Radical leader's connivance with the old political elite when his preferred ally, the socialists, had collaborated with the dictatorship. Was Azaña's discourse an attempt to defend the decision to emancipate the 'new republicans' from their Radical tutelage by going over to the socialists? Perhaps it was this and more. Azaña had glimpsed at the possibility of establishing the hegemony of the left, as the revolution could only be defended by new and virtuous men such as himself who were unsullied by doubts brought on by political experience. If that was the case, then republicans like Lerroux truly had no place within the Republic.

The Moderate Alternative

The benevolence of the Radical leader towards the new government lasted only until the latter's declaration of its parliamentary programme. In January 1932, it was evident that Azaña would sponsor a series of measures on divorce, the dissolution of the Jesuits, and the secularisation of cemeteries and funerals. Lerroux knew that whatever the merits of these reforms, they were not part of the legislation needed to implement the clauses of the Constitution. The latter included laws on religious congregations, the criminal responsibility of the president of the Republic, the Constitutional Guarantees Court, and the gamut of decrees that regulated the exercise of civil rights or the powers of representative institutions (such as electoral and public order acts). When the Catalan Statute – which was part of the remit of the constituent assembly – was sent to the Cortes, it was coupled with controversial legislation on land reform. Both were received by a wave of amendments that suggested an arduous parliamentary passage of at least several months. To make a dissolution an even more distant prospect, Azaña announced that because of female suffrage, a new electoral register needed to be compiled of all Spaniards over the age of 18.

The Radical response to these events was predictable. Lerroux proclaimed that his party's priority would be to moderate the Catalan State and the proposed agrarian reform; the rights of central government and private property had to be safeguarded. In February, he took the bold, if inevitable, step of formally moving his party into opposition; the Radicals were not willing to suffer the opprobrium that Lerroux felt the government's legislation would produce.[3] On 21 February, the former foreign minister told his audience in Madrid's bullring that the revolution was over and therefore the socialist presence in government was no longer needed since the Republic was not one of 'class' or 'party'. He stressed that the new regime could only be consolidated on the basis of tolerance, mutual respect and understanding that would make the Republic the natural 'political home of all Spaniards'. The Radicals, a 'liberal, democratic and republican' party, was the best means to achieve this noble goal, as it did not identify with any particular 'religious belief' or 'social class'. When they are called to government, Lerroux promised, the Radicals would become a 'dike' against tax rises, ill-considered land reform that did not provide adequate compensation for property owners, and a Catalan Statute that imperils national sovereignty and erodes civil and municipal rights. Having now broken with the government, the party's 'silences' were now over and it was prepared to take power. Lerroux demanded that Azaña clarify exactly what legislation was needed to enforce the Constitution, as the public did not want the Cortes to 'kidnap ... the sovereignty of the nation'.[4]

The demand for moderation and the expectation of a Radical government brought political dividends for the party. Lerroux's popularity rose among those who wanted a liberal Republic purged of anticlerical and socialist excesses. 'He will know', assured Melquíades Álvarez, 'how to protect freedom and maintain order'. The former reformist was not the only one to pledge their support for Lerroux. In a mass meeting in Barcelona, the Radical leader received the backing of key intellectuals and business leaders. In the capital, the Press Association elected him its president, and members of one of Spain's most prestigious cultural organisations, the Círculo de Bellas Artes, did likewise, a significant indication of growing dissatisfaction with a government containing liberal professionals including Azaña himself. Although Lerroux was careful not to attack the left republicans too harshly, he spared no effort in accusing the socialists of wanting to monopolise power and aiding those who attacked property and persecuted religion, thereby threatening 'social harmony' and even the 'existence of the Republic'. Moreover, he no longer hesitated to criticise aspects of the Constitution such as the absence of an upper chamber or technical committees that could support the work of government.[5]

Despite the claims of those who decried his abilities as a political leader, Lerroux was reaping the rewards of a strategy that created clear blue water between his party and his former republican allies anxious to position themselves firmly on the left. Although the Radicals themselves contained a not insignificant left-wing, Lerroux was conscious that the ideological complexion of the constituent assembly did not fully reflect that of Spain, and that many liberal and conservative voters felt bereft of representation. What the Radical leader did not recognise in early 1932 was the possibility that a serious competitor to his party might emerge from the right. After all, with Alcalá-Zamora now occupying the presidency, and Miguel Maura making no impact as leader of the Liberal Republican Right, it seemed as though there was no obvious rival to Lerroux for the moderate vote. Not only did the former foreign minister have good relationships with former monarchist leaders, but his appeals for Catholics to cooperate in the refashioning of the Republic secured him the goodwill, if not necessarily the active support, of most on the right.

On this assumption, Lerroux hoped to create a new republican federation with his party at its core. This would be the springboard to a parliamentary majority at the next general election. The continuing economic crisis suggested that victory was within his grasp. His calls for moderation took place in the context of deepening social conflict, spiralling unemployment, and more frequent strikes and business closures. The alliance between socialists and left republicans began to fissure at provincial level, as the latter's civil governors and mayors supported the police in confrontations with UGT militants. Indeed, some Radical-Socialists and left republicans began to question the continuing role of the socialists in government, agreeing with Lerroux that this only increased trade union militancy, impeded the efforts of the authorities to restore public order and deterred private investment. Significantly, left republican activists in localities with socialist mayors often defected to the Radical Party. This was especially true in the countryside, as proposed agrarian reform, welcomed with enthusiasm by UGT leaders because it allowed union-dominated collectives, provoked unease among republican smallholders and tenant farmers. They too increasingly looked to Lerroux for protection as for them the Republic had come to spread property ownership, not destroy it.[6]

Spain in Danger

The Catalan Statute extended protests against the government to those areas that had escaped the worst of the economic crisis. An extensive network of civil associations that included trade unions, employers' groups, educational institutions and professional bodies supported the campaign against autonomy led by republican provincial and local councils. Street agitation soon gave way to acrimonious parliamentary disputes. If discussion of agrarian reform was slow and tedious, carried out by bored deputies with mainly urban backgrounds, the debates on the Catalan Statute were passionate and shook the foundations of the government. The lack of confidence in Maciá, who demanded ample autonomy without repudiating Catalan independence, was felt among all parties as memories of his declaration of the Catalan Republic were still fresh. Moreover, few also forgot the subsequent struggle between the Provisional Government and the Generalidad (the new name for the Catalan administration), as Maciá took advantage of his 'pre-autonomous' status to seize powers from Madrid.

Within the parliamentary Radical Party, only Blasco-Ibáñez's Valencian deputies were not hostile to Catalan autonomy. Lerroux's opposition began with the draft text and its approval by catalanist dominated local councils; he then condemned the decision to hold a plebiscite in Catalonia on its contents on 2 August 1931. The referendum was an obvious attempt to put pressure on the Cortes and was organised by a Generalidad without legal guarantees; the overwhelming victory of the

Yes campaign was a formality. To the disgust of many deputies, Azaña then ruled that parliamentary discussion of the Catalan Statute was to take place within strict limits; the Cortes could neither reject the text for one of its own, nor amend the existing text to grant fewer powers than those stipulated in the Constitution. In other words, the terms of the San Sebastian Pact effectively rendered null and void the constituent power of parliament.

Struck by the scale of opposition to the Catalan Statute both inside and outside the Cortes, Azaña appealed to Lerroux to support the measure on the basis of the August 1930 Pact. In a parliamentary speech of 20 May 1932, the Radical leader reaffirmed his party's support for the principle of autonomy but maintained that the Cortes was entirely free to approve or reject the Statute. He condemned the catalanist text as invasive of central powers and opposed any concessions on public order, justice, finance and education. The Radical Party, he went on, would also support the continued ascendency of Spanish as the official language in communications between the state and its citizens, particularly in the courts and universities. He concluded that the Radicals would only support the Statute if there were a substantial reduction to the powers that the Generalidad had arrogated to itself. Outside parliament, Lerroux went further, adding that his party would support the inclusion of a procedure that would suspend the Statute if the political and economic unity of Spain were ever to be placed in jeopardy. While his words were received with enthusiasm by moderate republicans and agrarian conservatives, the ERC not surprisingly raged against what they saw as an attempt to defy the will of the Catalan people. Although Azaña managed to prevent the left catalanists from walking out of parliament, majority opinion within the Cortes remained hostile to the government's attempt to prevent a free discussion of the text. By the summer of 1932, passage of the Statute had paralysed, and the ERC preferred to give up on it entirely rather than return powers that the left catalanist dominated Generalidad had *de facto* enjoyed since the proclamation of the Republic. Moreover, opposition had become so intense that even the pro-government press accepted as an 'undeniable fact' the observation that the 'majority of Spain' was against autonomy; while it may be unwelcome, it was 'damaging and absurd to deny or ignore' this evident truth.[7]

The Sanjurjo Coup of August 1932

The deterioration of public order and the political storm over the Catalan Statute encouraged the gestation of a military conspiracy focussed on general Sanjurjo. Although he had accepted the Republic the previous year, socialist criticism of bloody clashes between the Civil Guard and the UGT in Castilblanco (Badajoz), Arnedo (Logroño) and other places in the winter of 1931–32 led to Sanjurjo being transferred from his command of the Civil Guard to the Carabineros, the customs police. Throughout this time, the general maintained his friendship with Lerroux, believing the Radical leader to be the personification of the true Republic of 14 April, and someone unwilling to sacrifice the national interest by agreeing to the demands of socialists or catalanists. Furthermore, Sanjurjo did not hide his disgust with Azaña's military reforms, slights of the officer corps and postings from his political chum, and Lerroux had to convince him to accept the post of director general of the Carabineros.

If Sanjurjo did not convey a particularly sophisticated analysis of the shortcomings of the Republic to the Radical leader, some of his comrades-in-arms were prepared to offer a violent solution in the first months of 1932. They saw Sanjurjo's prestige within the military as the magnet to attract those willing to stage a 1923-style *pronunciamiento* to overthrow the Azaña government. With the same naivety, they also sought to involve Lerroux in this madcap enterprise. After all, were republicans not inveterate conspirators? The Radical leader thought something was amiss when Sanjurjo invited him for dinner and railed against Azaña, telling him something that he already knew: a Radical government would not be poorly received by the officer corps. The veteran plotter suspected that he was being sounded out for his attitude towards a possible rebellion, but kept his silence having taken the precaution of bringing fellow Radicals Martínez Barrio and Azpiazu to the meal. Since the latter was a close associate of Sanjurjo, Lerroux used him to pass on the message that his scheming days ended in April 1931. He hoped to dissuade a general associated with his party not to ruin his reputation by getting involved in another one of the many comic opera risings that the republican had seen fail during his long political career.[8]

For Lerroux, the conspiracy was yet more evidence that Azaña had failed to consolidate the regime by the summer of 1932. It reinforced an optimism that the ever more popular Radicals were getting closer to power, as the creaking ship of government seemingly faced the imminent prospect of being torpedoed by the failures of Catalan autonomy and agrarian reform. Azaña's majority was at risk by splits and (above all), non-attendance in debates. The relations between the left republicans, the PSOE and ERC were fractured, even if at this stage not quite yet beyond repair. A rebellion would only serve to resuscitate a political corpse.

Despite this, Sanjurjo resolved to continue. Lerroux tried to stave off a rising by negotiating a change of government in a secret meeting with Azaña on 10 June, but the prime minister refused to join any administration without the presence of the PSOE. The Radical leader then received Sanjurjo in his hotel in Baños de Montemayor and became perplexed at the latter's explanation of the political nature of the conspiracy. The general had obtained the support of a ragbag of monarchist and republican generals and foresaw an initial military junta that would eventually appoint a government and hold elections. For Sanjurjo's monarchist backers, this would produce another constituent assembly that would consider the restoration of the monarchy. Increasingly alarmed, Lerroux informed Azaña via Martínez Barrio on 22 June that growing disillusionment within the army could provoke a coup against him. The prime minister, who was already aware of the conspiracy, demanded to know who was involved, and received a frosty response from a Radical leader not prepared to inform on Sanjurjo or expose his sources to danger on what was still (at this point) gossip. Lerroux again used Martinez Barrio as an intermediary to consult with fellow moderates Ortega y Gasset, Sánchez Román, and Miguel Maura, and they all advised him against revealing the identities of those suspected to be involved in the plot. In this manner, Lerroux was able to protect his political reputation without falling out with Sanjurjo.[9]

Having failed to negotiate an end to the republican-socialist coalition, Lerroux increased the pressure for its resignation. At a mass meeting in Zaragoza on 10 July, he assailed ministers while praising the Church and the military for loyally coming to terms with the 'injustices' imposed on them by the government. He warned however that 'within this silence ... seditious actions' might be under consideration in the army, actions that could not be suppressed by force as the reasons behind them did not 'lack foundation'. He dismissed the 'socialising experiments' and the work of socialist local councils, who he claimed were promoting disorder. A Radical government, he pledged, would re-establish 'harmony within the rule of law' and given the urgency demanded that Alcalá-Zamora appoint a new administration.[10]

Lerroux's appeal to the president provoked the wrath of socialist and left republican leaders. They accused the Radical leader of monarchist style dirty tricks. In doing so, his critics forgot how they themselves managed to take power in the first place. Lerroux's approach to Alcalá-Zamora was a logical one. The Constitution had instituted a 'double confidence' system that gave the president the right to appoint and remove the prime minister and Azaña conceded this point in a parliamentary debate nine days later when Lerroux resumed his offensive against the government. Responding to Azaña's gibe that voters ultimately determined the president's choice of prime minister, the Radical leader asked rhetorically why the government was afraid of calling by-elections for the numerous vacancies that had arisen in the Cortes. Although he did not explicitly break with the left republicans, he announced that the government no longer had his party's confidence.[11]

Azaña's 'Defence of the Republic'

On 10 August 1932, the long expected *pronunciamiento* finally took place. Restricted to Madrid and Seville, Sanjurjo triumphed in the latter but quickly realised that his putsch was a failure elsewhere. Attempting to flee to Portugal, the general was arrested in Huelva. Informed of the coup by José Valdivia, his contact within the police, Lerroux followed its lack of progress from his summer home in San Rafael. After Sanjurjo's arrest, the Radicals were quick to condemn the rebellion, although Lerroux did praise its leader for accepting its failure peacefully. When Sanjurjo was taken to Madrid for questioning, he insisted on taking full responsibility for the doomed venture, leading the Radical leader to compare him favourably to those romantic military leaders of his youth who accepted defeat with dignity and grace.

This did not imply that Lerroux considered the coup to be anything other than a political calamity. His fears that the republican-socialist government would be strengthened by his friend's stupidity were justified: henceforth Azaña identified his policies with the 'defence of the Republic'. With his oppositional strategy in tatters and under suspicion for his known association with Sanjurjo, Lerroux had no option but to support the purge of 'anti-republican' elements that included the closure of 114 conservative newspapers and the deportation of 138 alleged rebels to the colonies. The government took advantage of the post-coup *ralliement* to radicalise its agrarian reform programme, which did not now just include the expropriation of land owned by those implicated in the conspiracy, but also those owned by aristocrats more generally. Azaña had more freedom to indulge his socialist allies, and an accompanying decree designed to encourage cultivation gave the UGT estates in large parts of Spain, including Extremadura and Andalusia. To the dismay of many Radical deputies, the prime minister's 'defence of the Republic' also entailed the passage of the outstanding clauses of the Catalan Statute, and a gloomy Lerroux had to corral his parliamentary party into supporting the government.[12]

In doing so, the Radical leader was hoping that the post-coup bounce for the republican-socialist coalition would be a very short one, and it did not take very long for Lerroux to break his unwanted truce with Azaña. With the economic situation still bleak and social conflict rife, the Radicals resumed its calls for moderation by the end of the year, denouncing the government for placing the interests of the UGT above those of everyone else, and turning the cause for social justice into 'something disturbing and hateful'. Lerroux considered Azaña and fellow left republican leaders Domingo and Albornoz as socialist fellow travellers and began to re-consider whether there could ever be an all-republican administration in the future. His misgivings only intensified in December 1932 with the creation of the Spanish Left Republican Parliamentary Federation (FIRPE). This included supporters of the prime minister, Radical-Socialists, the ERC and Galician republicans but not the Radicals, despite the efforts of Martínez Barrio. This was the biggest indication yet that the future for Spanish republicanism was on the left, working with the PSOE.[13]

Meanwhile the Radicals held their own National Congress in October 1932 to revamp the party structure. This had remained largely unchanged since the dictatorship despite the surge in membership. Nevertheless, the attempts to build a stronger extra-parliamentary party were ineffective and it would never resemble the effective electoral machine that Lerroux had built in Barcelona at the start of the century. Indeed, the Radical Party increasingly looked like the dynastic parties under Alfonso XIII, where the links between the leader and local party committees were its deputies and provincial leaders, with the latter appointed by the leader himself. Therefore, the parliamentary party remained the Radicals' governing body in the 1930s, although Congress did appoint an Executive Committee to share decision-making with Lerroux.[14] After the Radicals took power in September 1933, they had access to the public purse, and the traditional means of maintaining loyalty soon supplanted ideas of organisational reform.

The rising Radical tide reinforced Lerroux's control of the party. His colleagues were well aware that his charismatic leadership and moderate strategy were the keys to electoral success. This meant little opposition to the leader's *de facto* monopoly over the party's resources or direction of policy. Therefore, the Radicals' democratic constitution did not prevent Lerroux having the final word on internal disputes or restrict his capacity to make nominations for party or public posts. Having appointed his provincial subordinates, the latter would invoke Lerroux's name to strengthen their own positions; they were the leader's representatives in local communities rather than the defenders of local interests at national level. Even so, the Radical Party remained the best-organised and electorally most successful republican organisation.[15]

The Consequences of Casas Viejas

The establishment of the FIRPE by left republicans may have left Radicals fuming, but Lerroux saw it as an opportunity to launch a no holds barred assault on the government in the hope of forcing fresh elections. The first test of this strategy came with the political fallout over the suppression of the anarchist insurrection in the village of Casas Viejas in Cadiz province in January 1933. Press accounts revealed that during the shootout between rebels and the police, an Assault Guard squad shot anarchists out of hand as a reprisal for the deaths of three policemen. Journalists then reported that the killing was based on orders given by Police Headquarters in Madrid, who were following instructions issued by Azaña and Casares Quiroga, the war and interior ministers. When the government attempted to shift responsibility onto their subordinates, various Assault Guards responded by issuing a sworn statement that they had received verbal orders 'not to take wounded or prisoners'. The scandal was compounded by the fact that the Assault Guard had been founded by Azaña to defend the Republic.[16]

Lerroux attributed such irresponsible orders to hotheads in the midst of battle and refused to call for a criminal investigation against ministers or senior civil servants, slapping down his parliamentary spokesman, Guerra del Río, in the process. But he did call for the resignation of the government on 3 February and warned that the failure to do so would mean that henceforth the Radicals would obstruct parliamentary business. For the Radical leader, Casas Viejas not only exemplified the failure to keep the peace legally, but also the stark differences between the merciless persecution of the CNT-FAI and the lenience shown towards socialist perpetrators of crimes. Lerroux accused ministers of 'completely' and 'utterly' failing in three key respects: the consolidation of the Republic, the legislative implementation of the Constitution and the maintenance of public order. With the left in power, he thundered in the Cortes, unemployment rose, the economy declined, press freedoms curbed and social legislation used for sectarian purposes. Martínez Barrio was even more vehement two weeks later when he famously accused the government of bringing 'shame, tears and blood'.[17]

Azaña sought to overcome the opposition of the Radicals by bringing constitutional legislation to the Cortes. A personal appeal by Alcalá-Zamora to Lerroux ended the obstruction of the passage of the bills related to public order, the electoral system, the Constitutional Guarantees Court and religious congregations, as their approval would permit the self-dissolution of the constituent assembly. The last measure proved to be particularly contentious, as the government intended to restrict seriously the legal status and activities of religious orders, and stipulated the end of Catholic college education by the end of the following school year (a 'miracle', Lerroux observed, 'worthy of faqirs'). Although the Radicals supported secular education, its education spokesman, Salazar Alonso, demanded that the deadline be extended as state schools did not have the spare capacity for thousands of extra pupils. Lerroux also wanted some legal room for manoeuvre to give any future government the opportunity to extend timelines and negotiate with the Church. Nevertheless, Azaña was obdurate and the legislation was passed, although a furious Alcalá-Zamora initially refused to sign the decree as an expression of his loss of confidence in the prime minister. But if a similar act of disapproval by Alfonso XIII was enough to remove governments in the past, Azaña was not prepared to give way and the president caved in.[18]

Lerroux concluded that while Alcalá-Zamora desired a change of administration, he feared 'the most hostile criticism' if he dissolved the constituent assembly. He was aware that the president preferred the government and the opposition to agree on the date of any future election. In effect, this meant that if the left republicans remained in coalition with the socialists, Azaña's successor had to come from those parties already in power. For that reason, after having withdrawn his confidence in the prime minister, he sounded out figures from within the PSOE and the Radical-Socialist Party, the most significant pillars of the outgoing government. Although perfectly constitutional, Azaña and others on the left were not impressed by these 'manoeuvrings of personal policy'. An Azaña inspired editorial in *El Sol*, entitled 'Once and no more' told the president to desist.[19] Without a dissolution, therefore, Alcalá-Zamora had no alternative to Azaña, and would have to wait for the implosion of the governing coalition.

This was not an unreasonable expectation. Although the premier's disciples remained disciplined, the Radical-Socialists were in turmoil as Domingo and Albornoz desperately worked to prevent its anti-socialist right-wing from joining the Radicals. These fissures prompted a militant response from the socialists, who were determined to protect the privileges they had received in government. Alluding to the prospect of a Radical administration, Prieto warned that any change in government outside the existing coalition would be 'unconstitutional'. Largo Caballero went even further, warning that the dissolution of the Cortes would be a 'coup' and Lerroux as premier would signify the victory of 'reaction' that would provoke a 'civil war'.[20] Since the left republicans had sacrificed their voters to the interests of the PSOE and the ERC, the coalition staggered on out of pure inertia, fearful that a dissolution of the Cortes would trigger an electoral apocalypse for Azaña and the Radical-Socialists.

There was plenty of evidence to suggest that left's chances of winning the next election were slim. Lerroux received a staggering 1,300,000 letters, cards and telegrams on his 69th birthday that March, and thousands of Spaniards paraded outside his home. A month later, the opposition triumphed in the local elections, winning 70% of the seats. While the Radicals obtained more councillors than any other single party, alarm bells rang at party headquarters in calle O'Donnell when they realised that the Catholic and agrarian right had won the most votes overall.[21]

Lerroux required no further prompting to push his colleagues further towards the centre-right in order to win a working majority at the next general election. In the summer of 1933, the Radical leader spoke openly of significant constitutional reform. However, this was not just about staving off the challenge of the CEDA or the agrarians. Lerroux was concerned that a growing number of Spaniards conflated the Republic with Azaña and the PSOE and drew the conclusion that they would be better voting for parties who did not identify with the new regime. He was indignant that the left refused to dissolve an out-of-touch constituent assembly that had completed its work; his dismay was compounded by the extraordinary fact that the Constitutional Guarantees Court decree prevented the new tribunal from re-examining the constitutionality of all legislation passed between April 1931 and June 1933, irrespective of whether or not these laws complied with the Republic's Magna Carta.

Significantly, it would be elections to the Constitutional Guarantees Court held that summer that finally put an end to the government. Most of its membership was chosen by local councillors grouped together in regional lists, with a minority selected by legal associations and university law faculties. Opposition parties obtained over two-thirds of the former, with the Radicals and the rightist parties sharing out the spoils equally; Lerroux's candidates won more votes than the leftist slate combined. It was a stunning defeat for Azaña, and suggested the extent to which his administration had failed to consolidate the Republic, as prominent figures associated with the monarchy and the dictatorship were returned on the votes of lawyers who had turned against Alonso XIII. Those elected included exiles like José Calvo Sotelo, Primo de Rivera's former finance minister, and even the imprisoned Juan March, the tobacco king of the Balearics.

These were bittersweet results for Lerroux. Although they dealt a heavy blow to the ruling coalition, he recognised the danger they posed for the Republic. On 6 September, he declared that he had no confidence in the government, and in an angry debate with Azaña accused the prime minister of putting the historic achievement of April 1931 in jeopardy. He hissed that if the left continued in power, the electoral defeat of all republicans was inevitable and both 'the Republic and the country would be lost'. To avoid that calamity, he announced that he would have no further dealings with ministers, saying that to calm the country and keep public confidence, 'I can no longer maintain any kind of relationship with that Government'.[22] Alcalá-Zamora immediately responded by asking Azaña to resign. The following day, 7 September 1933, the former muckraking journalist left the Presidential Palace as prime minister. Lerroux's difficult task was to give substance to the Radical slogan a 'Republic for all Spaniards'.

6

Prime Minister
(1933–1934)

In his memoirs, the CEDA leader José María Gil-Robles repeatedly stressed his ideological differences with Lerroux. 'There was a gulf', he wrote, 'between our ideas, [and] his friends and [republican] background were distasteful to me. Given his political position, my contact with him was strictly limited, determined only by the supreme interests of the nation'. Yet he did not hesitate to praise the Radical leader for his willingness to work with the Spanish Confederation of Autonomous Right-Wing Groups (CEDA) in parliament and then in government, noting that 'I always thought that Alejandro Lerroux was greater than his party... at all times when we sat opposite each other examining the problems of Spain, I could see his clarity of judgement, human feeling, loyalty to the task at hand, a noble heart and his deep patriotism'.[1] The agreement between both of them symbolised an elitist pact that would later generate close synergies between very distinct political movements.

It is certainly true that this *entente* would have been unthinkable without the common experience of opposition to the republican-socialist coalition. Common antipathy towards Azaña's policies reduced the political distance between a once leftist republican party and a Catholic movement more right wing than the dynastic parties that Lerroux had faced before 1923. Nevertheless, the CEDA was no reinvention of the old Catholic leagues or even the short-lived Christian right Social Popular Party of 1922–24. Its leaders and activists came from the liberal-conservative and agrarian organisations that formed the constitutional right under the monarchy. The closer identification of Catholics with the centre-right paralleled the Radicals' overtures to those on the former monarchist left in the hope of occupying the political space held by the Liberal Party until 1917.

Even so, a *rapprochement* between the Radicals and the CEDA only took place in November 1933. Until then, Lerroux saw the latter as a rival for the conservative vote, and when he became prime minister that

September, he faced opposition from both the left and the right. Thus at the same time as dismantling socialist patronage networks within the labour, public works and education ministries, he faced a confident CEDA determined to diminish the huge pro-republican majority produced in the previous general election of June 1931. Thanks to the polarisation of the two previous years, Lerroux's hope that the Radicals would constitute the main alternative to the left looked unlikely to be realised.

This was confirmed on the night of 19 November 1933 when the first round of the elections showed the extent of the collapse in the left republican vote. Lerroux reacted skilfully to break the electoral unity of his opponents on his right, separating the CEDA and the agrarians of Martínez de Velasco from those monarchists determined to end the new regime. By accepting that constitutional reform was necessary, the Radical leader hoped to enlist the former in his quest to consolidate the moderate Republic. That entailed jettisoning his earlier ideas of all-republican unity. Electoral coalitions could no longer provide the basis of government; any new administration, Lerroux now accepted, had to include former monarchists. This was only possible if Lerroux pushed his party further to the right and repudiated the idea of equidistance between his rivals on either side of the political spectrum. To prevent rightists from taking those millions of Spanish voters disillusioned with the Republic for their cause, the Radicals needed to demonstrate that conservative government was possible within the existing political system. This would mean discounting the intense hostility of a left that asserted proprietorial claims over the Republic. However, Lerroux would never have imagined that scarcely a year later this antagonism would lead to a rebellion.

The Scheming President

The Radicals did not have to wait until October 1934 to realise that they had nothing to gain by turning left. Alcalá-Zamora wanted the republicans and the socialists to agree about the need to hold fresh elections in order to avoid a unilateral – and therefore controversial – presidential dissolution of parliament. He therefore instructed Lerroux to form a government that included left republicans in the hope that it could secure a majority in the Cortes. The Radical leader's tenure of office thus began awkwardly, as he accepted the president's unconstitutional inference in the formation of his new administration. Lerroux believed that Alcalá-Zamora was desperate to justify any future election by pointing to the failure of parliament to produce a majoritarian government. The initial refusal of leftist republicans to work with the Radicals supports this interpretation. Alcalá-Zamora told Azaña that if he did not change his attitude, his one-time ally would organise fresh elections. The former prime minister then relented, and Lerroux took office on the basis that any change of mind by his reluctant new partners would lead to a dissolution. The Radical leader held all the cards: Azaña did not want to go to the country, while Alcalá-Zamora needed to ensure that any post-election government would not challenge the original decision to go to the polls.[2]

Following the tradition begun during the constitutional monarchy, Lerroux personally selected as ministers those left republicans who were closest to the Radicals. 'I looked for the most moderate', he later recalled, as 'I could not form a [politically] homogeneous Cabinet'. He deliberately excluded Azaña and Domingo. This Radical-led coalition was presented to the nation on 12 September, but few thought that it had a long shelf life. Azaña quickly warned that he would not support any reversal of his policies and stressed that his party opposed any measures to conciliate the right. Domingo went further and preferred to split his own party rather than vote with the government. Keen to maintain his political creditability, Lerroux announced his new government's programme to the Cortes on 2 October. He made few concessions to the left. The prime minister declared that he would facilitate the Basque Statute and relax secularisation measures. He promised to revive the economy by changing agrarian reform to promote smallholdings and weakening trade union collectives, as well as repealing the Municipal Boundaries Law, politically neutralising the labour arbitration boards and balancing the budget. Not surprisingly, he pledged to restore public order, but made clear his commitment to a more inclusive Republic by offering amnesty to those imprisoned or deported by the Azaña government (namely anarchists and monarchists), as well as reversing the dismissals of army officers and state employees deemed anti-republican or implicated in the failed coup of August 1932.[3]

While Lerroux knew that the PSOE would react with hostility, he was indignant that at the first opportunity his left republican allies supported a vote of no confidence proposed by the socialist leader Prieto. This 'parliamentary execution' had two objectives: warn Alcalá-Zamora that he should not use his constitutional powers against the leftist majority, and prevent Lerroux from holding an election. Both Prieto and Azaña believed that such a motion would force the president to dismiss Lerroux under Article 75 of the Constitution and nominate a different successor. This was a foolish interpretation. For one thing, the Radical leader had already announced his resignation before the vote was taken, and when Lerroux was in the Presidential Palace, the speaker of the Cortes, Julián Besteiro, declared that the parliamentary session had been suspended. More importantly, the no confidence motion did not comply with constitutional procedure. It only served to worsen relations between Azaña and Lerroux still further. 'You can trick me into taking [political office] once, twice, even three times', he noted, 'but I will never do it being treated like an idiot'. Time did not mellow his rage, writing in his memoirs that he had never previously suffered such 'cynical disloyalty [and] shameless betrayal'.[4]

Alcalá-Zamora did not attach much significance to the vote and decided to dissolve the Cortes. He was aided by the socialists' declaration that they had been 'expelled from Power' by the president and 'betrayed' by those left republican allies who had joined the Lerroux government. To put it another way, since the PSOE were resolved not to reconstitute the former governing coalition, a dissolution by a Radical administration appeared inevitable, especially as it was likely that Lerroux was the only major republican figure who could successfully head off the electoral challenge from the right.[5] Yet the Radical leader never received the call to lead another government. Instead, Alcalá-Zamora began an extensive round of consultations. Before 1923, it was common for the monarch to seek guidance among party leaders, former prime ministers and speakers of the Cortes. However, from June 1933, the president adopted the questionable habit of including non-party worthies in discussions. These talks were in reality a charade to provide legitimacy for a decision that he had made beforehand: Lerroux could not be prime minister.

Alcalá-Zamora first turned to Besteiro to lead an all-party government, but the socialist who had always spoken against the PSOE taking ministerial office, turned him down. He then offered the job to three 'neutral' figures: Manuel Pedregal, Gregorio Marañón and Felipe Sánchez-Román. The president wanted them to lead broadly based coalitions of socialists, left republicans and Radicals that would – crucially – accept the rationale for elections. They failed. To the growing anger of the Radical leader, Alcalá-Zamora then turned to another independent, the jurist Adolfo González-Posada. On the president's request, he completely ignored the Constitutional Court to declare that the motion of no confidence signified that Lerroux's ministers, but not the outgoing prime minister himself, could be asked to form a new government. This was a veto that an increasingly nervous Alcalá-Zamora hoped would pacify the left.

On the third day of consultations, Lerroux was dealt a bitter blow from an unexpected quarter. The president offered the premiership to his deputy, Martínez Barrio. His boss initially did not object, assuming that the socialists and the left republicans would dismiss the idea. But late that night, a flustered Martínez Barrio arrived at Lerroux's home with Azaña and Domingo to seek permission to form a government that included socialists as well as left republicans. The Radical leader reluctantly consented, conscious that Alcalá-Zamora was determined to exclude him from high office. This decision stunned his supporters and elated his opponents. In the end, the PSOE only agreed not to vote against Martínez Barrio, but a relieved president confirmed the creation of a Radical-left republican coalition. Lerroux did not hide his frustration with Alcalá-Zamora, although he consoled himself with the thought that his right-hand man now occupied the premiership. His faith was rewarded as Martínez Barrio obtained from the president the cherished dissolution of parliament, disabusing Azaña and Domingo of the notion that the constituent assembly would continue. Spain finally went to the polls on 19 November 1933.[6]

Although Lerroux finally got want he wanted, the undignified manner in which his deputy took office created a baneful precedent for the future. After Alcalá-Zamora's failed attempt to persuade Besteiro to take premiership, he acted without reference to political parties, giving the impression that the Constitution had granted him free rein in shaping Spanish political life to his own whims. Not only did the president want to impose a candidate of his choice as prime minister, but he violated the Constitution by insisting that his nominees had to form a particular kind of coalition government. The fierce rivalry between the parties allowed Alcalá-Zamora to take advantage of his ill-defined powers and create an administration of his choosing. The president always believed that since he was responsible for the exercise of his prerogatives, he had the right to use them in any way he saw fit; his power to give and withdraw confidence to ministers was used as a mechanism to make or break governments.

The appointment of Martínez Barrio also showed that Alcalá-Zamora did not respect the established lines of authority within parties. The self-sacrifice of Lerroux in September 1933 destroyed the elementary principle that party leaders formed governments. By allowing the president to choose his deputy as prime minister, Lerroux tacitly gave Alcalá-Zamora the right to meddle in the internal affairs of his party, undermining his control of the organisation. The Martínez Barrio government would mark the beginning of the end of Lerroux's Radical Party as the excluded leader no longer had a monopoly on patronage to reinforce his charismatic authority.

The November 1933 Elections

In order to form his government, Martínez Barrio accepted that the Radicals would not organise the next election. The key post of interior minister went to another 'neutral' figure, Manuel Rico-Avello. While Lerroux regarded him as a man of 'good will', 'noble character' and 'good intentions', he noted that Rico-Avello had little political experience. For the Radical leader, his appointment was due to Alcalá-Zamora, 'until yesterday a traditional *cacique* and now the guardian of electoral virtue'.[7] But Rico-Avello's presence also reflected Martínez Barrio's pledge to the left republicans that no party would be given an electoral advantage. The new interior minister was certainly conscious of what was expected of him, telling reporters that his role was like a football referee enforcing fair play on the field.

The government's promise of honest elections did not make sense to Lerroux. He knew that corruption still took place at local level as municipal authorities determined the results of numerous rural districts. Like everyone else, he was also unsure about how the millions of new female voters would act. He worried about the future of his precious liberal democratic Republic. On the left, the Radicals and their allies were confronted by a powerful socialist movement that had largely subscribed to an anti-democratic collectivist project; on the right, they were faced by the Rightist Union, a national electoral coalition made up of die-hard monarchists and the more moderate CEDA. Fragmentation accompanied political polarisation as the left republican parties disintegrated. Having lived through the crisis of the liberal monarchy between 1918 and 1923, Lerroux believed that Rico-Avello's notion of electoral fair play would inevitably produce a parliament that would not provide the strong governments necessary to consolidate the Republic. In this context, the Radical leader argued that it was essential that the government intervened in the electoral contest to create a Cortes where the forces of loyal centrist republicans were superior to those of the left and right. Only then would the risk of a sharp pendular movement from collectivism to monarchism be eliminated.

Such an attitude revealed the true nature of Lerroux as a Restoration politician. For him, general elections created parliaments that confirmed the confidence shown by the president to the governing party. The future of Spain could not be left to voters politically socialised by weak, divided and polarised parties. The evils of fragmentation had to be avoided by a single official electoral slate backed by the human and material resources of the state. This did not mean that the Radicals and their allies should not campaign to win votes; rather government intervention would only be decisive if Lerroux's candidates matched the energy of their opponents. This was not a cynical betrayal of his democratic credentials; the Radical leader was the only republican who could justly boast of a long record in the struggle for the vote. But he knew that a passive interior minister would not produce clean elections; it would simply ensure that corruption in localities lacking effective political competition would favour somebody else. If it was going to happen anyway, Lerroux reasoned, it was surely better that any fraudulent practises should serve the noble objective of producing stable government. In any case, Lerroux believed that the days when a government could easily 'make' elections were long gone. He also shared the respect that dynastic monarchists had showed towards unfavourable electoral results produced by a mobilised electorate and proper party competition. Faced with defeat, their reaction was either to mitigate its scale through new parliamentary alliances or wait until the government had discredited itself. The latter was Lerroux's preferred strategy from December 1931, bringing him all too briefly into power less than two years later. If Lerroux remained essentially a politician from the Restoration era, he did not share the vices of the socialists and the left republicans, who inherited from those who fought for power during the turbulent revolutionary years of 1868 to 1874 the conviction that elections were only legitimate if they won. For Azaña, Domingo and the PSOE, the popular vote was only a means to confirm – not question – their own political agendas, which were conflated with the Republic. If elections endangered their hold on power, they could conceive of no other option than that of breaking with the 'corrupt' regime and 'saving' the Republic by use of force. By definition, this meant that their enemies could never legitimately take office, irrespective of whether they obtained a parliamentary majority. To avoid such an awful outcome, the socialists and the left republicans were prepared to use the same tactics of electoral manipulation used by monarchists under Alfonso XIII; indeed, they had already done so in June 1931.

Lerroux's worst fears began to be realised in the early stages of the electoral campaign. Although the prime minister was not wholly ineffective, his lack of experience against a mobilised PSOE and a confident Rightist Union was telling. Martínez Barrio would later defend his poor performance by stressing a supposed desire to run a clean election, but at the time he believed that he would secure a clear Radical victory by simply being in power. To assuage the mounting concerns of his Radical colleagues, Lerroux threw himself into the campaign, but the party leader was much less confident than the prime minister, predicting that centrist republicans would have to obtain the support of conservatives to govern. Since he was determined to make the Radicals the largest single party, he rejected any national electoral pact with the left republicans, and authorised joint electoral slates with conservatives in provinces where the PSOE appeared dominant. Moreover, Lerroux increasingly used rightist language in his speeches to lure voters away from the CEDA. At his final campaign rally in Madrid, the former foreign minister told his followers that they should not become obsessed with labels. If it is right-wing to prioritise the consolidation of a regime that had 'come at great sacrifice' by 'appealing to those willing to accept republican legality' and ensuring that 'reforms are carried out at a pace that reflects the country's needs', then 'the Radical Party is right-wing'.[8] But despite his efforts, Lerroux could not prevent a comprehensive conservative victory in the first round of voting. The latter took 206 out of 377 allocated seats, with the Radicals obtaining barely 75. Lerroux did much better than his rivals on the left: the PSOE won less than 30 seats while Azaña was left with a derisory rump of five deputies.[9]

The result surpassed the expectations of rightist leaders, including Gil-Robles, who had not expected that conservatives would dominate the new parliament. Lerroux, on the other hand, was furious with Martínez Barrio, and blamed his deputy for running a 'stupid' campaign that could inflict a fatal blow on the Republic. The Radical leader was conscious that if the Rightist Union was regarded as an enemy of the Republic, its spectacular victory could be construed as a plebiscite against the new regime. Unlike other republican leaders who were too stunned to react, Lerroux moved quickly to prevent this narrative from taking root. Taking advantage of the fact that his party had largely survived the republican catastrophe, he told journalists that those who had pursued revolutionary dogmatism and collectivist experiments, satisfied anti-Catholic cravings and defended the damaging prolongation of parliament, were paying the electoral price. Resistance to broadening the bases of the support for the Republic, he fumed, had left her bereft of the support from the majority of Spaniards in less than three years. Lerroux appealed to the victors not to begin 'a movement to restore the monarchy' but to 'enter the Republic'. If they did so, he promised that the Radical Party would work with them to create a strong centre-right majority government capable of liberal and conservative change. Gil-Robles, Martínez de Velasco and Cambó responded to this overture positively, as they saw the election results as a demand for a change of direction rather than as a plebiscite against the Republic. Indeed, Martínez de Velasco instructed his thirty or so deputies of the Agrarian Party to make an explicit declaration of loyalty to the Republic.[10]

Lerroux's strategy nearly collapsed when Martínez Barrio made the unrealistic demand that conservative leaders make republican 'expressions of faith'. Miguel de Unamuno, part of the Radical electoral slate for Madrid, captured Lerroux's thoughts better when he remarked that 'it was enough' that the right 'obeyed the regime' after the series of 'legal outrages' perpetrated by the constituent assembly between 1931 and 1933. Nevertheless, Martínez Barrio ignored the mood music of his party leader, and announced that the Radicals were prepared to enter an electoral alliance with left republicans and socialists in those provinces where a second round of elections was going to take place because no candidate had obtained the necessary 40% vote threshold. Lerroux quickly criticised his deputy, refusing to walk 'arm in arm' with those 'responsible' for the electoral disaster, and threatened to resign if the party's National Committee adopted Martínez Barrio's proposal at its meeting of 22 November. The evening before the crucial vote, the Radical leader make clear his direction of travel when he met Cándido Casanueva, a friend and close associate of Gil-Robles, at his home. The latter promised CEDA support for a Radical government, and both politicians agreed that their parties should fight the second round together in those constituencies where the Catholics were not already in alliance with monarchists. Lerroux's approach prevailed within the party and reaped the electoral rewards: the centre-right electoral coalition won 63 out of the remaining 95 seats, with the Radicals finally ending up with 102 deputies. Nevertheless, the CEDA remained the largest party with 115 seats.[11]

Lerroux had overcome the most difficult situation yet faced by the Republic by widening divisions between the accidentalists of the CEDA and monarchists. Yet this feat was predicated on delivering substantial constitutional reform. The Radical leader faced the difficult task of satisfying conservative demands while maintaining those changes that they regarded as welcome and legitimate. This was not, despite the claims of their leftist opponents, the politics of surrender. The objective remained the nationalisation of the Republic. For the regime of 1931 to survive, it had to be released from any particular political agenda. Nevertheless, although Lerroux had worked hard to take his party to the centre-right, his pact with former monarchists generated new internal tensions, especially in those regions where the right was the Radicals' main rival. The new government's political honeymoon was short.

Martínez Barrio Splits the Radical Party

Despite the compelling parliamentary arithmetic, Lerroux's prospective CEDA-backed minority administration faced a double challenge before it could take office. The most tragic was the anarchosyndicalist insurrection at the start of December which produced 125 deaths and 200 seriously injured. This revolutionary response to the electoral result was at that point the bloodiest rising in twentieth century Spanish history. Less violent, but equally serious, was the pressure of leftist leaders on Alcalá-Zamora to dissolve the Cortes before a government supported by 'enemies of the regime' could be formed. Martínez Barrio, the outgoing prime minister and Lerroux's less than loyal deputy, was sympathetic to these attempts to overturn the electoral verdict of November. He suggested that Lerroux should sponsor a Radical-left republican coalition government that would call fresh elections if it were defeated in a parliamentary confidence vote. His boss was not prepared to listen to such 'drivel' and, with the approval of the president, finally formed his second government on 16 December 1933. The new parliamentary speaker was Santiago Alba, the former liberal monarchist and now Radical politician. An experienced figure – he first entered the Cortes at the same time as Lerroux and Melquíades Álvarez in 1901 – Alba was chosen by Lerroux to provide substance to his vision of extending the Republic to all who were prepared to work for her loyally. He proved to be an inspired choice, as Alba would prove to be an excellent mediator between Radicals and conservatives, mainly because of his friendly ties with the Agrarian Party.[12]

The composition of the new government was the first step towards the construction of a solid centre-right majority. Apart from the Radicals, it included the liberal democrats of Melquíades Álvarez and two associates of Alcalá-Zamora, Pita Romero and Cirilo del Río. Yet the star signing for Lerroux was José María Cid y Ruiz-Zorrilla who despite his impeccable republican lineage – scion no less of the prime minister of the First Republic – represented the Agrarian Party. In sum, these ministerial appointments guaranteed the votes of around 150 deputies, although the parliamentary backing of the CEDA and the Lliga was still necessary for an overall majority. Nevertheless, as Gil-Robles shared the same aversion to radical swings of the political pendulum as Lerroux, the CEDA leader was prepared for the moment to eschew office and back the new government from the backbenches as long as the Radicals delivered on its electoral promises of political change.

It was not his allies but his own deputy that provoked the first trouble from within the government. Martínez Barrio refused to join the cabinet when he heard that Cid had been offered a job. Apart from his refusal to work with rightists, the former prime minister was piqued at Lerroux's choice of Alba as parliamentary speaker, since constitutional tradition suggested that the former monarchist was now the front-runner to replace the septuagenarian as Radical leader. Lerroux was determined to prevent the emergence of a leftist faction within the party and threatened Martínez Barrio that he would refuse to form a government if his deputy remained aloof.[13] This was sufficient to produce a U-turn from the latter, but despite joining the cabinet, he refused to come to terms with the new situation and his public criticism of government policy fed rumours of an imminent party split.

The prime minister had little sympathy for Martínez Barrio, who was firmly told to cast any doubts about policy aside and follow party discipline. For Lerroux, his deputy was the last person who had the right to lecture him about the dangers to the Republic, as the new government was the product of 'inexorable reality' and 'patriotism' caused by the former prime minister's disastrous brief spell in power that had produced the electoral defeat. Even Martínez Barrio acknowledged openly that the results of November 1933 entailed at best an all-republican government with the support of the right. Yet by the beginning of 1934, Lerroux began to prepare his party for the prospect of sharing power with CEDA leaders tired of living on 'parliamentary charity'. He did not fear this eventuality, seeing it as a significant step towards incorporating the CEDA within the Republic, which would ensure a full parliamentary term and essential constitutional reform. Most important of all, it would show that the Republic was inclusive, as in the context of a 'free and just' political system, it was 'legitimate' that the right had the same opportunity as their leftist opponents 'to serve the Patria'. After all, Lerroux reasoned, the Radicals had previously governed with adversaries such as the socialists and catalanists, and had even supported the elevation of a renowned monarchist like Alcalá-Zamora to the presidency. Why 'should we feel repugnance for striking a noble deal [with] former conservative elements, the majority of whom had never previously been actively involved in politics?'[14]

Martínez Barrio thought otherwise. He could only conceive of a 'Republic governed by the republicans'; only those involved in the original coalition of April 1931 had the right to hold power. In a speech given in Madrid's Victoria Theatre on 21 January 1934, he told his ministerial colleagues in the audience that they could not operate with 'full authority' if they had to negotiate 'daily' with their conservative allies. But what was the alternative? Martínez Barrio urged the government that it 'should dream' of having the support of 'the majority of the Chamber' and if this did 'not accord with parliamentary realities, present its resignation'.[15] To put it bluntly, this was merely a variant of the tune played by left republicans in the aftermath of their electoral catastrophe: parliamentary government was to be discarded in favour of fresh elections with the president's blessing. This was not an option that Lerroux was ever going to entertain, and in February, his disillusioned apprentice prepared his departure from government by giving a candid interview in *Blanco y Negro*. Martínez Barrio complained that minority government could not bring 'authority' and 'prestige' as it represented 'daily capitulation' to the right. A centre-right administration led by Lerroux may be feasible in terms of parliamentary logic, he went on to say, but it did not have the 'backing' of 'public opinion'. Therefore, 'as a man of the left', he felt that he could longer remain a minister, although he reiterated his loyalty to Lerroux and criticised the socialists' decision to prepare an insurrection.

The fact that Martínez Barrio's one-time allies were organising the overthrow of a democratically elected government would not have been news to *Blanco y Negro* readers. Remarkably, Largo Caballero and Prieto had already revealed their revolutionary intentions publicly, with the former finance minister even making his declaration in parliament. After the executive committees of both the PSOE and UGT had concluded that the ruling centre-right administration was both anti-republican and anti-socialist, they created a committee to co-ordinate a rising that would depose Lerroux and establish a new government that would manage the 'transitional period towards full Socialism'. At this stage, the only disagreement between the conspirators was whether they should wait until the CEDA took office. As Martínez Barrio himself admitted, he chose to destabilise the government at a time when 'the whole world knew that the workers' organisations were moving towards a revolutionary objective'; he had no doubt that for socialist leaders 'an explosion was inevitable'.[16]

The *Blanco y Negro* interview damaged the relationship between the Radical Party and the CEDA and therefore threatened the government's majority. Lerroux fired his deputy on 3 March 1934 as part of a more general Cabinet reshuffle prompted by Alcalá-Zamora's determination to force the Radical education minister Pareja Yébenes out of office after the latter committed the cardinal sin of ignoring the president's suggestion to appoint some of his friends as university rectors. To the surprise of Martínez Barrio, his formulaic pronouncements of loyalty did not impress the parliamentary party which gave the prime minister its full confidence on 27 April, despite previous internal grumblings about legislation that temporarily gave the poorest priests and clerics a modest pension.[17]

The breach between the prime minister and Martínez Barrio widened in the following fortnight. The prime minister became more irritated at the former minister's depiction of himself as a sacrificial lamb to the right. More ominously, Martínez Barrio had already begun to organise a new organisation, the Radical Democratic Party, openly courting Radical deputies like Sánchez Román and the Radical-Socialists under Félix Gordón. On 16 May 1934, Martínez Barrio formally left the Radicals. Lerroux never forgave him for the split.[18]

The creation of the Radical Democrat Party was a blow to the prime minister, but it could have been much worse. Martínez Barrio hoped to attract half of the Radical parliamentary party to his side including those from his powerbase in Andalusia, Valencian deputies of the Blasco – Ibáñez tradition, and (given his rank as Grand Master), Freemasons. In the end, only 17 joined the Radical Democrats, and the government kept its overall majority. Most Radicals understood why their leader had reached out to the right, and did not see it as a betrayal of the party's traditions or policy since 1931. But the split did weaken the Radical Party's role as the axis of the centre-right coalition and a moderating influence on the CEDA. Ironically, it actually increased Lerroux's dependence on his allies, although the lack of internal opposition would create fewer obstacles to closer relations.

The End of Lerroux's Second Government

To complicate matters further, the prime minister's relationship with Alcalá-Zamora began to deteriorate markedly in the spring of 1934. When he took office, Lerroux intended to involve the restless president in affairs of state, abandoning Azaña's attempts to reduce him to a constitutional cypher. He not only consulted Alcalá-Zamora over government bills, but he also permitted ministers to communicate directly with the president as the prime minister regarded them as better placed to inform the president of the details of proposed legislation. Yet this courtesy was misconstrued by Alcalá-Zamora as a licence to intervene in the minutiae of government business. Lerroux soon repented a decision to allow the president to participate in Cabinet meetings, as Alcala-Zamora's interminable contributions threatened to monopolise the discussions. Moreover, frequent contact with ministers only served to alienate them from their head of state. Few appreciated his interference in their work, and the president's penchant for manipulation, smears and insinuation made ministerial office a burden rather than a reward. As Lerroux perceptively observed, the president's growing isolation reflected his 'demanding and possessive' personality that displayed a clear 'lack of confidence' in the 'abilities of others'.[19]

Alcalá-Zamora's sense of superiority over ministers was born out of greater political experience based on an encyclopaedic knowledge of public law. Although he shared with Lerroux a desire to recalibrate the Republic along liberal lines after two years of leftist government, his growing interventionism was based on an arbitrary definition of powers that undermined the legitimate role that the double confidence system gave to the government, parliament and the electorate. For exasperated party leaders, the president's political activism seemed motivated only by partisanship. The manner in which he exercised his prerogatives exposed major errors in his understanding of the political situation, a lack of confidence in his governments and a brazen disregard for the crucial role of political parties in a parliamentary democracy.

Yet we should not forget that Alcalá-Zamora first made his political career in the factionalism of the last years of the Restoration period. His late conversion to republicanism did not alter his fundamentally personalistic view of politics. He saw it as his duty to incorporate former monarchists into the Republic, and never accepted the failure of his Liberal Republican Right party. Its successor, the Progressive Party, remained the same tiny band of notables who had followed him before 1923. As a politician lacking a popular base, he did all he could to prevent parties circumscribing his room for manoeuvre by encouraging political fragmentation within the Cortes. In this, he benefited from Lerroux's leadership style. In footballing parlance, if Alcalá-Zamora led from the front, the prime minister preferred to act as a sweeper, co-ordinating the efforts of his ministerial colleagues and preventing any internal disputes from threatening the cohesion of his coalition government. Much to the consternation of his younger and more forceful subordinates, the veteran politician soon found that the demands of the president and party management – Lerroux did not delegate the latter – consumed ever larger amounts of his energy and time.

A clash of personalities helps explain why the amnesty law turned a dispute about the relationship between the president and his government into a full-blown constitutional crisis. The measure had formed part of the election manifestos of the Radicals and the Rightist Union, although Lerroux saw amnesty somewhat differently to Gil-Robles. He believed that it should apply to the left, namely to anarchosyndicalists who had been pushed into revolt by the sectarianism of their socialist rivals. Yet the most polemical feature of the legislation was the proposed annulment of the punishments imposed on high-ranking members of the Primo de Rivera dictatorship and the Berenguer government; this would allow monarchist exiles and those persecuted by Azaña such as José Calvo Sotelo and Juan March to resume their political lives in Spain. It also commuted Sanjurjo's prison sentence and ended the detention and deportation of those suspected of involvement in the August 1932 coup.

For the prime minister, the purpose of the amnesty law was not to make a moral statement about the nature of guilt of those encompassed by the decree. He simply wanted to put an end to the wearisome matter of responsibilities, which punished some but not others for the same kinds of activity. For example, was it justice that Berenguer and his ministers faced trial for defending the constitutional monarchy against the republican insurrection of Jaca and Cuatro Vientos? Why were some associates of Primo de Rivera sentenced while others (like socialist leaders) did very well under the Republic? Lerroux also saw amnesty as a second chance to those who (in his mind at least) had not risen against the Republic but against the *modus operandi* of the Azaña government. The prime minister believed that a liberal and accommodating Republic would make any further appeal to violence futile.[20]

Alcalá-Zamora had a more realistic view of the mollifying virtues of amnesties. He agreed with Lerroux that the Azaña government was to blame for the revolts of the previous three years, and certainly did not want the responsibilities issue to bedevil Spanish politics further.[21] Yet the president firmly opposed the return into the armed forces of officers expelled by administrative order for serving the dictatorship in the 1920s or taking part in the August 1932 coup. With the support of leftist parties and Miguel Maura, he declared them a threat to the Republic. However, Lerroux and his parliamentary supporters did not yield, arguing that these dismissals were arbitrary and partisan, and conservatives wondered why the government should announce an amnesty that was less generous than the one given by the constitutional monarchy to rebel socialists and republicans in 1917. Characteristically, Lerroux attempted to assuage Alcalá-Zamora's concerns, assuring him that convicted officers would not return to the army and Sanjurjo would be packed off into exile. He even accepted the president's suggested amendments to the legislation. But Alcalá-Zamora refused to sign the bill after it passed the Cortes, and urged parliament to think again. When the government dismissed this stratagem, a reluctant president finally gave way, although his signature was accompanied by a long dissenting statement. Lerroux interpreted Alcalá-Zamora's unconstitutional behaviour as a withdrawal of confidence and resigned on 28 April 1934. His government had lasted scarcely four months.

Lerroux's self-immolation ended a constitutional crisis. His conservative allies, appalled by Alcalá-Zamora's actions, saw the president as a significant roadblock to the delivery of centre-right reform. His sectarianism, they reflected, was shown by the fact that he did not employ similar methods to frustrate the laws of the republican-socialist administration, including controversial measures restricting civil liberties. After hearing the news of Lerroux's resignation, the Lliga leader Cambó sounded out the speaker Alba and other centre-right party leaders in an attempt to save the government. He proposed that they pass a parliamentary motion expressing overwhelming support for Lerroux that would be seen as a condemnation of the president. If they could secure three-fifths of deputies to support them, Alcalá-Zamora could be constitutionally dismissed, and the vacancy would be offered to Lerroux. This scheme met with approval with all except the Agrarian leader Martínez de Velasco, and the CEDA's Casanueva was delegated to sound out Lerroux. However, despite their friendship, the Radical leader wanted nothing to do with it. Obsessed with the instability of the First Republic, he thought it essential that Alcalá-Zamora serve out his full constitutional term. Moreover, the idea that the president could be sacked on the votes of monarchists was a difficult pill to swallow. Seeing that it was a hopeless task, Casanueva desisted, although not before warning the outgoing prime minister that 'he does not know Don Niceto' and that the president will not thank him for his loyalty. Keeping Alcala-Zamora in his post, Lerroux's friend averred, condemns the Republic 'to perdition'. The Radical leader would later have plenty of time to reflect on this shrewd prediction.[22]

On losing the premiership for the second time, Lerroux could not look back on a very fruitful period in office. He did manage to consolidate his partnership with the conservatives by suspending the bans on religious education and clerical pensions, and negotiated a *modus vivendi* with the Vatican. In non-religious matters, he passed the amnesty law and ended socialist control of labour arbitration boards and the rural labour market. There was also a minor international triumph with the occupation of Ifni, an African territory south of Morocco and opposite the Canary Islands. Roughly equivalent in size to Vizcaya province, the Spanish claim to the area dated from the Catholic Kings of the fifteenth century and was confirmed by the Wad-Ras Treaty with Morocco in 1860. Nevertheless, it could only be made effective after the end of the Rif war in the 1920s and Lerroux's successful negotiations with the French prime minister Gastón Doumergue, which secured the tolerance of the dominant power in the region. In a modest sense, the Radical leader's old dreams of African expansion were realised; unlike most other prime ministers, he could point to an increase in Spanish territory under his watch.[23]

Samper's 'Summer Siesta'

The fall of Lerroux created a thorny political problem. As his demise was due to the actions of the president, it seemed unthinkable that Alcalá-Zamora would turn to the Radical leader to form another government. The alternatives were Gil-Robles, as leader of the largest parliamentary party, or the main opposition party, the PSOE, which would expect fresh elections. Since it was known that the president did not favour either option, Lerroux expected that he would return to office swiftly having scored a bloodless victory over the head of state. He was therefore perplexed to receive a visit from one of his former ministers, Ricardo Samper, who wanted his consent to form a government. 'A long-standing republican, a prestigious intellectual and democrat from Valencia, a good lawyer [and] an eloquent orator', the Radical leader wrote of his political ally, a man of 'much worth'. Samper had been his contact man with the party's Blasco-Ibáñez faction in Valencia and a person of 'order' and 'governmental spirit'.[24]

For all his personal merits, Samper's nomination provoked fury within the Radical Party, as memories of the Martínez Barrio government were all too fresh for those who wanted to maintain party unity. But Lerroux saw a Samper administration as an interim measure that would allow the president to save face; he decided to support his subordinate as prime minster in the hope that this would rebuild his relationship with Alcalá-Zamora. In the meantime, he was confident that he could control the government from the outside with Samper's blessing. This did not seem unrealistic. The new prime minister's cabinet was the same as its predecessor, with even Salazar Alonso, a bitter opponent of Alcalá-Zamora, remaining as interior minister. With the socialists openly conspiring against the government and the new fascist Falange active, Lerroux saw Salazar as a safe pair of hands to meet the threat from paramilitary bands of the left and right.[25]

The Radical leader knew that leadership was not one of Samper's talents, and indeed this was the very reason why the president favoured him as prime minister. With the departure of Lerroux, the government ceased to be a coherent entity, as the greenhorn Samper could not impose his authority on ministers. Indeed, he felt overwhelmed and did not try to defend the prerogatives of his office, allowing Alcalá-Zamora to co-opt the powers of the prime minister. The president led cabinet meetings and shaped the legislative agenda, while Samper struggled to smooth over the increasingly fierce clashes between Alcalá-Zamora and his ministers. In particular, the president's determination to ensure a balanced budget provoked complaints from Manuel Marraco, the finance minister, as the

Radical wanted to continue with a public works programme to alleviate unemployment. By the summer of 1934, disenchanted ministers paid daily homage to Lerroux at his home, and the Radical leader stiffened their resolve, dismissing any talk of resignations under presidential pressure. This backing was especially important not just to Marraco but also Salazar Alonso, as the Interior minister despaired of Alcalá-Zamora's refusal to permit a search of the socialist *Casa del Pueblo* in Madrid for weapons. Lerroux himself was mystified at Alcalá-Zamora's order of priorities, asking why he was insisting on a balanced budget if the Republic was unable to maintain confidence in the economy due to an inability to keep public order.[26]

The political situation only deteriorated further during the summer of 1934. The workers' left continued their preparations for a revolutionary uprising. The PSOE had formed a Workers' Alliance with the communists and part of the anarchosyndicalist movement to organise the insurrection, which would take the form of a revolutionary general strike. In those areas where the Workers' Alliance was strong, attacks on property was already taking place on a daily basis. Socialist mayors also encouraged or sponsored the boycott of public events held by centre-right organisations, and political strikes were endemic. Even a reluctant Samper concluded that these acts were but a prelude to insurrection. The most serious was the violent attempt by the rural branch of the UGT to prevent the collection of the harvest in June 1934. Its leaders did attempt to spark a rising, but the government declared the strike illegal and saved the harvest. This setback did not end the conspiracy, as that September the authorities uncovered an enormous stash of weapons stolen from state arms factories and deposited with the Asturian UGT by Prieto and Juan Negrín. These were not the first weapons taken from public stores. Other seizures included pistols and machine-guns taken from police warehouses in 1933 when Manuel Andrés was Azaña's police minister. The authorities feared that an insurrection was imminent. Soon after the discovery of the Asturian arms dump, Lerroux warned Samper to suspend the transfer of the remains of republican martyrs Galán and García Hernández to a crypt under the Puerta de Alcalá in Madrid as the Workers' Alliance planned to disrupt the ceremony with a mass demonstration. The insurrection would start, the Radical leader informed the prime minister, with the arrest of Alcalá-Zamora and the government, as their presence at the celebrations had previously been publicised.[27]

If things were not bad enough, the Samper government faced a significant challenge to its authority in the Basque Country and Catalonia. In the north, the Basque Nationalist Party (PNV), with the backing of leftist parties, illegally attempted on 12 August to restrict elections to Basque provincial councils to nationalist controlled local authorities. In the northeast, the situation was more serious as the catalanist Esquerra had joined the revolutionary conspiracy. Using its majority in the Catalan parliament, the Esquerra passed a law that transferred to the rabasaires, tenant vineyard farmers organised in an Esquerra controlled union, the land they cultivated. Aided by the Lliga, aggrieved landowners took the Catalan government to the Constitutional Court in Madrid, and succeeded in getting the law struck down as an infringement of powers reserved to the central state. This only escalated the crisis, as the Esquerra defied the sentence by passing an identical law and withdrawing its deputies from the Cortes. In this constitutional battle, the catalanists could count on the support of the socialists and left republicans; Azaña told parliament that the Catalan authorities were the only truly republican power left in Spain. Samper sought to end the conflict peacefully with secret negotiations with Luis Companys, the Generalidad prime minister, but the latter had already committed himself to the socialist-led insurrection. By September, catalanist paramilitaries were openly on the streets and the *escamots*, an Esquerra militia, attacked the Barcelona provincial court. Even more unsettling for the government was the fact that the distinction between the police and the separatist militias began to erode as Companys appointed members of the latter to public order positions.

For Lerroux, Samper's inability to deal with the nationalist challenge was the final straw. The government survived a vote of confidence on 4 July on condition that it ended the Catalan crisis by forcing the Generalidad to respect the decision of the Constitutional Court. Lerroux was obliged to deal with Gil-Robles directly to prevent the CEDA from withdrawing its support from Samper, but he tired of the prime minister's 'summer siesta' which he attributed to the paralysing influence of Alcalá-Zamora. The Radical leader was in a quandary. Convinced that a CEDA entry into government would provoke a left-wing rebellion, he was not too enthusiastic about Gil-Robles' demands for a presence at the cabinet table, but neither did he want to lead yet another minority government because the socialists had 'vetoed' the entry of his conservative allies. With the backing of his deputies, Lerroux began conversations with other parties in September to explore the possibility of a new majoritarian centre-right administration. Since he knew that the president would not withdraw his confidence in Samper, he made a compact with his allies that they would withdraw their support for the government when the Cortes reopened on 1 October. The days of a caretaker prime minister were finally at an end.[28]

When it became apparent that he had no choice, Alcalá-Zamora asked Lerroux to form a government. The Radical leader allocated seven ministerial posts to his party with Samper obtaining the foreign ministry as a reward for his continued loyalty. The other six went to his coalition partners, including three for the CEDA. All those chosen by Gil-Robles had republican backgrounds; José Oriol Anguera de Sojo, a former Supreme Court prosecutor, was handed the labour portfolio; Manuel Giménez Fernández and Rafael Aizpún were given agriculture and justice respectively. The list did not please Alcalá-Zamora, but his efforts to reduce the presence of the CEDA came to nought as Lerroux was not prepared to make a 'humiliating offer' to the largest party in the Cortes, especially when the president's attempted proscription of the CEDA provoked fury among Gil-Robles and his colleagues.[29] Lerroux appeased Alcalá-Zamora by dropping Salazar Alonso and finding room for the president's friend Martínez de Velasco. On 4 October 1934, Lerroux formed his third government. The socialists now had their pretext; the insurrection was not long in coming.

7

A Conservative against Anarchy (1934–1935)

There were tumultuous scenes within the communications ministry in Madrid during the night of 6 October 1934. César Jalón, its new Radical minister, told his officials that all contact with Asturias had been lost. Gumersindo Rico, the head of Telefónica, the state telecommunications company, reported that the last known message from the province stated that revolutionaries had taken control of the mining region; Civil Guard posts opposing their advance towards Oviedo and Gijon had been 'swallowed up'. After ensuring that the guards protecting the ministerial building from snipers were safe, Jalón returned to his office to more bad news: the Generalidad had also rebelled against the government. 'We were all emotionally overwhelmed', he wrote in his memoirs, 'Catalonia had risen!' He did not underestimate the gravity of the Catalan revolt, but felt more concerned about the Asturian revolution. '[It is in] Asturias, Asturias!' Jalón stressed, where 'blood will flow'. His mental state was not improved by subsequent messages of uprisings in Vizcaya and Guipúzcoa. An exasperated minister also saw that those around him 'became considerably depressed' and 'desolate'. Yet this funeral atmosphere was transformed after a radio message given by the new prime minister. Forty years later, Jalón could still recall how 'that speech by Alejandro Lerroux, fanned by the fiery language of the days of his youth' raised the morale of all who heard it with him; the oratory of the 'old titan, that paladin of Spanishness [*españolismo*] touched the hearts of all good men', and his 'warm, emotional yet calm' words brought 'succour to millions of sleepless, [and] restless households'. The insurrection, Lerroux declared, had not triumphed in most provinces, and the forces of law and order were poised to crush the rebels. The nightmare looked like it was ending.[1]

Although these promises were premature, one should not dismiss Jalón's recollections of October 1934 as those of a party sycophant. Praise for Lerroux's handling of the most violent episode in Spanish politics in nearly sixty years went well beyond the Radicals. He was no longer a mere party leader but a symbol of anti-revolutionary Spain and the personification of the liberal democratic Republic against those who would not accept their defeat at the polls in November 1933. Of course, the rebels and their apologists intensified their criticism of Lerroux as a traitor who had sold the Republic to her enemies. The socialists reiterated the claims first made by Pablo Iglesias that the Radical leader was merely a populist demagogue acting on the orders of the most reactionary elements of the bourgeoisie.

Even so, Lerroux's elevation to the status of national hero by many Spaniards did not offset the bitterness he had felt during those difficult days. While he expected a revolt from the extreme left, he was indignant at the news that his former republican allies had reacted to his appointment as prime minister by breaking off all relations with the government. This was a deliberate act by Azaña, Sánchez-Román, Miguel Maura and even Martínez Barrio to make up an alibi in case of a rebel victory.[2] Soon after left republican parties withdrew from politics, the new interior minister Eloy Vaquero informed Lerroux of the first clashes between the police and leftist militants in Madrid and Oviedo following the declaration by the Workers' Alliance of a revolutionary general strike throughout Spain. He was also told that the government did not have any contingency plans for the rebellion as the previous month, Samper – acting on the advice of Alcalá-Zamora – had dispersed military units sent to León as a precaution. Had such a force been available for immediate transfer to Asturias, it is possible that the miners would have thought again before rising; it is certain that the fighting would have been ended more quickly with less bloodshed.

The October Revolution

Irrespective of the desertion of left republicans and Samper's negligence, Lerroux did not hesitate when confronting a rebellion 'against a legitimate Government that had the confidence of the Cortes and the Head of State'. Rapid suppression was essential before it spread to other parts of Spain, and the prime minister was prepared to use the army if the police could not do it alone. This was a matter of life and death for the Republic; if the socialists, Catalan separatists and even former republican colleagues had repudiated the rule of law and broken the Constitution with 'ill-considered and fierce' declarations, then they were no longer opponents 'separated from us by ideological differences' or different views towards the government, but 'sworn enemies'. This was no exaggeration, and Lerroux's bellicose attitude towards the left republicans was more than justified. Earlier than summer, its leaders had met Alcalá-Zamora twice in an effort to persuade the president to appoint a government of 'republican defence' that would call new elections to ensure a 'truly republican' parliamentary majority. In return, the Esquerra would end the ongoing Catalan constitutional crisis. If Alcalá-Zamora did not accede, Diego Martínez Barrio warned, left republican parties would no longer display any loyalty towards the current regime; the president would have to take responsibility for the 'risk' of a 'rising'. This threat was repeated on 6 October with the revolution already underway; a Martínez Barrio government, it was claimed, was the only way to save the Republic. Understandably, Alcalá-Zamora dismissed these ultimatums as evidence of the 'mad fervour to regain power' by the losers of the previous year's elections.[3]

Needless to say that on this particular matter, Lerroux agreed unreservedly with the president. The Catholic right was not fascist, he stressed to all who would listen, and it owed its parliamentary strength to legal and democratic activities. Moreover, not only had it always obeyed the Republic, but it had even come to its aid after November 1933 when the CEDA had broken with the monarchists to work with the Radicals. Gil-Robles, Lerroux underlined, may not have liked the Constitution but he respected it, and the prime minister contrasted the CEDA leader with those on the left who pontificated about the sanctity of the December 1931 text only to later violate it. Deriding the arguments of left republicans and socialists about the need to hold fresh elections, he pointed to the fact that the existing composition of the Cortes was the consequence of the failures of the Azaña government (including a non-proportional electoral law), socialist isolationism and Martínez Barrio's disastrous 1933 election campaign. For all its talk about the Republic in danger, the left should have followed basic democratic practice and acted as a responsible and constitutional opposition in order to win back power legally. Instead, he noted with sadness, it reacted to the loss of power by reverting to its 1930 attitude of impugning a political system that it could not control; the refusal to see the CEDA in government was mere subterfuge for a patrimonial view of the Republic. For Lerroux, his leftist critics 'believed that power belonged to them permanently'.[4]

With his political opponents favouring the bullet over the ballot box, Lerroux obtained Alcalá-Zamora's signature for the declaration of a state of emergency on 6 October. He quickly realised that his own life might perish with the democratic Republic as revolutionary gunmen hidden on roofs and terraces shot at the prime minister when he arrived at the interior ministry in Madrid's Puerta del Sol to direct operations. After being informed that the building was also under threat from assault by armed militias, he received a report that the Generalidad had raised the standard of revolt in Catalonia. Companys' declaration of a Catalan state within a new Federal Republic and his invitation to other rebels to form a provisional government in Barcelona led Lerroux to believe that the Catalan capital was the hub of the conspiracy and the prime minister immediately ordered general Batet, the head of the Fourth Division, to declare martial law and take total control of the region.[5]

Lerroux then turned to the alarming situation in Madrid. After learning that the mayor Pedro Rico had joined the rebellion, he placed the Agrarian leader Martínez de Velasco in control of the city council to secure the loyalty of the municipal police. Working with Civil and Assault Guards, the local cops cleared the city centre of leftist militants and silenced the snipers. By the end of 6 October, the prime minister also received encouraging news from Catalonia as the government had taken back control of the streets of Barcelona and troops were surrounding the Catalan government building. Yet the situation was seriously deteriorating in Asturias, and the authorities elsewhere in Spain began reporting serious armed clashes. Lerroux had no option but to declare martial law throughout Spain to preserve order.

As one of Spain's most experienced politicians, Lerroux knew that the battle of the airwaves was as important as the struggle for control in the streets. In order to counteract rebel propaganda the prime minister decided to speak directly to the nation on the radio. After hurriedly preparing a text, he broadcast from the interior ministry at 10 p.m. that night. His speech reflected the principles and values that guided the government in its struggle against the revolution. It was another example of his genius as an orator, and its tone explains why liberals and conservatives welcomed it so enthusiastically:

> At the present time the rebellion, which has managed to disturb public Order, has reached its peak. Fortunately, Spanish citizens have overcome the foolish madness of the misadvised, and the [revolutionary] movement, which has made few serious and painful appearances throughout the country, remains circumscribed to Asturias and Catalonia because of the heroic activity of the forces of law and order.
>
> The Army are the masters of the situation in Asturias and normality will be restored there tomorrow [7 October]. Forgetting the responsibilities of his post, the prime minister of the Generalidad has permitted the proclamation of a Catalan State [*Estat Catalá*] in Catalonia.
>
> Given this situation, the Republican Government has taken the decision to declare martial law throughout the country. On making

this public now, the Government declares that it has waited until all the options that the law had placed in its hands were exhausted without humiliating or undermining its authority. In the hours of peace, it spared no expense to reach a compromise; on declaring a state of war, it will apply martial law energetically but without weakness and cruelty.

Be sure that before the social revolt of Asturias and the unpatriotic and rebel position of the Catalan Government, the whole country's full soul will rise in an eruption of national solidarity in Catalonia, like in Castile; in Aragon, like in Valencia; in Galicia, like in Extremadura; in the Basque Country like in Navarre and Andalusia. [All provinces] will place themselves on the side of the Government to re-establish not only the rule of the Constitution, the [Catalan] Statute and all Republican laws, but also the moral and political unity that makes all Spaniards a free people with a glorious tradition and glorious future.

All Spaniards will feel a real sense of shame of the madness committed by a few. The Government asks you not to find a space in your heart for any feelings of hate towards any of the peoples of our Patria. The patriotism of Catalonia will know how to impose itself on the separatist madness and will know how to preserve the freedoms that the Republic, under a Government that is loyal to the Constitution, has given her [Catalonia].

In Madrid, like everywhere else, the fervour of citizens accompanies us. With that, and under the rule of law, we are going to continue the glorious History of Spain.[6]

The contrast with the proclamations of Lerroux's former republican allies could not be clearer. With these words, Lerroux made a vigorous defence of freedom based on the rule of law. While he was excessively optimistic in order to sustain the morale of his supporters and depress that of his enemies, the prime minister nevertheless admitted that the rebellion would not be over in a matter of hours. As he spoke, shootouts continued in the suburbs of Madrid and panic paralysed commerce and public transport. The police and volunteers from centrist and rightist parties stepped in to ensure the continued supply of essential goods and services, and on the morning of 7 October, a few city centre shops reopened.

Lerroux did not sleep until he received word of the surrender of the Generalidad that same morning. The catalanist rebellion had been brief but violent: 50 dead and 150 seriously injured. By then, an exhausted and stressed prime minister had returned home to receive a depressing update from the military authorities in Oviedo and Gijon. The old man burst into tears in front of colleagues and journalists.

Lerroux had reached his lowest point. His spirits revived when he returned to the interior ministry later that day. The crowds awaiting him were very different to the groups that attempted to attack the building 24 hours earlier. They wanted to salute not murder the Radical leader, and the Puerta del Sol was filled with enthusiastic cries for Spain, the Republic, and for Lerroux. This was followed by a seemingly never-ending procession of anti-revolutionary figures from across the political spectrum who wanted to thank the prime minister and volunteer their services. Among them was the Falangist leader José Antonio Primo de Rivera. Lerroux had never previously met him, although he knew both his father and grandfather. The fascist effusively praised the work of the old republican, and offered the assistance of his youthful subordinates in exchange for pistols. Unlike Manuel Azaña and José Giral less than two years later, the Radical prime minister firmly rejected the idea of arming paramilitaries, as the maintenance of public order could not be entrusted 'to those who did not work for the State or those not subject to the discipline of the armed services'. Primo de Rivera took this disappointment well, as he told journalists afterwards in the Puerta del Sol that Lerroux had acted vigorously to defend the unity of Spain. Although sporadic gunfire could still be heard in the city, the public came out to applaud Lerroux as he made his way home that evening. In scenes reminiscent of 14 April 1931, his car could barely move as it attempted to leave the Puerta del Sol; the prime minister shook hands, waved and made himself hoarse shouting cries to Spain and the Republic.[7]

The Consequences of October

This spontaneous tribute was the first of many. With leftist deputies absent, the Cortes met on 9 October to pass unanimously credits to increase police numbers; the first vote of confidence in the government was also approved amid cheers from even the monarchist benches. The end of the Asturian revolt a week later produced public demonstrations of support for the prime minister and the forces of law and order throughout Spain. As the saviour of the Republic and democracy, countless local councils named Lerroux their 'adoptive son' and 'honoured citizen'. Various well-off supporters organised a public subscription for the Radical leader with a target of one million pesetas. This was a kind and extremely timely gesture, as Lerroux's personal finances had been much eroded by a focus on politics and largesse on a grand scale to party friends and acquaintances. Such was the prime minister's popularity that the original figure was easily surpassed, and Lerroux donated much money to those who fought the revolution, as well as the widows and orphans of those who died for Republican democracy. He also contributed to the reconstruction of areas – principally Asturias – that suffered physical damage as a consequence of the socialist-led insurrection. For a romantic revolutionary like Lerroux, the scale of destruction in Oviedo was a shock. In a visit to the Asturian capital, he thundered against the material 'attack . . . against art, against science, against religion, against tradition, against wealth, against work, against all the spiritual values that make up the patrimony of civilised Humanity'. He was referring to the attacks on educational establishments like the university and its library, the cathedral, the episcopal palace, the Campoamor Theatre and the provincial branch of the Bank of Spain that was successfully broken into 'with the deliberate . . . intention to force open its deposit boxes for the millions [of pesetas] that they contained'.[8]

Albeit at a heavy price, the suppression of the revolution had positive consequences. With the exception of continuing clashes with rebel bands in the mountains of Asturias and León, and the frequent discovery of arms, money and jewels stashed by the revolutionaries, political violence declined markedly. Confidence in the economy also rose, and investment rebounded strongly, although continuing doubts about political stability –the socialists after all remained the main party of opposition – meant that it remained lower than before 1931. Although no political organisation had been illegalised, Julián Besteiro's efforts to persuade the PSOE to abandon the revolutionary road were fruitless; more generally, the extreme left and the Esquerra also remained outside the realms of constitutional politics. The left republican parties did return to parliament some weeks later, but few forgot their permissive attitude towards the revolt.

There was no credible alternative to the ruling centre-right bloc. The dramatic events of October completed the Radical Party's conversion to conservatism. Irrespective of previous electoral pledges and the 'outsider' backgrounds of its leaders, the revolution had fundamentally changed the landscape of Spanish politics; the Radicals now firmly identified with other moderate republicans and rightists. The prospect of sharing power with the left republicans was unthinkable barely a year after it had briefly taken place.

Polarisation between revolutionary and anti-revolutionary camps intensified over the punishments meted out to the rebels. For Lerroux, exile normally followed failed insurrections, but few insurgent leaders imitated the examples of Indalecio Prieto and Josep Dencás, councillor of the interior in the Catalan regional government. The police had netted not just the Workers' Alliance revolutionary committee (including its chief Largo Caballero), but also the leaders of the Asturian rising. In addition, Manuel Azaña was arrested in Barcelona accused of being the head of the provisional government cited by Companys on 6 October. This claim did not lack foundation. At a public meeting on 30 August, the former prime minister called for a revolt if the CEDA entered the cabinet, and his close friend and confidant Carlos Esplá had joined Dencás military committee. Azaña only pulled out of the insurrection in Catalonia when he became alarmed at its increasingly separatist character.[9]

The sheer number of armed rebels caught by the authorities in Asturias, Catalonia, Madrid, and the Basque Country and elsewhere made matters more difficult for the government. Asturias witnessed open warfare with 4,286 dead and wounded. Attacks on property in rebel held territory was common, and around fifty priests, policemen and rightists had been murdered. Military courts and emergency tribunals permitted under the terms of the Public Order Act of 1933 worked hard to process the thousands of cases, but unsurprisingly mass trials could take weeks if not months. Nevertheless, the military courts produced the first 23 death sentences that October.

Those passed against Catalan police commanders, and especially against Enrique Pérez Farrás, the man who led the defence of the Catalan government building, provoked the most political controversy. An aggravating factor in his case was the killing of one government soldier and the wounding of two others during surrender negotiations. Article 102 of the Constitution allowed the government to request a presidential pardon based on a Supreme Court ruling but Lerroux and his ministers decided against clemency. Although the prime minister did not support the application of the death penalty in civil trials, he was a firm advocate of its use in military courts. Even in his revolutionary days, Lerroux remembered what had happened during the First Republic, when its abolition sparked the collapse of military discipline and intensified the conflicts within Spain and Cuba. While the prime minister had the backing of other centre-right leaders, the left mobilised to save the lives of those facing a firing squad. The existence of such a campaign indicated that Republican democracy was still very much alive despite the imposition of martial law, and Lerroux was placed in an awkward position when he received a visit –'almost an assault' in his recollection – of Farrás' family accompanied by the daughter of the recently deceased catalanist icon Francesc Macià. The pleas of the condemned man's wife and daughter visibly touched the prime minister, but Lerroux remained firm in his refusal to grant clemency.

Farrás' relatives had better luck with Alcalá-Zamora. Although the president also supported the death penalty in military trials, he feared that executions would only create martyrs and discredit the Republic in the same way that the lack of mercy shown to its own heroes Galán and Hernández after the Jaca uprising of December 1930 had delegitimised the monarchy. He called on Lerroux and reminded the prime minister of Sanjurjo's pardon earlier that year. The Radical leader refused to accept the comparison with Farrás, as the August 1932 coup had caused no deaths. While Lerroux understood Alcalá-Zamora's concerns, he argued that the sheer scale of the revolutionary violence of October meant that clemency would be misconstrued as weakness, if only because the insurrection's leaders had yet to show any remorse for their actions. Indeed, the socialists and their allies openly celebrated the attempt to rid Spain of 'fascism' and did not repudiate future revolutionary action.

Dealing with the penal consequences of the revolt overshadowed the other work of the government and undermined its cohesion. Its priorities were economic recovery, balanced budgets and constitutional reform, as from December 1935 the original text could be amended by a simple parliamentary majority. But Alcalá-Zamora used the Farrás affair to shake the unity of the ruling centre-right coalition. After submitting Samper to an interminable speech in the Presidential Palace, the Foreign minister cracked and called for Farrás to be pardoned. In order to keep his Radical colleague in government, Lerroux referred the case to the Supreme Court but the nation's most senior magistrates confirmed the original death sentence. The president, determined to save the Republic from the apparition of catalanist martyrs – the Esquerra had already labelled Farrás as the 'hero of Catalan freedoms' – was not to be outdone. On 31 October, he ignored constitutional propriety and told the cabinet that public opinion expected Farrás to be spared as passions had cooled. Alcalá-Zamora fretted about the impact of the left's campaigns for clemency in Spain and abroad, and pointed to Fernando de los Ríos' mobilisation of international socialist opinion against the government. If the civil leaders of the insurrection were to be shown mercy, the head of state told his ministers, it would be impolitic not to show the same grace to its military commanders. In any case, the president announced that he had the right to issue a pardon, and did not accept the Supreme Court's ruling. If the government refused to change its position, he threatened, another government would be found. To the frustration of his coalition partners, Lerroux gave way, and pardons were granted to Farrás and twenty others. In the end, only two executions took place for the murder of policemen.[10]

Alcalá-Zamora's interest in Farrás was strictly political. A few months later on 1 February 1935, a military court condemned to death Diego Vázquez, a sergeant who deserted to command one of the rebel columns in Asturias. Lerroux sought to pass responsibility for a pardon to the president in order to save his administration. The cabinet referred the case to the Supreme Court, which confirmed the original verdict. Yet to the prime minister's surprise, Alcalá-Zamora did not intervene and the execution went ahead. He realised that the head of state's vaunted humanitarianism was merely a tactic to ensure his popularity among Catalan nationalists. Nonetheless, Vázquez's fate was an exception. The Farrás case created a precedent and by the spring of 1935, the public clamour for firmness had diminished. Lerroux felt a 'spiritual conflict' in approving death sentences 'coldly against the pity and horror of the entire country that previously demanded implacable justice'. He also did not want Alcalá-Zamora, who was prepared to intervene to save the lives of socialist rebel leaders, to monopolise the politics of compassion. The next crisis over a death sentence was not long in coming. Predictably, a military tribunal decided that the socialist Ramón González Peña should die for leading the revolt in Asturias. Lerroux secured the support for a pardon among his Radical ministerial colleagues, although he had a harder time convincing his parliamentary party. Yet on 29 March 1935, the three CEDA ministers resigned in protest, and the government collapsed.[11]

A Reforming Government

The departure of CEDA's ministers over pardons was predictable given the pressure placed on Gil-Robles by monarchists over the preceding five months. On 5 November 1934, a Calvo Sotelo-inspired parliamentary debate over the Samper government's failure to prevent the insurrection prompted the CEDA leader to demand the heads of Lerroux's now foreign minister and war minister Diego Hidalgo. The prime minister acquiesced, and he decided to the take on the war ministry himself, finally satisfying the 'rather puerile' and frustrated military ambitions of his youth. He may not have had the technical background for the post, but Lerroux identified more with the military than any other republican leader. He saw it as his mission 'to restore their morale, to rise their depressed sense of internal satisfaction' following Azaña's bruising tenure of office. He was optimistic, for as well as having 'authority and prestige' as prime minister, his party was popular with the army.[12]

In this as in other matters, Lerroux had to overcome the thorny problem of Alcalá-Zamora if he was going to bring back into active service those officers deemed by Azaña as too 'lukewarm' towards the Republic. The first clash was over general Millán Astray, the founder of the Spanish Legion. When the president objected, Lerroux pointed to his many war wounds 'in service of the Patria' where 'the bullets did not discern whether he was a republican or a monarchist'. The prime minister then decorated generals Batet and López-Ochoa, commanders of the operations in Catalonia and Asturias respectively, and (more controversially) Franco, who directed the military campaign against the insurgents. He also made the future Caudillo head of the Army of Africa, as well as bringing Joaquín Fanjul and Emilio Mola back into the fold. Lower down the ranks, Lerroux restored to the air force Franco's brother Ramón, the once revolutionary pilot of 1930–31. None of this implies that openly republican officers fell into disfavour; on the contrary, many were promoted and given prestigious postings. Lerroux only wanted to base appointments on merit rather than politics.

So rather than seeing the prime minister's policy towards the military as the triumph of reaction, it reflected his deep conviction that the Spanish army still possessed 'a frankly liberal spirit'. Lerroux assumed that the majority of the officer corps were 'indifferent to the form of government' with only a minority divided among monarchists and republicans, 'the latter being much smaller in number than the former'. Given this state of affairs, he argued, the idea of making the army 'fervently republican' was a 'ridiculous pretension '. Lerroux was only thankful that it 'had not turned firmly monarchist' by the time Azaña left the war ministry. He was neither naïve nor intent on handing over the military to the Republic's enemies. Broadly speaking, the command structure inherited in 1933 remained unchanged. The prime minister simply wanted to address grievances thereby winning over 'the liberal ... majority, indifferent to the different forms of government', in order to neutralise the two politicised wings of the military. By treating officers with intelligence and empathy, 'one can obtain the loyalty of gentlemen and veterans, and the obedience of both the mature noble officer and the young generation coming up in the new atmosphere of loyalty to the Republic in the military academies'.[13]

Apart from a revised appointments policy, Lerroux's other proposals for military reform reveal a modernising vision equal or even superior to that of Azaña. He envisioned a reorganised and professionalised unified national police force based on the Civil Guard, the creation of a fully integrated national defence ministry, the establishment of a motorised brigade, a state monopoly on the manufacture and sale of arms and most ambitiously of all, a feasibility study into one of his long-standing pet projects, the construction of an underground tunnel that would link the peninsula with north Africa through the Strait of Gibraltar.[14] But given the multiple demands on the old man's time, these ideas remained on paper.

A more pressing concern was Catalonia. The revolt by the Esquerra placed Lerroux in a difficult situation. The region was under martial law, but the prime minister had pledged in his 6 October manifesto to preserve Catalan autonomy. He could not easily restore the regional parliament, as its leader and the majority of its deputies had supported the seditious movement. His alternative was a transitory administration approved by the Cortes in January 1935. This was run by a governor general who exercised the powers of the Generalidad with the assistance of an executive council composed by centre-right politicians. This improvisation gave the Cortes an opportunity to revise the 1932 Catalan Statute and repatriate certain powers such as policing. The government did not suspend autonomy, and the commission entrusted with transferring non-affected services to Barcelona continued to operate.[15]

The prime minister selected Manuel Portela Valladares, a former Liberal minister and Barcelona civil governor before 1923, for the post of governor general. They had met in the Catalan capital in 1910 and remained in friendly contact until the 1920s. They bumped into each other again while on holiday in Galicia during the summer of 1933, and Lerroux thought him ideal for the post some eighteen months later. He regarded the former monarchist as precisely the kind of politician that the Republic needed in 1935 because of his 'experience and [comfortable] economic background, which protected him against wickedness' as well as being an 'skilful, energetic and active' man who 'knew well the social and special problems of Catalonia'.[16] In other words, as a seasoned non-party figure, Portela could bring together all sides in the Catalan imbroglio, and indeed, he carried out his duties as governor general with such success that he obtained the post of interior minister in April 1935.

Portela became part of a minority Radical administration under Lerroux, which took office during the parliamentary recess. Although Alcalá-Zamora hoped that the prime minister would govern again without the CEDA, Lerroux only saw it as an interim measure while he negotiated a new pact with Gil-Robles. Just before the opening of the parliamentary session in May, a relieved Radical leader announced that the CEDA would contribute five ministers to a new coalition government and for the first time, Gil-Robles took office as war minister to demonstrate definitively the legalism of the Catholic right. Both Lerroux and Gil-Robles assumed that the CEDA leader would take over the premiership after he had proved his loyalty to the Republic as the civilian head of the army. Inevitably, the president attempted to dissuade the Radical leader from sharing power by raising the spectre of the leftist reaction. But Lerroux did not retreat. This was a key feature of the prime minister's plan to integrate the conservatives within the Republic. As early as December 1934, he had warned his parliamentary party that the Radicals would have to back a Gil-Robles government as a reward for the CEDA's backing during the previous twelve months.

Lerroux also took the opportunity to incorporate veteran leaders of the old Liberal Party into his administration. Apart from the political experience that they provided, their followers bolstered a Radical Party still recovering from the loss of Martínez Barrio's followers the previous year. In particular, the former monarchist minister Joaquín Chapaprieta accompanied Portela into government as finance minister. Since Lerroux wanted to balance the books, he needed an expert to work out the details of the necessary tax rises and spending cuts. As a former Liberal himself, Alcalá-Zamora was – for once – delighted with the Radical leader's choice of ministers, and the presence of Portela and Chapaprieta in the cabinet softened the blow of the disintegration of his dream of a Radical-led 'conciliation government' that included Martínez Barrio.[17]

Lerroux's determination to overcome the president's opposition to the CEDA did not however signify that he wished to eliminate Alcalá-Zamora's influence on government policy. Even as the two men quarrelled over pardons in the autumn of 1934, the prime minister wanted the head of state to play an active role in constitutional reform. Taking advantage of this, the president presented a detailed set of proposals to the first three cabinet meetings of 1935. In response, the Radical leader appointed an inter-party ministerial committee to harmonise Alcalá-Zamora's suggestions with those of the ruling centre-right coalition. Led by Joaquín Dualde, the Liberal Democrat education minister, it issued a report that was approved by the government on 13 June and presented to parliament three weeks later. The reform bill was a substantial piece of legislation, affecting 41 of the most controversial articles of the Constitution. It proposed to abolish the anticlerical clauses, as well as reaffirming the rights of property. It also envisaged a wide-ranging transformation of the Republic's political architecture with the creation of a Senate, the re-centralisation of tax-raising powers and the policing, and a clearer demarcation of the powers of the Republican president, government and parliament. The bill passed to committee stage, with a revised text due to ready for further parliamentary scrutiny in 1936. In the meantime, the administration set itself the task of revising the electoral law, and provincial and local government regulations; the latter was approved with the intention of holding municipal elections by the end of 1935.[18]

This ambitious reform programme was predicated on the stability of the centre-right government, and that summer few believed that it was in imminent danger. The Radicals remained its hub. It was the second largest parliamentary grouping in the Cortes, essential for any viable ruling coalition. The party also controlled most of the provincial administrations and about a third of local councils. Yet its greatest asset remained Lerroux. His personal relationship with Gil-Robles cemented the political compact between the Radicals and the CEDA. This was 'considerate' and 'affectionate' with 'mutually recognised courtesies' that reflected Lerroux's typically paternalistic style with a man half his age. The best example of this was a public tribute to Gil-Robles in Salamanca on 23 June. Addressing the audience, Lerroux explained that his concordat with the Catholic right was not opportunistic but rather an instrument that would guarantee the much coveted consolidation of the Republic. 'I will not abandon this coalition', he promised, if the conservatives 'continue to collaborate with me'. Furthermore, he stressed that the *entente* between the two parties should be extended at provincial and local level to ensure that both parliament and the president complete their terms of office.[19]

For Lerroux, this happy outcome could only come to pass if the CEDA became republican through constitutional reform and Alcalá-Zamora accepted Gil-Robles as prime minister. Achieving the latter was more difficult. Quite apart from the president's frequent interference in the business of government, the CEDA leader became tired of Alcalá-Zamora's manifest hostility towards him. While Lerroux partly attributed the less than harmonious relationship between Gil-Robles and Alcalá-Zamora to the former's youth and political inexperience, he held the veteran president primarily responsible. Lerroux could not understand why the head of state, despite being more right-wing than himself, derided the CEDA leader as a 'dangerous reactionary'. The Radical leader also believed that Gil-Robles had more than demonstrated that such insults were unjust, and that only the experience of government would allow the CEDA to abandon its 'doctrinal rigidities', acquire 'versatility' and definitively join the Republic. Being rightist should be no barrier for a party in a liberal democracy, as it was only natural that 'the [political] pendulum' would later resume its 'synchronic swing' and lead to more leftist governments. The constitutional crisis of April 1934, Lerroux argued, was a warning that Alcalá-Zamora's continued use of the presidential prerogative against the CEDA could create a 'dangerous political situation'. The prime minister also watched with dismay as the president continued to dabble in the internal affairs of the parties, noticing how Alcalá-Zamora attempted to cultivate Giménez Fernández, the CEDA agriculture minister in October 1934, insinuating on various occasions that he was a possible future prime minister. Allergic to large and disciplined parties that reduced his political room for manoeuvre, the president seemed to be looking for a Martínez Barrio of the CEDA.[20]

Loyal Collaboration

The centre-right coalition looked firm. On 9 September 1935, Gil-Robles responded to Lerroux's gesture in Salamanca with a public telegram of support. Read out at a Radical Party meeting in Barcelona, it referred to their alliance as 'loyal collaboration' for a common undertaking that 'being national is above party differences or interests'. For the prime minister, these words confirmed that his parliamentary majority was secure. The president remained the problem. Alcalá-Zamora saw the consolidation of the ruling bloc as a threat to the exercise of his powers. He ceased to regard Lerroux's Radical Party as a possible instrument of political change, dismissing the still republican party as just another liberal-conservative entity. For the president, his prime minister had damned himself on 25 August with a speech in Baños de Montemayor, when Lerroux ruled out announcing any agreements with the socialists or their republican allies. Far from convincing Alcalá-Zamora to bow to the inevitable and accept the CEDA leader as a future prime minister, the public declarations of unity between Lerroux and Gil-Robles only served to intensify Alcalá-Zamora's fears that he was being forced to submit to the latter to prevent a dissolution of parliament.[21]

The president's response to Lerroux's efforts at reconciliation was correspondingly blunt: he sought to undermine the prime minister's leadership of the Radicals as a means to decouple the party from the CEDA. The president made ever more indiscrete comments to Radical ministers about their boss in a clumsy attempt to ferment internal dissent. He also warned conservative leaders against working too closely with the veteran politician, as the 'moral infection' that afflicted the Radicals could strike their parties too. Alcalá-Zamora was prepared to grasp at any straw to discredit his prime minister.[22]

8

Much Ado About Nothing
(1935–1936)

Miguel Maura liked to escape to Lerroux's retreat in San Rafael to elude Madrid's oppressive summer heat. In 1933, he had an added incentive to go into the mountains. With the republican-socialist coalition government on the ropes, the Radical leader invited him to his home ostensibly to coordinate their tactics against Azaña. Maura quickly realised that Lerroux wanted to go further; his host saw the premiership within his grasp and wanted to make the former monarchist his party deputy in order to make the Radicals more attractive to moderate voters. He promised Maura a generous allocation of parliamentary seats and ministerial posts and even recognised that he treated his father Antonio badly a quarter of a century earlier.

Although the interior minister of 1931 appreciated the gesture, he flatly refused: 'I cannot work with you in any government today, tomorrow, or the day after tomorrow'. It was not Lerroux who was the problem, he explained, but 'the utterly disagreeable people who surround you, and who will eventually ditch you'. A stunned Radical leader asked 'What are you saying to me, Miguel, my friend? . . . Who are you talking about? For better or worse, I have old friends who have been my loyal companions in the struggles during the heroic years, and now I have to reward and attend to them. You know, my dear Miguel, that I always value and take care of my friends. Have some committed peccadillos in the past? What am I to do? That for me, as the French say, is the *rançon de la gloire* [price of glory]'. Lerroux's explanation did not convince. 'The glory of yourself, Don Alejandro', replied Maura, 'but not me. I have had nothing do with your past and I fear for the future if it is anything like [your past]'. This was too much for Lerroux. He criticised Maura for suggesting three years earlier that he could not be trusted with the post of justice minister in the Provisional Government for fear that his cronies would sale sentences. The awkward conversation came to end abruptly without agreement.[1]

Maura's qualms did not preclude him standing alongside Lerroux for Madrid or his followers agreeing electoral pacts with the Radicals that November, but this anecdote shows well what Lerroux's allies of 1931 thought of the Radicals' moral standards. In their eyes, the supposed venality of the party made it unsuitable for government. Yet in reality *realpolitik* shaped Maura's ethical outrage against Lerroux; the Radical leader was the most significant obstacle to the emergence of an alternative popular conservative republican movement. Given Maura's own political past, it is somewhat ironic that his denunciations of Radical sleaze only served a broader agenda to delegitimise Spain's constitutional experience before the Primo de Rivera coup of September 1923. The left in particular argued that April 1931 represented a clean break; Azaña was just one of many who dismissed the political traditions and practises of the past as the systematic plunder of public resources by the powerful few. Despite being republican, Lerroux's party was the embodiment of old corruption. As the socialist leader Largo Caballero cruelly put it to journalists when he heard that Lerroux was about to form his first all-Radical government in September 1933: 'Only the Radicals? . . . then just round up eleven gypsies from Peñuelas [a Madrid slum district] and everything will be sorted'.[2]

Such slander aroused Lerroux's fury. The fact that the Radical Party contained morally dubious individuals who used public positions for their own interests hardly made it exceptional in Spanish politics or even within the Spanish republican movement. The 'weaknesses' so often attributed to the Radical leader were in reality inevitable concessions to reality. As Max Weber recognised, the professionalisation of politics during a transitory phase where most public posts remained unpaid produced a culture where the charismatic leader could only safeguard the loyalty of his closest followers through material and non-material rewards. Lerroux modernised the clientelist practises of the early nineteenth century in the sense of making the economic benefits of public service available to those previously excluded from politics. As we have seen, favours and recommendations characterised Lerroux's *modus operandi* from his days as a revolutionary agitator in Barcelona. Party members at all levels wrote or visited his home in calle O'Donnell in the hope that they could benefit from the legendary generosity of Don Alejandro.

Lerroux's largesse was not restricted to public funds. He liberally distributed his own money for party purposes. Even harsh critics like Alcalá-Zamora and Prieto recognised that he 'donated' money with 'open hands'. Lerroux created 'pensions for widows of fallen comrades' and those 'old republicans without means' as 'no-one in need went without'. His house even became known as a 'little hotel' because (among other reasons), it provided a roof to desperate friends and their families. This was also true of his chalet complex in Gudillos, where those suffering from tuberculosis could recover in the mountain air. Among the beneficiaries was Joaquín Vila, an old but impoverished party chum from Barcelona, whose family was given the task of managing the estate. But Lerroux's munificence was not restricted to Radicals. To the disgust of some, he also gave José Primo de Rivera a job in his administrative team. The eldest brother of the dead dictator had been sacked from a bank as an enemy of the Republic when the left was in power despite being apolitical and close to retirement.

Lerroux's recourse to patronage on a grand scale generated continual problems of finance. Excluding the Radicals' somewhat patchy record in local government, the party spent most of its history in opposition, forcing Lerroux to rely on his own money and donations that he could obtain from wealthy backers which often came with strings attached. Changing political circumstances led to periods of personal debt in which the Radical leader struggled to meet the financial demands of his party and its press. The massive growth of the Radicals after April 1931 only complicated matters further as increased income did not satisfy the all the expectations of his enlarged clientelist network. As well as disappointed and disgruntled petitioners, Lerroux found that favours did not always grease the wheels effectively. His memoirs are full of complaints about the ingratitude shown by those he had helped. This does not imply that the republican ever seriously considered changing his way of doing politics. There is little evidence that Lerroux was interested in endowing his party with an efficient bureaucracy sustained by membership dues, press income or affiliated societies. Nor did he consider that the state should directly pay its politicians more.[3]

The Radicals did not even bother to hide their appropriation of public funds after the predictable howls of protest from political opponents. However, this was not the main reason for the party's reputation for corruption. Lerroux was the only republican to create a truly national organisation that could challenge a socialist movement with its snout similarly in the public trough. The Radicals were the only moderate party during the Republic that had a realistic chance of winning enough seats to lead a government. This was not an achievement to which such paladins of virtue as Miguel Maura and Manuel Azaña could lay claim. After all, the conservative politician owed his career to the influence of his father rather than any popularity among the voters, while the left republican leader entered the Cortes in the 1931 and 1933 elections less due to the efforts of his own miniscule party than to agreements reached with the Radicals and the socialists respectively. Ultimately, the Radicals rebutted accusations of rapacity by their actions in government from 1933. There was no descent into an inferno of financial iniquity. The customary re-distribution of state posts and rewards provoked the understandable protests of those on the left who had previously enjoyed the fruits of power. While it is true that Alcalá-Zamora also privately thundered against Radical corruption, this had more to do with his general animus towards the party. CEDA leaders were pleasantly surprised to discover when working with Lerroux in government that their allies' infamous reputation was not justified. As Gil-Robles recalled in his memoirs, the president's complaints were nothing more than 'vague accusations', 'generic allusions' and 'never . . . concrete cases'. Lerroux was furious with a head of state known as a 'model cacique' who still treated the Cordoban districts of La Carolina and Priego 'as his own fiefdom'. How could someone who flagrantly used his own powers of patronage to keep together his exiguous band of political brothers accuse others of immorality?[4] Alcalá-Zamora was hardly a credible champion for clean government.

Estraperlo

Before he went into his prime ministerial office, Lerroux generally rose early to deal with personal correspondence at home. On a cold morning in January 1935, he opened a large envelope with a foreign postmark and began to read its contents. The first lines of the letter left him dumbfounded; he turned immediately to the last page to learn the identity of its author: Strauss. He did not recognise the name, but read the document in full, with curiosity increasingly giving way to dismay.

The story it told was explosive. It revealed that Lerroux's nephew Aurelio and various friends, all holding government or state company positions, met with Daniel Strauss, a German with a Mexican passport during the spring and summer of 1934. The latter wanted to distribute in Spain his roulette game, *estraperlo*, which had made a lot of money in Amsterdam and Ostend. Although games of chance were illegal, Strauss argued that his invention was based on speed and calculation rather than luck. After the failure of an approach to the Catalan authorities, the foreign businessman spoke to Juan Pich y Pon, Lerroux's close friend in Catalonia who had responsibility for the merchant navy within the Samper government. Sniffing an opportunity for profit, Pich contacted Aurelio Lerroux and the latter agreed to join the board of a new company that would market *estraperlo* in return for using his political influence to get a gaming licence from Samper and his interior minister Salazar Alonso. In the letter, Strauss claimed that he handed over money and gifts to Radical politicians as part of his lobbying, and given Lerroux's continued sway over the Samper administration, it seems unlikely that his son kept him out of the loop. As was to be expected, the government legalised *estraperlo* and Strauss installed the game in San Sebastian's Gran Casino. Nevertheless, during the night of its inauguration on 12 September 1934, the civil governor closed down the premises on the orders of Salazar Alonso. Various players had complained that the house always seemed to win, and an inspection of the roulette wheel revealed an electric device that could control the outcome at the push of a button. The following day, the interior minister began a police investigation and banned *estraperlo*.[5]

In his letter, Strauss claimed that after he failed to get the casino reopened, his business partners urged him to take advantage of Salazar Alonso's departure from the interior ministry in October to install the game at the plush Hotel Formentor de Pollensa in Majorca. Play began for ten days that December until Eloy Vaquero, the new interior minister, closed it again after receiving a tip-off from Gil-Robles. Strauss concluded his missive with a demand for 400,000 pesetas in compensation. He complained that the gifts and kickbacks had ruined him, and threatened to go public with all the juicy details of his relationship with Aurelio and other Radicals if he did not get what he wanted.

An alarmed prime minister immediately talked to those implicated in this case, and they confirmed their dealings with Strauss even if they denied profiting from them. While Lerroux latter dismissed the affair in his memoirs as an 'imprudent lapse without importance', he took it very seriously at the time, ordering a secret investigation into Strauss.[6] This uncovered that his lawyer was a French left republican deputy called Henri Torres, who was also a member of an international assistance committee for the October 1934 rebels. Torres made contact with Lerroux's faithful attorney Dámaso Vélez via Gastón Cohen in Madrid, and told him that his client was prepared to go to the courts if no compensation was forthcoming. The prime minister sought to reach an agreement through Vélez, but when Cohen refused to compromise, Lerroux brought off negotiations and vowed not to give in to blackmail.[7]

Strauss took his revenge. He spelled the beans to Martín Luis Guzmán, a Mexican journalist close to Azaña, while his lawyer Torres met Prieto in his Belgian exile. Events moved quickly. Guzmán brought Strauss and Prieto together at the Brussels International Exposition, and kept Azaña abreast of developments. The socialist leader took the initiative: in the Belgian capital, he discussed *estraperlo* with José Centeno, a close presidential adviser, and suggested that a detailed report of the Strauss affair be sent directly to Alcalá-Zamora. As Prieto was determined to exact full political advantage from Strauss' dealings with the Radicals, he dismissed the option of taking the allegations to the police and made sure that the names of Radical figures unconnected with *estraperlo* were included in Centeno's account. This landed on the president's desk on 5 September, although it is possible that Alcalá-Zamora was forewarned of its contents, as the president insinuated during a conversation with the prime minister in August 1935 that Strauss had met Aurelio in Lerroux's San Rafael residence.

In any case, Alcalá-Zamora did not hesitate to make use of the political dynamite placed at his disposal. He first raised the Strauss dossier with Samper and Juan José Rocha, a Radical minister close to Lerroux, before informing the prime minister himself on 16 September that he had received an envelope sent 'by recorded post requiring acknowledgement of receipt'. He could not therefore ignore its contents, the president continued, and although it did not contain firm evidence that a crime had been committed, there was enough to suggest that Lerroux's entourage were involved in shady activities. These comments by an experienced lawyer betrayed why Strauss decided to tarnish the political reputations of the Radicals rather than seeking justice in a courtroom. The prime minister rejected the allegations of the dossier, referring to German-Mexican's attempts at blackmail and the results of his police investigation. This revealed that Strauss had a criminal record and been subject to two international expulsion orders. At this stage, Lerroux remained unconcerned about his political survival, regarding Strauss as a crook with little credibility. Courtesy of information supplied by Spanish diplomats in the Netherlands, he could also tell Alcalá-Zamora of Guzmán's relationship with Strauss, suggesting that the charges were a political set-up by the left to destabilise his government.[8]

The prime minister was therefore surprised to learn on 18 September that the president wanted him to go public over the accusations, subtly suggesting that it would be best in order to forestall a leftist campaign in parliament. Lerroux remained resolute, deriding the moral authority of those with less than spotless records in government who had flagrantly broken the law less than a year earlier in October 1934. He was not prepared to publicise a subject that could provoke a torrent of rumours against his own nephew as well as his party. When the president insisted that it had to be done, Lerroux stormed out of the meeting suspecting that the president wanted a political scandal. His relationship with Alcalá-Zamora never recovered.

The Radical leader's reaction may have been disproportionate, although it is true that the president's motives are difficult to fathom. If, as he claimed later, he was simply worried about being involved in a political cover-up, then he could have handed over the dossier to the government for their opinion. If he had no confidence in Lerroux's ability to deal with the allegations competently and thought it a legal issue, then he could have created a new government to carry out this task. Certainly, the republican president did not normally accept complaints directly from aggrieved citizens and Alcalá-Zamora should have returned the dossier to Strauss' lawyer suggesting it was a matter for a judge. He could have even simply thrown it in the bin. He did none of these things. His scarcely concealed desire to use Strauss against the prime minister made him complicit in blackmail.[9]

Living One Hundred Years in Two Hours

Alcalá-Zamora did not dismiss Lerroux after the spat of 18 September. The prime minister's resignation took place two days later following the departure from the cabinet of navy minister Antonio Royo-Villanova. His decision to quit in protest over the transfer of various public works programmes to the Generalidad ended the participation of the Agrarians from the government. Although the president indicated that Lerroux could continue without his junior coalition partner, the prime minister regarded their presence as essential. Moreover, since Chapaprieta's cost-cutting measures envisaged reducing the size of the cabinet from thirteen to nine, Lerroux wanted to carry out a more thorough government reshuffle with the approval of the president.

The ball was in Alcalá-Zamora's court. If he wanted a new prime minister, the only alternative was Gil-Robles. Since the PSOE had excluded themselves from power, the possibility of a minority leftist administration calling an election was political fantasy. After the obligatory consultations, the president decided to overcome this self-imposed dilemma by disregarding parliament altogether. When his attempts to interest Santiago Alba in the job were rebuffed, and the political world expected the return of Lerroux or a Gil-Robles government, the president pulled a rabbit out of the hat by asking Chapaprieta to form an administration on 25 September. Since the finance minister had not formally joined the Radicals, Alcalá-Zamora expected the Cortes to accept a non-party figure. If it refused, Chapaprieta would dissolve parliament.[10]

The president's arbitrary exercise of his constitutional prerogatives left centre-right leaders stunned and bewildered. His actions were the clearest indication yet that Gil-Robles would never be offered the premiership despite leading the largest parliamentary party. Although Alcalá-Zamora has been dismissed as a mere 'paperback' Alfonso XIII, veteran monarchists such as Romanones and Abilio Calderón struggled to recall an occasion when the monarch acted in a similar manner. Even a staunch republican like César Jalón noted that while the king sought to throw his '*golden lasso*' to overcome the fragmentation of the dynastic parties, no-one 'could dare to defend' how Alcalá-Zamora could 'only pause for a minute [in the pursuit of] of his destabilising preoccupations' or 'the incision of his scalpel in the entrails of the moderate parties'.[11] Given the circumstances, was there any other option to that of impeaching the president to force his resignation? If the necessary three-fifths of parliament could not be mustered for such a motion, the centre-right bloc could prepare for a new national poll by accelerating electoral reform and dropping unpopular austerity measures. At the most favourable and least divisive moment, the ruling coalition could then force through a dissolution of parliament. An united left might win a few seats, but a common electoral slate that encompassed monarchists as well as Radicals would be enough to secure a parliamentary majority, keep those who rebelled against the Republic in October 1934 outside government, and if there were enough votes, force Alcalá-Zamora out of office.

This could be the only basis for centre-right support for a Chapaprieta government. Anything else would endanger the cohesion of the ruling bloc. The presidential proscription of their leader brought the Radicals to the brink of departure from government. Understandably, the party initially refused to support Chapaprieta, and Gil-Robles had to use all his powers of persuasion to convince Lerroux to enter the new cabinet as foreign minister. As compensation for losing the premiership, the Radicals also gained two ministerial posts, but in conversations with the CEDA leader and Chapaprieta, Alcalá-Zamora did not hide his antipathy towards the supposedly dubious character of Lerroux's closest associates and wished they had left office.

On 2 October, the president told the new prime minister informally of the existence of the Strauss file on the pretext of 'asking advice'. The latter was stupefied that he had not been informed previously, as he would have refused power. Chapaprieta was well aware that Alcalá-Zamora wanted him to accept 'the responsibility of dealing with the Strauss papers'. Since any formal presidential *démarche* would elevate the political significance of the affair, the prime minister advised him the following day to drop the matter discreetly. But this only encouraged the indefatigable head of state to leak indirectly details of the dossier to the public. In the first parliamentary debate on *estraperlo*, the monarchist Antonio Goicoechea announced that his followers had heard the allegations from 'rumours' spread by the 'highest authorities'. When the Latin American press published still secret extracts of the file, Lerroux suspected the source to be the president's press chief Emilio Herrero, a contributor to Prieto's *El Liberal* who was also close to foreign correspondents. Alcalá-Zamora was not the only possible suspect. In order to avoid any nasty surprises, Lerroux secretly informed leading figures within his party of the dossier. During Chapaprieta's investiture on 1 October, the Radical deputy Basilio Álvarez remarked that his leader's new job was strange, as 'if D[on] Alejandro Lerroux did not sin politically, why the demotion?' In the same debate, the Agrarian Royo-Villanova criticised Alcalá-Zamora's decision to appoint a new prime minister given that his predecessor continued to enjoy a parliamentary majority, and alluded to the moral opprobrium that monarchist statesmen Romero Robledo and Antonio Maura received in their day, quoting former Liberal prime minister Moret's aphorism that 'these accusations . . . are not made against people but against a regime'.[12]

In order to express the extent of their disgust with the president, the Radicals organised a public tribute to Lerroux in Madrid on 9 October and encouraged other parties to participate. Given that the new government was barely a week old, this was a foolish act that could only be interpreted as a direct attack on the president and risked turning him leftwards. Yet Lerroux agreed it should ahead. Not only did he want to demonstrate that his leadership of the party remained as strong as ever, but also that his former coalition partners had not deserted him. Nevertheless, he was aware of the risks and tried to convince Alcalá-Zamora that the occasion had little political significance. This was rather difficult to believe as Lerroux was flanked on the platform by the whole government, the speaker, and other centre-right leaders, as well as 180 deputies. Before such an impressive turnout, Gil-Robles declared that the maintenance of the ruling bloc was his primary political concern, and warned the president that any dissolution of the Cortes would be his last. He concluded by praising Lerroux's capacity for self-sacrifice. In his reply, the Radical leader picked his words carefully except when he called for obedience to the 'highest' authorities, as they demanded 'the utmost of respect' not 'for the men [who occupy these offices] but for the rule of law'. This was a distinction that he knew would trouble the querulous Alcalá-Zamora and sought to disguise the slight by raising a glass to the 'Head of State . . . for the Republic and for Spain'. None of those who attended the event noticed the allusion and a relieved Chapaprieta telephoned Alcalá-Zamora to praise Lerroux's restraint and professions of loyalty, and the president even called to congratulate his reluctant new foreign minister on the speech.[13]

This happy state of mind only lasted until Alcalá-Zamora read press accounts of Lerroux's words. At the following day's cabinet, he blasted Chapaprieta's myopia and made ironic asides to Lerroux about Strauss, including a barbed comment that he will leave the presidency 'with a clean conscience and with my head held high'. On 11 October, the head of state informed Chapaprieta that he could no longer withhold the dossier and wanted the government to act. On the prime minister's request, Alcalá-Zamora told Gil-Robles and Martínez de Velasco the following day, and refused the CEDA leader's entreaties to drop the matter. Confronted by presidential stubbornness, the prime minister and his two senior ministers decided to forward the dossier to the Supreme Court prosecutor without publicity. Ultimately, they did not want to be accused of covering up a scandal 'uncovered' by the president and committed under a minority Radical government in which they had not served.[14]

As Lerroux argued that he had nothing to hide, he not did object to the involvement of the Supreme Court but refused to countenance the resignation of those Radical ministers implicated in the dossier as this would be tantamount to an admission of guilt. But on 18 October, any lingering hope that the political damage could be contained disappeared. Chapaprieta and Gil Robles were alerted to moves to raise Strauss in parliament and it appeared likely that Azaña would mention *estraperlo* at a forthcoming mass meeting in Comillas. To avoid being implicated in the scandal, Gil-Robles issued a seemingly innocuous press release that only served to stoke the fires of speculation further. It did not prevent Azaña from making vailed references to Strauss in Comillas and failed to protect the Radicals' allies from the rising political heat. The CEDA leader convinced Lerroux that the quickest way out of the crisis was for the Radicals to reaffirm their fitness for office and confront their critics in the Cortes. On 22 October, Pérez Madrigal, a party backbencher, called on the government to make a statement which prompted the opposition to demand a parliamentary commission of inquiry to determine political responsibilities. When the Lliga leader Cambó feared that Gil-Robles and Chapaprieta were prepared to succumb to this pressure, he rose from his seat to denounce what he regarded as an unconstitutional act that would subvert the separation of powers and turn the Cortes into a French Revolution style 'Public Health Committee'. He then raised the 'extremely malevolent precedent' of the 'responsibility commissions' between 1931 and 1933, when parliament became judge and jury.[15]

In an attempt to avoid both a parliamentary investigation and a split with his coalition partners, Lerroux presented the allegations as a conspiracy of lies cooked up by a blackmailer in cahoots with the opposition. He read in parliament a letter written by Guzmán to Strauss that underlined Azaña's interest in his grievances. However, his centre-right allies still voted for a parliamentary investigation; Gil Robles saw it as the best way to delineate responsibility and bring closure. As the CEDA leader did not want to hold the debate on the scandal along party lines, he chose not to press home the advantage that no current ministers – the only ones politically responsible to the Cortes – were involved or demand proof from Lerroux's accusers. This was a great error: a partisan left/right scrap would have produced more heat than light, and the government could have used its majority to guillotine the debate by turning it into a vote of confidence. Had Chapaprieta then referred Strauss' allegations to the courts, no one could have accused him of a cover-up.

Instead, the investigation began on 23 October and the Supreme Court prosecutor told to hand over the available documentation. As the prime minister observed, 'bitterness' and 'passion' characterised the attitude of the parliamentary commission, as 'their partisan spirit raised [the political temperature] rather than reduced it'. Concluding their work in barely three days, investigators admitted that they could not prove that any crime had been committed, or even that *estraperlo* was illegal. But they had 'the moral conviction' that there existed 'conduct and ways of operating that are not in tune with austere or ethical standards'. The parliamentary report provided a list of implicated individuals including two Radical deputies, Salazar Alonso and Sigfrido Blasco-Ibáñez, mid-level figures who had dealings with Strauss like Pich y Pon and Aurelio Lerroux as well as Eduardo Benzo and José Valdivia, the senior interior ministry officials who dealt with the *estraperlo* licence application. Yet investigators only questioned Salazar Alonso and Blasco-Ibáñez, and the report failed to explain precisely what they had done wrong. Nevertheless, after this political naming and shaming, the cabinet decided to disown the officials on the list just before the parliamentary debate of 28 October due to the 'sensitive' nature of their positions.[16]

That day the Radicals faced a political trial in the Cortes. The details of the Strauss case faded into the background as the party's enemies voiced grievances that in some cases dated from the beginning of the century. 'In two hours I lived a hundred years', Lerroux remembered, as he tried to fend off the bitter attacks of his opponents. Although he expected an onslaught from the left, he was surprised and hurt by the interventions of José Antonio Primo de Rivera and the monarchists given his party's role in securing amnesty for their association with the dictatorship. The significant exception was Calvo Sotelo, who identified Alcalá-Zamora as the cause of this parliamentary hullabaloo.

The humiliating climax was a secret vote on the Strauss report that cleared Salazar Alonso but condemned Blasco-Ibáñez. The Radicals left the chamber in protest when votes were subsequently held on implicated officials who could not defend themselves in parliament. When Aurelio Lerroux and Rocha (whose brother had carried out some legal work for Strauss) refused to leave their posts, the prime minister stepped in to force them out, appointing two other Radicals in their place.[17]

Only after the parliamentary trial came to end did the judges take over. On 2 November, the Supreme Court appointed Ildefonso Bellón as a special investigative magistrate. After his 'meticulous enquiry', he filed charges of fraud and bribery against Strauss and influence peddling and misfeasance against those officials who worked with him, including Lerroux's nephew. Bellón stressed that these latter crimes were acts of intention, not commission, as the police closed the casinos immediately. The bribes, the magistrate concluded, consisted of two gold watches worth around 5,000 pesetas in total, but the invoices provided by Strauss did not reveal their recipients, and the dates of purchase – December 1934 – did not tally with his later statements. Furthermore, Aurelio Lerroux's name did not appear on the game license for the Formentor Hotel and Bellón dismissed Strauss' figures for the losses he sustained over *estraperlo*. He also accepted the validity of technical and legal police reports that recommended the legalisation of the game, and pointed to a demonstration of the roulette wheel that took place within the interior ministry. Bellón recorded the astonishment of the high officials who watched Strauss present his game, and Benzo asked how one could make money from it. The inventor replied that it was all about speed and the inevitable errors of judgement made by casino gamblers enjoying themselves. This differed to later reports about what actually happened in the casinos, as these suggested that the house always won. Bellón ruled that Strauss attempted to get a license for a game of skill when in reality he wanted to install a rigged roulette wheel. The case file emphasised that if was not for the swindle, *estraperlo* did not violate Spanish law, and established that ministerial approval had only been given for the game to be played in San Sebastian, not in Majorca. Bellón pointed to an unsigned document issued by Salazar Alonso on 25 August 1934 and another signed by Benzo authorising 'a trial' on condition that bets did not exceed five pesetas. Although the magistrate concluded that there was enough evidence for charges, the allegations were not serious enough to demand a secured bail bond for any of the defendants. For Bellón, the case was a 'poor man's Stravisky', a reference to the far more significant financial scandal that rocked France in 1934.[18]

Tayá-Nombela

The political dust from the Strauss affair had not yet settled when the Tayá-Nombela scandal erupted. Antonio Tayá was a shipping agent known to Lerroux from his days in Barcelona as a Pi y Margall federalist. Tayá never joined the Radical Party and drifted away from politics to concentrate on his increasingly lucrative business activities after 1914. The Radical leader did not hear his name again until May 1935 when Guillermo Moreno, the prime minister's principal private secretary, handed him a voluminous file containing Tayá's claim for state compensation for his Africa Occidental maritime company. In 1926, the firm obtained the right to run the colonial shipping lines in the Gulf of Guinea, but the dictatorship cancelled the concession on two occasions in 1928–29 alleging breach of contract. Tayá claimed that the suspension of service and the consequent losses were due to the malicious actions of the colonial authorities who kept his ships in port and withheld promised subsidies in order to aid a competitor. After the Council of State, the supreme consultative council, argued against the rescission of contract, the Supreme Court concurred, adding in November 1930 that Tayá should receive compensation for the state aid that Africa Occidental did not receive. Yet less than a year later, the first payment of 500,000 pesetas was blocked on the orders of the new Provisional Government, and in February 1932, the republican-socialist coalition under Azaña once again annulled the contract. These decisions were made at the highest political level, as the relevant government department, the General Directorate of Morocco and the Colonies, reported directly to the prime minister's office. After this fresh reverse, Tayá took his case back to the courts and the Supreme Court reversed the decision on 25 April 1935, ordering the complainant to be indemnified in full. Nevertheless, when the General Directorate of Morocco and the Colonies stalled on carrying out the sentence, an exasperated Tayá launched an appeal to the prime minister's office less than a month later. Guillermo Moreno told Lerroux that Africa Occidental demanded seven million pesetas for unpaid subsidies between 1930 and 1935, but state lawyers were appealing against the figure. The principal private secretary advised the prime minister to commission an expert evaluation of the services provided by the company as the basis of a negotiation with Tayá in the hope that this would end the dispute with less cost to the government. With Moreno and Tayá's friend the left-wing Federalist deputy Melchor Marial acting as intermediaries, Lerroux met Africa Occidental's owner, who stressed his willingness to settle to avoid further financial pain in his ruinous legal battle with the state.[19]

After reading details of the case carefully, the prime minister sympathised with Tayá's plight. He agreed with Moreno that the government should accept the Supreme Court's ruling, adding that the contract be restored to Africa Occidental. To enable the company to meet its contractual obligations, a magistrate working with an accountant from the finance ministry determined the amount of unpaid subsidies between 1928 and 1935 to be three million pesetas, and stipulated that it come out of the Guinean colonial budget. This was less than half of Tayá's claim, and it could have been the end of the matter, as the prime minister had the constitutional right to resolve this type of administrative dispute. But Lerroux recognised that Alcalá-Zamora was against paying any compensation, and the president had requested that no decision be made until the Council of State had pronounced on the settlement. The Radical leader was hardly an expert on administrative procedure, but he knew enough to grasp that was an attempt to torpedo the agreement, but once again, he decided to indulge Alcalá-Zamora in the vain hope of winning his favour. As feared, the Council of State's pronouncement did muddy the waters as it stated that the government should not pay for services that it did not receive and specified that any compensation had to be based solely on losses suffered by the company. Moreno advised the prime minister to disregard this non-legally binding judgement, as the final bill could be even higher, but an undecided Lerroux created a ministerial committee under Chapaprieta, Gil-Robles and Royo-Villanova to make a final recommendation after taking the ruling to cabinet on 9 July.[20]

Senior officials within the General Directorate of Morocco and the Colonies were furious at the government's willingness to come to terms with Tayá. Its inspector general, Antonio Nombela, and his secretary José Antonio de Castro accused Moreno of misleading the prime minister in order to profit personally from plundering the colonial budget. Tayá, in turn, accused these civil servants of disobeying the Supreme Court judgment of that April. Nombela and Castro were close political associates of Alcalá-Zamora, as the president had managed to place many of his friends within the colonial department in 1931. The change of government two years later did not harm their careers, as Samper promoted both men to the top of the General Directorate of Morocco and the Colonies as part of a general administrative reorganisation that only increased the influence of the head of state. After Lerroux's return to power in October 1934, clashes between his prime ministerial office and the colonial department increased as the former sought to hive off the latter's duties to a reconstituted overseas territories ministry that had been originally abolished in 1899. Underlying this administrative conflict was a power struggle between colonial officials and Radical post holders over the production of cocoa and coffee in Spanish Guinea, as well as the export of tropical timber and the concessions of public works and maritime transport contracts. What made this dispute politically serious was Alcalá-Zamora's championing of his allies within the General Directorate of Morocco and the Colonies. He spuriously objected to a decree regulating the production and importation of cocoa from the neighbouring island colony of Fernando Poo, while sponsoring the unopposed appointment of Luis Sánchez-Guerra, the brother of his secretary Rafael, to the post of public works inspector general in Spanish Guinea. Thus the president's attempt at empire building was frustrated by Lerroux after discovering that the colonial department had formulated a prohibitively expensive infrastructure plan for the West African colony without his knowledge or approval.[21]

Royo-Villanova was not involved in this turf war, and he was the only member of the cabinet committee to study the papers of the Tayá case. With the support of Gil-Robles and Chapaprieta, he reported to the cabinet on 11 July that Moreno had handled the matter competently. But as the subject came up at the end of the meeting, Luis Lucia, the minister taking the minutes, did not properly record the backing of the cabinet for the prime minister's office. That did not seem to matter at the time, as Lerroux told Moreno to order the General Directorate of Morocco and the Colonies to pay Tayá. On 12 July, Nombela refused, and complained to Alcalá-Zamora, Lucia and Gil-Robles that the colonial budget was being fleeced. Moreno instructed Lucia to confirm in writing the cabinet agreement, but he refused, and to add to the political pressure Alcalá-Zamora called Lerroux to express his opposition while Gil-Robles demanded to look at the case file on 13 July. After the Radical leader handed it over and suspended the payment, the CEDA leader proposed in cabinet three days later that compensation should only be based on the Council of State's judgement. At 3.2 million pesetas, this turned out to be more than the original settlement and Lerroux sacked Nombela and Castro, ordering the General Directorate of Morocco and the Colonies to pay up on 13 September.[22]

With the *estraperlo* scandal dominating the headlines, Nombela waited until 28 November to retaliate. That day he sent parliament a note – simultaneously published in the press – demanding that his 'honour be restored' by the revocation of his dismissal as inspector general. He not only accused Moreno of defrauding the public purse but claimed that Lerroux had acted illegally by compensating Tayá. Significantly, Federico Fernández Castillejo of Alcalá-Zamora's Republican Progressive Party presented these allegations to the Cortes having accompanied Nombela to a meeting with Chapaprieta a fortnight earlier to demand a full parliamentary investigation. But after the earthquake of Strauss, the prime minister was not keen for Nombela's campaign to gather momentum and proposed in cabinet on 28 November to send the former inspector general's note to the political graveyard of the parliamentary petitions commission. This was rejected by Gil-Robles, as the CEDA leader was convinced that Nombela was out to get him and Lucia, and insisted that the Cortes look into the charges in further detail. As in the *estraperlo* imbroglio, Gil-Robles also called on Lerroux to anticipate the opposition and ask for a parliamentary commission; the Radical leader did so in the Cortes on the following day. Not all deputies were impressed. Breaking protocol, the former minister Royo-Villanova stood up to protest against a ruse designed 'to cast further shadows on Mr. Lerroux' at the cost of destroying parliamentary democracy:

> Is Parliament going to be at the mercy of anyone who comes to bring us matters that are outside our competence? What is this about? [On one occasion] a foreign man, who one day instead of going to the Courts, goes to the President of the Republic and presents, in my judgement irregularly, an accusation. Now it is something more scandalous: a civil servant [comes] a few months after losing his position and who coincidentally ... has lost all hope of getting it back ... How can we, just because some man makes an allegation, paralyse the legislative work [of parliament] to nominate a Commission, just like last time?

He went on to suggest that the matter be dealt with by the parliamentary petitions commission as the government was already conducting an internal inquiry, and that any political responsibilities should be discussed on the floor of the Cortes. Having just left government, Royo-Villanova promised to take part in such a debate, as 'I will answer for everything ... that took place, and I will also respond for all those people ... who continue to have confidence in Mr. Lerroux'.[23]

The former minister's speech did not prevent a parliamentary investigation. On 7 December, this concluded that Lerroux was innocent and confirmed the dismissals of Nombela and Castro. Yet the enquiry heard evidence from Nombela without calling Tayá, and also ruled that Moreno had authorised the original payment to Tayá without cabinet authorisation on 11 July. The report pleased no one. Radical deputies rejected its findings of culpability with the support of the Liberal Democrats, the Lliga and the PNV. The left did not get a condemnation of the whole government, while monarchists were disappointed that Lerroux was off the hook. As if the situation was not chaotic enough,

Lucia remarked in parliament that the agreement to pay Tayá had taken place at the end of cabinet 'with the ministers about to leave the room', which led to a vehement denial by Royo-Villanova. This was followed by an altercation in the corridors of parliament between Lucia and his fellow CEDA deputy and ex-justice minister Casanueva, who later apologised to Lerroux for the comments of his party colleague. This sorry spectacle provoked disgust among even seasoned observers of Spanish politics. As the centrist *Ahora* put it, 'the average citizen will have their head in their hands [with bewilderment] as they recall the existence of magistrates' courts, the complaints' boxes in the Palace of Justice [and] administrative investigations; he will suspect that all that is immaterial when Congress of Deputies... can intervene and be judge and jury'.[24]

The fact that parliament eventually confirmed the Nombela report did not help Lerroux. The debate ended on 8 December with a resounding victory for the opposition. They managed to present the affair as one of fraud exposed by an honourable civil servant. With an increasingly pessimistic Radical leader believing that the centre-right bloc would split over the issue, he instructed his parliamentary spokesman Rafael Guerra del Rio not to hold up the vote on a symbolic motion of censure against the former prime minister and Moreno. Lerroux himself had decided not to participate from the government bench and went home on the evening of 7 December. His withdrawal prompted dismay among his coalition partners and many within his party, who pleaded with him to return to stave off defeat. Lerroux presented his decision to leave parliament before the end of the debate as an act of dignity in the face of unmerited criticism. His disconcerted followers saw it as a confession of defeat. The Radical leader's action was comprehensible: the Nombela allegations were a deliberate attempt to destroy his reputation by inflating an insignificant issue into a major case of corruption. But a parliamentary speech which would have exposed the hollow nature of the accusations against him and rallied the government's supporters could have limited the damage to his leadership and his party.[25]

Alcalá-Zamora Commits Political Suicide

The parliamentary humiliation of the Radical Party brought to an end Chapaprieta's brief spell as prime minister. The negotiations to find his successor were more tortured than usual due to Alcalá-Zamora, as the president's determination to end Gil-Robles' tenure as war minister ended the possibility of a Martínez de Velasco administration. With Lerroux banished to political purgatory, the former prime minister blessed the deal agreed by the speaker Santiago Alba and the CEDA leader to support each other if either was called to the presidential palace. But Alcalá-Zamora was no longer interested in prolonging the life of the present parliament. He was looking for a dissolution, and offered Miguel Maura and Portela Valladares the opportunity of jointly wielding power. This was madness; apart from a mutual antipathy, the two men could barely muster ten deputies between them. After this move failed with a break in relations between Maura and the president, the latter turned exclusively to Portela, suspended the parliamentary session and announced that his new government would organise fresh elections. The prospect of a national poll broke the unity of the former centre-right bloc as the smaller parties – the Lliga, Agrarians and the Liberal-Democrats – agreed to serve Portela alongside Chapaprieta. They followed the logic that if a dissolution was inevitable, it was better that the left did not have the opportunity to call elections. Portela was under strict instructions from the president not to ask the Radical Party or the CEDA to join the government; in any case, neither organisation was prepared to offer ministers. When Radicals Manuel Becerra and Joaquín de Pablo-Blanco agreed to accept office under Portela, they had to leave the party.

The Portela government was a key marker in Alcalá-Zamora's strategy to establish a new centrist political force on the ruins of the Radical Party. From April 1935, he had dreamed of having the loyalty of a large bloc of deputies who would underwrite his political activism. Even if another election did not win a majority for his centre party, it would alter the parliamentary arithmetic enough to permit the unrestricted exercise of his presidential powers until his term expired in December 1937. It would also provide the platform for his return to front-line politics. There is little doubt that Alcalá-Zamora used the two scandals to further his ambitions and break the unity of the ruling centre-right coalition in the autumn of 1935. Despite being cast into the political wilderness, Lerroux continued to be the main obstacle to the president's pet project and Portela used every trick in the governmental book to weaken the former prime minister's hold over the Radical Party. Struggling to come to terms with Strauss and Nombela, the veteran republican witnessed how Portela dangled the fruits of power in the faces of demoralised Radical deputies who feared that a rapid return to government was impossible due to the now toxic reputation of its leader.[26]

Lerroux refused to wave the white flag of surrender. He did not consider retirement just yet. That November he published a detailed plan to reactivate the stalled process of internal party reform, and just before Christmas the Radicals held a special congress that reaffirmed Lerroux's leadership, while granting Santiago Alba a prominent place in the projected reorganisation, a clear sign that he was being groomed for the succession. Delegates also confirmed the alliance with the CEDA. Although in trouble, it was still assumed that the Radicals had a future in Spanish politics; the party would remain an essential part of any future centre-right majority government. By the beginning of 1936, Lerroux had successfully contained the attempts by Portela to steal the party's best talents as only twelve accepted government jobs, leaving the Radicals with a parliamentary grouping still in excess of sixty.[27]

As December progressed, Alcalá-Zamora's hopes of a realignment within the centre-right looked doomed to failure. The minor parties within the Portela government were not prepared to come together within a new centrist grouping, let alone fight an election against their old Radical and CEDA allies. Cambó and Chapaprieta hoped that Portela would reconstruct a broad centre-right coalition as the government faced the real prospect of a broad electoral pact between leftist parties that included communists as well as left republicans and socialists. It was political suicide to run alone as the voting system awarded 75–80% of the seats to the winning slate in multi-member constituencies. This was a dilemma of Alcalá-Zamora and Portela's making as the sudden closure of parliament prevented an electoral reform bill from reaching the statute book. Lerroux drew up the legislation during his final government after closely consulting his centre-right partners. Reflecting his great political experience, it proposed reducing the scale of victory for the victors, eliminating electoral thresholds and the second round, and reducing the size of constituencies with more than ten members, as it was in these districts where the results were least proportional to the votes cast. Had these changes been introduced in time for the crucial elections the following February, the final composition of the Cortes would have better reflected the close outcome of the poll.

In December 1935, Portela did not foresee the consequences of the failure of electoral reform as no one within the government wanted to go to the country immediately. But as Alcalá-Zamora did also not want his prime minister to work with the CEDA or reopen parliament, the smaller parties began to peel away from the administration. Soon Portela's cabinet only consisted of friends and cronies of the president. In order to avoid submitting his government to a parliamentary vote of confidence that would surely be lost, the prime minister obtained the president's approval to call fresh election. 'Nothing is less parliamentary', wrote Lerroux, 'nothing less politically dishonest, electorally less honourable or more risky than that decision'.[28]

The electoral campaign began on 7 January 1936 in circumstances that did not favour the centre-right generally or the Radicals in particular.

Quite apart from a predictable dip in popularity after over two years in government, they faced an electorate tired of the suspension of constitutional guarantees following the October 1934 revolution. The green shoots of economic recovery had yet to translate into a fall in unemployment, and Chapaprieta's austerity measures provoked fierce protests from civil servants. To make things worse for Lerroux, the Strauss and Nombela scandals made him an easy target for his enemies and the Radicals a less attractive electoral partner for other centre-right parties. The dissolution of parliament ended the former prime minister's hopes for party reform, and open conflict erupted within the Radicals' provincial organisations during the selection of candidates. Lerroux's late intervention could not compensate for Alba's lack of authority, and some of those who lost out in internal squabbles joined the depleted ranks of Portela's centre party. Those who remained had to fight an election in which their leader was not just a 'traitor' for the left, but also 'the executor of the Spanish proletariat' responsible for 'drowning in blood' the 1934 revolution. It was evident that for Lerroux and his former ministers at stake was not just their seats but also their freedom, as the Popular Front promised to hold to account those 'criminally responsible' for the 'repression'.[29]

The Radical leader therefore had no doubt that the Radicals should contest the election alongside those in government during the October insurrection: the CEDA, Agrarians, Liberal Democrats and the Lliga. As no vote could be lost in the battle to prevent a Popular Front victory, Lerroux obtained the approval of his national committee to enter electoral pacts with the monarchists, despite their generally hostile reaction to the Strauss and Nombela scandals. Predictably, a weakened Radical Party encountered more difficulty making agreements with other parties than in previous elections when they were in government. Conscious of his damaged reputation, Lerroux delegated the task to enter the Anti-revolutionary Bloc to Alba, but this only suggested to conservatives that the republican's long political life was finally ending. Complicating matters further was the CEDA's decision to negotiate pacts with Portela in fifteen leftist strongholds at the expense of the Radicals. Lerroux thought it an error for Gil-Robles to underestimate the value of his party as a partner, while negotiating with those who had little chance of success. He also criticised his former minister's efforts to maximise the number of CEDA candidates within the Anti-Revolutionary bloc in order to dominate the next parliament, stressing that as the left-wing of the electoral coalition, the Radicals could attract republican voters hostile to both the Popular Front and the Catholic right.

In the end, in the Radicals reached agreement with the CEDA in 18 out of the 60 multi-member constituencies. Lerroux had 23 candidates within the Anti-revolutionary Bloc and 44 others fighting alone with a negligible chance of victory. Pre-poll forecasts suggested that the Radicals would not win more than twenty seats. Lerroux himself stood for Castellon, where the party won in 1933, and for insurance accepted an offer from Cambó to be included in the Barcelona slate of the Catalan Front for Order. So, in what would be his last ever election, the old man returned to the city where he first tasted political success, although his mission was very different to that of 1901: he had to convince his voters to go conservative.[30]

The outlook for the Radicals was as gloomy as the prospects for Spanish democracy. Lerroux thought that even if the centre-right won, there would be a merciless struggle to the death between revolutionaries and anti-revolutionaries. The country faced a 'problem, which is not the nature of its [political] regime, but whether it would exist at all'. Even a normally circumspect Alba gloomily noted that there was no longer a 'middle way'. The Radicals' campaign combined its defence of a liberal parliamentary Republic with anti-revolutionary rhetoric. In Barcelona, Lerroux explained that his alliance with the CEDA and moderate republicans was consistent with 'a vision of civilisation that has property and family as its base'. He did not apologise for working with the Catholic right, as he preferred a 'liberal and Christian Republic to a demagogic and communist Republic'. The Radicals were continuing in their task of building a grand 'liberal and conservative... republican bloc' that would prevent the victory of the revolutionaries of 1934, the 'moral and material ruin' of Spain, 'the renunciation of all feelings of humanity', 'the most awful barbarism' and even 'our very own existence as individuals'. The Radical leader and his followers went to vote on 16 February 1936 convinced that their futures were on the line.[31]

The February 1936 Election

For Lerroux, the early hours of 17 February were as bitter as his triumphs in the 1931 and 1933 elections were sweet. As the first results came in, it became obvious that he had failed to be elected for Barcelona. In Castellon, the CEDA and the Popular Front relegated him to third place, but at least the Radical leader had garnered enough votes to force a second round. He was unaware of how exactly his party was doing nationally, but it seemed evident that most of those candidates who stood as part of the Anti-revolutionary Bloc had a good chance of success. But soon the count descended into chaos. As the polls closed on 16 February, unorganised groups of Popular Front supporters illegally began to congregate around the counting centres. Ostensibly celebrating the increasingly clear triumphs of the left in urban areas that placed the Popular Front in the lead, they jumped the gun to proclaim victory a few hours later. Consequently, jubilation turned into demands for the immediate release of revolutionaries from prison as well as control of local councils. By the afternoon of 17 February, leftist crowds called for Popular Front leaders to take power. With declarations still pending in many areas, these increasingly violent demonstrations posed a threat not just to public order but also to the integrity of the final election result itself. Portela, who was interior minister as well as head of government, faced the difficult if necessary prospect of forcibly dispersing the supporters of those who could be in government within weeks.

On the morning of the 17th, the Portela government decided to declare a state of war [*estado de guerra*] to take back control of the streets and ensure the peaceful completion of the count. However, Alcalá-Zamora forced the prime minister to declare a state of alarm [*estado de alarma*], which meant that Portela, and not the army, remained responsible for preserving order. This prompted repeated attempts by the prime minister to resign, but the president held firm and it appeared that Portela would remain in office until the official declaration of the result on 20 February. But further street violence led the prime minister to desert his post 24 hours earlier. This left the government leaderless at a critical juncture in Spain's history, and Lerroux – like most Spaniards – decried Portela's 'flight' or 'bunk'. The Radical leader attributed the prime minister's decision to the electoral failure of his candidates, but correctly pointed out that he had to remain in office temporarily until the situation had been clarified and public safety guaranteed. Not even Portela's most fervent supporters, Lerroux averred, 'can find arguments to defend his actions', and took pride in his very different reaction to the October 1934 revolt.[32]

The Radical leader was as surprised as everyone else by the strong performance of the Popular Front which left the election result on a knife-edge when Portela abandoned office on the morning of 19 February. Still, he suspected that later declarations in traditionally conservative areas would favour the Anti-revolutionary Bloc. This did not spare Gil-Robles of criticism. The Radical leader argued that the inability to turn votes into seats was due to the CEDA leader's partisan approach in the pre-election negotiations, 'overconfidence' and 'excessive arrogance' that undermined the cohesion of the Anti-revolutionary Bloc, also claiming that the 'right should not have vacillated, haggled on candidates, and dismissed cooperation'. The outcome was uncertainty until the second round. As a shrewd electoral operator, Lerroux knew that in very close contests, not even the official declaration was definitive since 'electoral reruns can influence, sometimes decisively [like in February 1936] the composition of the [parliamentary] Chamber'. Moreover, 'it would be very different indeed' if these contests 'took place under a different government to that which organised the general election'.

The former prime minister was pointing to Alcalá-Zamora's decision to ask Azaña to replace Portela. In the mind of the Radical leader, this only facilitated the 'dubious and disputable' victory of the Popular Front. He argued strenuously against it when asked by the president during the normal round of consultations, asserting that a new government could not be formed in the middle of an election count with the outcome still uncertain. Instead, he pressed the president to exercise boldly his constitutional powers until the crisis was over. Lerroux would never understand why in that 'most critical hour' he gave the premiership to a left republican whom he did not trust and who had scorned the rule of law by fighting the election with the leaders of a rebellion. Gil-Robles had been denied the opportunity to govern for much less. The Radical leader maintained that rather than choose Azaña, Alcalá-Zamora should have selected a respected political figure who would have completed the election count impartially, contained the 'avaricious avalanche of the Popular Front' and resisted 'the inevitable outbursts that were taking place in the streets'. If that meant provoking the revolutionary general strike threatened by the extreme left if the Popular Front were denied power, then at least the rebels would have confronted 'a legitimately constituted power'. These were serious accusations, but Lerroux did not appreciate the desperate political straits that Alcalá-Zamora found himself in after Portela's sudden departure. All of his political friends were already in the cabinet, and none of them was willing to take power in those desperate circumstances except the military men.[33]

The Azaña government took office on the afternoon of 19 February. For the next few days, Lerroux received reports concerning 'the most elemental and shameless ploys' undertaken by the new authorities to 'force the scrutineers [of the count]' in several key provinces to produce 'a falsified parliamentary majority' for the Popular Front. The Radicals were convinced that leftist chicanery denied them four out of the eight seats that they believed were theirs in the first round. Another three seats were later lost following a ruling by the leftist dominated parliamentary electoral commission. Without these irregularities, Lerroux complained, 'any parliamentary majority would have been in doubt... or precarious' for anyone claiming victory. Certainly, Azaña's accession to power eliminated any possibility of 'the legitimate triumph of those candidates of the republican electoral coalition hostile to the Popular Front'. It was little comfort that Radical voters generally supported Lerroux's anti-revolutionary stance. In 51 of the 57 constituencies where comparisons can be made, they all or mainly voted for centre-right electoral slates, which won 700,000 more votes than in 1933.[34]

The End of the Democratic Republic

Out of parliament, Lerroux could only observe the last months of the Republic as a privileged outsider. Refusing to leave politics, he spent his time trying to rebuild the Radical Party in grim times. This is not to suggest that the disappearance of the longest surviving republican party was inevitable; the left republicans had suffered a similarly catastrophic defeat in 1933 and were now back in government. The main problem was that the Radicals (together with the CEDA), were the main targets of leftist violence that disrupted their legal political activities after 19 February. To make matters worse, the Azaña government overturned Radical majorities on local councils; political reprisals combined with the lack of income meant that any recovery remained a chimera.

Far from staging a remarkable political comeback, Lerroux soon found that his own life was in danger. As the *bête noire* of socialists and communists, the Radical leader had to endure regular demonstrations outside his home with protesters chanting 'Lerroux Must Die!' and waving placards graphically depicting his funeral. On 13 March, the police intervened to prevent arsonists from firing his home. In this context, it is tempting to regard leftist demands for Lerroux's imprisonment as a positive step to ensure his safety.[35] In any case, the government seemed to worry less about what leftist vigilantes could do to Lerroux than what the old man could do to its hold on power as the interior ministry disregarded the former prime ministers' protests to change his police escort in order to keep a better eye on his movements. The left also humiliated Lerroux in other, more petty, ways. These included Popular Front local councils withdrawing the honours granted to him by previous centre-right administrations. Concerned friends and party colleagues urged him to leave Madrid, but Lerroux was determined to stay put and face any criminal investigation that Popular Front leaders had promised former ministers involved in the suppression of the October 1934 insurrection.

Nevertheless, the Radical leader's zeal for the political fight much diminished following a car accident during a drive back to Madrid from

San Rafael on 15 May. Lerroux was still recovering at home when he heard rumours of a military uprising. He could not contain his scepticism given memories of Sanjurjo's foolish escapade in August 1932, but stressed that he would never conspire 'as long as republican legality remained in place'. This did not signify any change of attitude towards the left republican government, as 'we are suffering a more or less disguised Dictatorship' whose acts of constitutional vandalism included 'the illegal dismissal' of his long-time rival Alcalá-Zamora from the presidency. Lerroux pleaded with his supporters to 'remain united' and 'have nothing to do with fascism [and] falangism' because 'salvation' lay with 'the law and freedom'. Only if the Popular Front intended to abolish democracy would the Radicals cooperate with a rebellion to restore 'the rule of law' and 'legality'.[36]

Epilogue

Exile and Return
(1936–1949)

On 28 June 1949, the press announced that Alejandro Lerroux had died of a heart complaint in the early hours of the previous day. He was eighty-five. He died 'in the bosom of the Catholic Church' and 'comforted by the spiritual assistance' of his parish priest and friend, father Moreno. But the news was no surprise to many of his friends and acquaintances in Madrid. Many had already come to pay their last respects to his nephew Aurelio and his wife. Lerroux no longer resided in calle O'Donnell, so they headed to 4 Marqués de Villamejor, adjacent to the central thoroughfare of the Paseo de la Castellana, where the former prime minister lived following his return from Portuguese exile in July 1947. They brought 'countless flowers' to go alongside the numerous 'telegrams of condolence' received 'from all the provinces of Spain'. Although the family tried to prevent his funeral becoming a political act, let alone an anti-Francoist gathering, the backgrounds of the mourners suggested the opposite.

Among them was Juan Ignacio Luca de Tena, the chief-editor of *ABC* and friend of Lerroux from their days in the Press Association. At 6.15 p.m. on 27 June, he witnessed the coffin being carried into the Concepción Church from a modest hearse. Among the crowd following the body were fellow monarchists Count Romanones, Gabriel Maura, Natalio Rivas, Joaquín Calvo Sotelo, Juan Pujol, José Martínez Acacio, the widow of general Cavalcanti and the Count of Vallellano. While the ceremony did not have the pomp of an ex-prime minister's funeral, other attendees included the Cortes speaker, the carlist Esteban Bilbao, and Madrid's mayor, the former CEDA deputy José Moreno Torres. Their presence ameliorated the hostility emanating from monarchists towards a regime encountering serious internal and external problems. These critics also included former republican ministers who believed that the return of a king would be the best way to restore constitutional politics such as Rafael Guerra del Río, Cirilo del Río, Vicente Iranzo, José María Cid, Diego Hidalgo, César Jalón, Ramón Feced and a host of others who had served Radical governments or supported them from the backbenches. Perhaps the most poignant example of this was the appearance of generals Luis Castelló and Mariano Muñoz Castellanos, close associates of Lerroux in the war ministry who fought on different sides during the civil war.

Recalling the funeral, Luca de Tena's hostility towards the Republic diminished slightly. He acknowledged that 'History would have radically changed' if that regime 'had consolidated under a presidency held by don Alejandro Lerroux', a man 'profoundly liberal in spirit and action' who alone among the victors of 1931 sought to 'liberalise, democratise and make bearable' the political earthquake of 14 April. That explained the reaction to his death: 'nearly every one of us were monarchists at Lerroux's [burial]. Just imagine saying to don Alejandro on 14 April 1931 that among the chief mourners in his funeral would mainly be ... adversaries of that form of Government that had been the hope and goal of his life!'[1]

Nevertheless, Luca de Tena's memory was selective. He had forgotten that among the congregation were also old men who represented a dwindling ideal that Lerroux embodied best in his later years: liberal constitutionalism. Since the Franco regime was an explicit repudiation of this tradition, it could never consider the former prime minister as one of its own. As defenders of the rule of law, centre-right moderates who governed under both the constitutional monarchy and the Republic could not identify with the Caudillo. At best, they had to put up with his dictatorship, obeying it as the unavoidable consequence of a political catastrophe.

This sums up Lerroux's attitude towards the Nationalists during the civil war. His support for Franco was reactive; in no way does it suggest a deep commitment to what would be forty years of authoritarianism. After all, it was not the first civil war in modern Spanish history, and constitutionalism had always survived. Without wanting to become a martyr, Lerroux's decision to back the July 1936 rebellion was a logical confirmation of his political trajectory. He was the prime minister who had defeated the revolutionaries of 1934 and fought against the Popular Front in February 1936. He and his supporters suffered the consequences of electoral defeat as they were harassed and hounded in the months leading up to the fratricidal conflict. Had Lerroux stayed in Republican Madrid in 1936, it is likely that he would have shared the same grisly fates of José Martínez Velasco and Melquíades Álvarez, the leaders of the Agrarians and the Liberal Democrats, as well as other Radical and CEDA politicians. Their murders were evidence – if any were needed – that the rule of law no longer existed in the Republican zone. But the Radical leader's initial backing for the rebels did not imply that he approved of the subsequent process of 'Falangistisation' that transformed a cause that at the outset Lerroux thought was a republican defence of order. How else could he had acted that bloody summer, when the head of the Council of National Defence [*Junta de Defensa Nacional*] in July 1936 was general Miguel Cabanellas, the most prominent Radical within the military? Why would Lerroux doubt Mola or Franco, the two leading generals of the rebellion whom he had earlier rescued from political ostracism, even placing the latter in charge of the forces that vanquished the revolutionaries of 1934?

Taking Sides

Lerroux did not make his usual sojourn to Baños de Montemayor at the beginning of June 1936. The resort manager warned him of disturbances in the spa town and could not guarantee his safety. The Radical leader decided to go to Portugal instead in order to continue the writing of his memoirs in peace. He had started work on them that spring, although due to the failings of his long-time secretary Sánchez Fuster, his papers were in a chaotic state. Both his wife Teresa and nephew Aurelio were relieved at the change of holiday destination as they became ever more alarmed at the decline of public order in Madrid that prompted the family to place its money, precious items and bonds in a safety deposit box within the Bank of Spain.

On the morning of 13 July, Lerroux heard of the kidnap and murder of José Calvo Sotelo, the leader of the National Bloc. The Radical leader's family panicked when they realised that policemen were among the perpetrators. His wife demanded that they leave Madrid immediately for San Rafael, and returned only on 16 July to prepare their luggage for journey to Portugal the following week. After lunch the next day, when conspirators in Melilla were on the brink of revolt, Martín Báguenas, an old police friend involved in the planning of the rebellion in Madrid, warned Lerroux that he should leave the capital immediately. Taking heed of this advice, the family took their belongings back to San Rafael, although Sánchez Fuster preferred to stay behind in Madrid. With the head of his protection team bringing the passports, Teresa asked her husband to go to Portugal the following day, 18 July, while she would follow with Aurelio and their daughter-in-law three days later. She hoped that they would all be back in Spain a month later.

Lerroux set off early the next morning unaware that the garrisons in Spanish Morocco and the Canaries had already risen against the government. His destination was the Curia hotel-spa in the Portuguese Buçaco mountains, and he reckoned it would take the entire day to arrive. While travelling west he noticed a heavy police presence on the Avila-Salamanca road, but reached the frontier without incident at 1 p.m. After a long wait and a baggage search, he crossed into Portugal and reached the hotel at 7 p.m. It was only then that he read the first reports of the rebellion in the local press. His heart fluttered when he saw reports about fighting near his home at the Guadarrama Pass where he had left his family hours earlier. Afterwards, he received a phone call from general Cavalcanti who wanted to know his reaction to the rebellion. Lerroux replied that although he was not involved, he would not oppose it, although his only focus was locating the whereabouts of his family. This remained his main preoccupation until they were reunited three weeks later on 11 August.

By that date, it was evident that the failed military rising had turned into civil war. Lerroux issued a public note of support for the insurgents, and on Spain's National Day of 12 October, pledged his allegiance to the recently elevated Nationalist leader Francisco Franco. In the latter missive, he refused to recognise the 'apparent legality' of the Popular Front government, as this was based on 'an artificially rigged [election] result'. Leftist ministers, he went on, were ultimately responsible for the violation of civil rights to the point that 'the life, the home, the property and the conscience of each citizen was protected only by the individual means of defence available to him'. This was the inevitable consequence of the decision on 19 July to give up the monopoly of legitimate force by distributing weapons to Popular Front parties and trade union organisations. Consequently, the Caudillo was merely doing the same as he had done in October 1934, saving the 'ethical and moral principles that underpin the nation, society and civilisation'.[2]

Lerroux dismissed Republican propaganda that portrayed the war as a conflict between democracy and fascism. While recognising that possession of the principal organs of state gave the left a moral legitimacy abroad, he could not accept that 'Popular Front Spain has a democratic character' as it would 'take an effort of imagination or hypocrisy that goes beyond reasonable limits'. It was absurd, he argued, to conflate 'communism' with 'democracy' while at the same time labelling those liberal politicians who opposed the Popular Front as 'authoritarians'. Using similar arguments to Gregorio Marañón and Clara Campoamor, the exiled Radical warned that the left republicans have been disembowelled by the revolutionary forces of socialism interested only in the 'dictatorship of the proletariat'.

Lerroux did not fail to realise than an attempt to defend the Nationalist cause from a liberal democratic perspective sounded incongruous, but appealed to international opinion to recognise that the rebels represented the Spanish army which was but 'the people organised and armed by the nation' to defend 'the law and rights' besmirched by revolutionaries. The Nationalist movement was but as an 'interim power' created by the destruction of the rule of law by the Popular Front. Moreover, he insisted that the army had acted in defence of the Republic, using its flag, national anthem and acclamations. He may not have been directly involved, but when dealing the communists, the military rebels faced 'the battle standard of one dictatorship', and 'raised that of another dictatorship', the army. With democracy crushed in a struggle between two dictatorships, he had to take sides, and inclined towards the latter.[3]

However, the continuation of the war and the 'fascistisation' of the Nationalist zone placed Lerroux in an increasingly uncomfortable position during the course of 1937. He supported Franco on the basis that he led a strictly military dictatorship that would only last until victory was secured, public order restored and 'disappearance' of 'the dangers' that had caused the war. With Primo de Rivera's dictatorship in mind, he wanted neither a prolongation of exceptional measures nor the institutionalisation of an authoritarian regime. With 'the dangers' eliminated, Franco should give way to a 'regime of responsible liberty and organised democracy that guaranteed ... order and authority' and stabilised society 'on the paths of progressive development and social justice'. Lerroux no longer thought of a liberal democracy but of a Republic that combined aspects of his hosts' Salazarism with representative institutions. This, he hoped, would help heal the wounds of the civil war and stamp out demands to exterminate the political enemy. The conflict had to be won, but once it was over, the vanquished should be reincorporated into the 'common *Patria*'.[4]

Did all this mean that Lerroux had renounced liberal democracy? His 1937 memoir *Pequeña Historia* shows that this was not the case. He accepted that it had not worked well in Spain 'whether with Monarchies or with Republics', even if he did not clarify why the latter always ended so quickly. In any case, and reflecting sadly on the course of his own political career, he implored an end to the dynamic of 'going through life coming and going from the Monarchy to the Republic, from the Republic to the Dictatorship, and from the Dictatorship to the Monarchy'. There needed to be an end to the sacrifice of so many generations 'who succumbed heroically, tragically and futilely in the task'. This could only come, he wrote, with the realisation that constitutions in themselves do not create democracies and freedoms. Without deep roots, Spanish constitutionalism had co-existed with openly dictatorial governments and 'oligarchies of various kinds, organised in political parties'. Like the republican he was, Lerroux reasoned that reforming representative government to reconstruct a legal and institutional system within Spain that would guarantee individual freedoms and facilitate popular participation was not the priority. Rather, he called for nothing less than the remaking of a people incapable of governing itself in order to build a democracy founded on a common ideal of mutual respect. This was the mission of his 'regime of responsible liberty and organised democracy'; it had to plant the seeds of 'culture' that would eventually produce the flowers of freedom and democracy.

As a lifelong patriot, it was axiomatic for Lerroux that any regime that emerged from the military dictatorship would not slavishly imitate a foreign model. With its foundations based on 'the depths of tradition', this new political system would be shaped by 'the spirituality of a common civilisation', even if it remained ultimately rooted in 'present realities'. His vision was not a static one, as it essential to promote 'moral and material prosperity' through peaceful, gradual and patient change. Even during the dark days of 1937, he dismissed as 'sectarian prejudice' the argument that freedom, democracy and parliamentary government were in terminal decline and mocked those who sought to revive authoritarian institutions that had 'failed' in the past.

Lerroux's criticism of those within Nationalist Spain who wanted to use the war to sever Spain's link with the values of western civilisation could not be more explicit. Carlist or Falangist conceptions of organic democracy, guilds and corporations may have been 'essences' that 'do not evaporate', but they were also pure 'political archaeology'. If communism was the 'complete denial of our [human] personality', Spain should not adopt 'fascist or Nazi' models either, irrespective of the supposed achievements of Mussolini and Hitler: 'If we are right in being Spanish patriots above everything, then perhaps we already have the solution that our necessities demand'. Lerroux did not have a problem if the Francoist authorities thought the answer lay in organic democracy and a corporative parliament. But he reaffirmed his devotion 'until the end of my days, because of conviction and decorum' in 'a republican, democratic, liberal and parliamentary regime'. As this required 'the people to be educated again' to ensure that freedom could be exercised 'completely' and enjoyed 'to its greatest extent', he did not hesitate to call for the present generation to make sacrifices so that it could 'live without sun to allow the rain to fertilise the earth'. Someday, he dreamed, 'the sun of liberty' would rise and 'shine again on Spain'.[5]

A Tolerant and Inclusive Leader

Lerroux's wartime writings are valuable in that they dispel the myth about his supposed intellectual vacuity. These are not the words of an opportunist who sacrificed everything to get political power for nefarious or corrupt ends. They are the thoughts of a seasoned statesman committed to constitutional politics who managed to prosper originally as an outside critic of 'the system' and later as the leader of an electorally successful political movement that mirrored his strengths and ambitions. There were failures: he could not make the Radical Party the national equivalent of the Barcelona machine that provided his first taste of political victory during the 1900s. While his party served as a vehicle for power in the 1930s, he was never able to establish an effective organisation capable of sustaining lasting loyalties outside election campaigns. He also clung to romantic notions of revolution for far too long, not adjuring the faith until the last years of the constitutional monarchy; a radical firebrand until 1910, his ambivalent attitude to dynastic politics for the next decade may not have brought the system down but it scarcely strengthened it. Yet this hardly makes him unique among republicans. If one compares his direction of travel with those republicans who came before and after him, we find that Lerroux came to terms with constitutionalism much more quickly; once that step was taken, his main priority became the legal pursuit of power by the Radical Party.[6]

Lerroux's distain for long-winded political programmes and dense intellectualism can be easily explained. He was a born organiser scornful of the narrow doctrinal disputes that characterised Spanish republicanism after the restoration of the monarchy in 1874. He discovered that effective leadership was necessarily grounded in ambiguity, and used this insight to construct the most formidable republican movement in Spain before the civil war. Although his less successful political rivals accused him of a lack of principle, the very reason for his popularity among the electorate was his ability to convey simply his vision of a modern Spain. From his youth in Madrid to enforced exile in Portugal, Lerroux believed that a Republic was the best way to democratise the nation. He entranced audiences with talk of civil equality and the end of privilege; the state would serve the many not the few. His evocation of the cross class 'republican *pueblo*' against the 'monarchist oligarchy' and its malevolent 'caciques' was so powerful because it was sincerely believed; conviction slowed the journey towards a more liberal and inclusive politics that was taken by others like Melquiades Álvarez.

Yet with time Lerroux combined his ideas about the Republic and democracy with a growing appreciation for civil liberties and tolerance;

a 'live and let live' attitude[7] eroded his youthful quasi-religious passion for equality and fraternity. He no longer saw the state as an instrument through which one party could remodel society according its ideological whims; rather than seeing revolutions as midwives to the new society, Lerroux feared them as being more destructive than creative. By 1923, he argued that positive and lasting reform could only come about slowly, and that elections and parliaments were more useful tools for change than bullets and barricades. This conclusion took him to the brink of accepting office under Alfonso XIII before the political crisis provoked by the Annual disaster of 1921 and Primo de Rivera's *pronunciamiento* two years later relieved him of the arduous task of transforming his anti-system Radical Party into a respectable candidate for government. Nonetheless, his reversion to the old shibboleths of Spanish republicanism during the subsequent dictatorship was more apparent than real. Although Lerroux was the leading figure in the Republican Alliance, he never severed his ties with such liberals as Romanones, Melquíades Álvarez and Santiago Alba and indeed worked with them to find an exit from authoritarian government that would restore constitutional government as peacefully as possible. The Republic was no longer the *sine qua non* of Spanish democracy.

It is in this context that we should place the Radical leader's ambivalence towards the Republican-Socialist Alliance and above all his telling silences that Alcalá-Zamora and Azaña simplistically attributed to his 'lack of preparation' for government. For better or worse, Lerroux did not compare unfavourably to the average republican or socialist politician, and unlike them had many years of political experience behind him. His reluctance to speak out in the last days of the monarchy and within the Provisional Government was a way to avoid making uncomfortable commitments to others in the Alliance whom he had to work with in his role as Spain's most prominent republican leader. This was obvious after 14 April 1931, when the euphoria of taking power induced his partners to turn leftwards while a more cautious Lerroux took his party in the opposite direction, losing power and influence in the process.

So how should we understand the Radical Party during the Second Republic? Was it left-wing, centrist, or right-wing? Throughout this period, the party used all these labels tactically. Sometimes it emphasised radicalism to underline its origins and retain the loyalty of the faithful. On other occasions, it sounded conservative to attract the centre-right vote. With the party system in flux, ambiguity was a virtue, not a vice. Yet this should not be mistaken for a lack of strategy. Lerroux never wavered in his objective of making the Radical Party the most significant centrist voice of the Republic against the siren calls of the PSOE and its left republican allies. This was not historically unique; the Radical Progressive Party sought to do the same in the 1873 Republic.

The commitment to moderation ensured that the Radicals became the most important republican party in the 1930s. Of course, errors were made. Antipathy towards the Liberal Republican Right – mutual it needs to be said – and Lerroux's efforts to keep Azaña within the Republican Alliance contributed to the eventual hegemony of the socialist-left republican coalition within the constituent assembly. In a parliament where former monarchists were thin on the ground, Lerroux decided that the Radicals would be the conservative wing of the constitutionalised revolution of 1931, and eschewed the opportunity to denounce unreservedly its anti-liberal and anti-democratic spirit. Struggling to decide whether the party should move firmly to the right or conciliate the left republicans in the hope of peeling them away from the socialists, Lerroux allowed his right-wing flank to be occupied by others who did not share his commitment to the Republic. His hesitation carried a heavy electoral price, as the Radicals could not take advantage of the conservative tide in November 1933 to become the largest party in the new parliament.

In the aftermath of this shock electoral result, the impromptu pact with the CEDA and the Agrarians demonstrated the extent to which his strategy was neither opportunistic nor merely centrist. By then the Radicals no longer occupied an equidistant position between left and right. The departure of Martínez Barrio and the October 1934 insurrection accelerated the shift to the right that had already begun. That the majority of a once leftist party followed its leader in this journey cannot be attributed simply to his leadership or internal discipline. The partisan Constitution of 1931, and the failures of the left republican-socialist coalition government, convinced the Radicals that liberal democracy and its longstanding commitment to social harmony would be better served with a centre-right coalition rather than collaboration with those who had polarised Spanish society by deepening the 'class struggle'.

Many who knew Lerroux after 1918 stressed his clarity of judgement, and this was on display in November 1933 when he turned the republicans' electoral defeat into a new opportunity for the Republic. His genuine commitment to liberal democracy was shown during the desperate days of October 1934, when he overcame the most violent insurrection in sixty years without turning to authoritarianism. Although some observers compared Lerroux to André Tardieu, the moderate republican leader who dominated French politics in the early 1930s, he was more like his idol Georges Clemenceau, the left republican patriot who led France to victory over Germany in 1918. A fervent anticlerical in his youth, 'The Tiger' ended his career as leader of the conservative

National Bloc in reaction to revolutionary strikes of the 1900s and the Bolshevik Revolution of 1917. Lerroux may not have been a war leader, but he fought on numerous political fronts against multiple enemies. When dealing with the unremitting hostility of left republicans, he had to remain watchful of Alcalá-Zamora's efforts to torpedo his efforts to integrate the Catholic right while defeating the revolutionary aspirations of the anarchosyndicalists (December 1933) and socialists (1933–1934). If that was not enough, he had to confront the challenge of Catalan and Basque nationalism (summer and autumn 1934). It is therefore one of the great ironies of the short history of the Republic that Lerroux was sunk by a minor case of corruption (*estraperlo*) and a non-scandal (the Nombela affair). As even Portela recognised, both episodes only became politically significant due to 'the stupid trumpeting from the highest level'[8], or presidential intrigues intended to destroy Lerroux's leadership and the cohesion of the Radical Party. After making an enormous effort to construct the a centre-right ruling bloc, Gil-Robles threw it all away in an effort to preserve the reputation of the CEDA without realising that without his Radical allies, he had little chance of forming a government.

A great opportunity to consolidate the Republic had been lost. By the summer of 1935, it appeared that Lerroux had finally managed to escape the political quarantine of the Republican-Socialist Alliance. No longer did he need to remain silent about his hopes of a moderate Republic in order to remain in office. Unlike in 1931, his party played a key role drafting constitutional reform that promised a more liberal and democratic political system. His supporters understood this project, and the vast majority voted for the centre-right coalition in February 1936 rather than Martínez Barrio's leftist alternative. Lerroux had carved out his own political space and made the Radicals the anchor of the Republic.

So for this political historian, it is puzzling why Lerroux's reputation has remained low relative to other republicans like Alcalá-Zamora or Azaña. As Juan José Linz has demonstrated, the Radical leader's political career is instructive when analysing the consolidation of democratic regimes. In his pioneering work on the Radicals forty years ago, Octavio Ruiz Manjón stressed that Lerroux's tolerant and inclusive remedy to heal the wounds opened by the 1923 military coup was founded on the values of 'generosity' and 'consensus'. Derided in the 1930s as the remnants of a dying outdated liberalism, these ideals later became the basic ingredients of the 1978 Constitution, Spain's most successful Magna Carta.[9]

A Sad End

Lerroux's 'loyal and disinterested' pledge to the Francoist cause did not ingratiate him with the victors of 1939. Persecution at the hands of the left did not count for much. In the early months of war, socialists confiscated his calle O'Donnell home, destroyed part of the furniture and forced open the safe, confiscating 'various thousands of pesetas in cash, a handful of jewels and other valuables'. The Madrid PSOE quickly converted the building into its eastern district base, and even used its cellars as a prison. Yet these were not the only examples of revolutionary justice against the 'butcher' of October 1934. After militiamen arrested Sánchez Fuster, Lerroux's secretary revealed the details of his employer's bank accounts and safety deposit boxes in order to save his own life. When opened, the government confiscated nearly one million pesetas, and the Republican press used 'Lerroux's Treasure' as the basis of a smear campaign against the Radical leader with the participation of a terrified Fuster.

What happened to relatives and associates was even worse. His aged widowed sister Adriana lost her sight in prison after being arrested in Valencia on the orders of Ángel Galarza, the socialist interior minister. At least she survived, unlike many of the party's former ministers, deputies, mayors and councillors who perished in Republican Spain. They included his old friend Juan José Rocha, who died in Montjuich, the very prison that had been the focus of Lerroux's furious pen forty years earlier.[10]

Some Radicals who managed to cross the lines into Nationalist Spain found to their surprise that they were under investigation. Although membership of the Radical Party did not incur punishment under the terms of the Law of Political Responsibilities of February 1939, the same was not true of Freemasonry, which included Lerroux and other Radical figures among its number. This helps to explain why the Francoist authorities refused to allow the former prime minister to return to Spain at the end of the war. Instead, the military authorities occupied his Madrid home until 1941, and on departure took what was left of the furniture and library. As his estate in Gudillos was close to the front during the war, it served as a refuge for Falangist troops who amused themselves by drinking his wine cellar dry and smashing whatever took their fancy. When the fascists moved on, others came to pillage the remains. Abandoned to the elements, the Civil Guard had to intervene to prevent the main building from being demolished by a gang who sold construction materials on the black-market.[11]

In 1940, Lerroux's ill wife finally managed to return to Madrid in order to receive treatment from the family doctor. She located the remnants of the family's property and rented a modest flat to await the arrival of her husband. Lerroux remained in a small hotel in Estoril that he had occupied in 1937, living off income obtained by writing articles in the Latin American press. But the old politician could not come home, despite Teresa narrowly avoiding death in February 1941. Subject to a Law of Political Responsibilities investigation, his assets were frozen for three months, and when the case was closed, the Special Tribunal for the Repression of Freemasonry and Communism, created in March 1940, charged him for joining a Masonic lodge. Before the Spanish consul in Lisbon, Lerroux responded by stressing that his membership was purely passive, even if he admitted paying dues between 1886 and 1934. He refused a deal that would have involved naming other brothers, irrespective of the fact 'I had shown . . . that I was never in a position to learn Masonic secrets'. Acquittal only came in 1945 due to his contribution 'to the cause of order'.

His wife, tired of constant dealings with Francoist investigators, died on 11 March 1943 with Lerroux forcibly absent.[12] Her death affected him deeply. When at last he returned to Spain in 1947, the regime forced the exhausted and sick man to declare that he would remain outside politics. The once celebrated politician spent the rest of his life at home awaiting death. With his final breath two years later, the liberal Republic perished.

Notes

Introduction: The Truth Betrayed – Alejandro Lerroux and his Critics
1 Joaquín Romero Maura, «*La rosa de fuego*». *El obrerismo barcelonés de 1899 a 1909* (Madrid: Alianza, 1989).
2 Octavio Ruiz Manjón, *El Partido Republicano Radical (1908–1936)* (Madrid: Tebas, 1976).
3 Nigel Townson, *The Crisis of Democracy in Spain: Centrist politics under the Second Republic, 1931–1936* (Portland: Sussex Academic Press, 2000).
4 Andrés de Blas, 'El Partido Radical en la política española de la Segunda República', *Revista de Estudios Políticos*, nº 31–32, 1983, 137–164.
5 Paul Preston, *A People Betrayed: A History of Corruption, Political Incompetence and Social Division in Modern Spain* (London: William Collins, 2020). Subsequent citations come from chapters 2 to 11.
6 *The Sunday Times*, 1 March 2020.
7 *The Times*, 22 February 2020.
8 *The Sunday Times*, 1 March 2020.

1 The Forging of a Rebel (1864–1899)
1 Pío Baroja, *Galería de tipos de la época* (Madrid: Biblioteca Nueva, 1952), 162–164.
2 S. A., *Estado del Cuerpo de Ingenieros del Ejército en 1876* (Madrid: Imprenta del Memorial de Ingenieros, 1876); Alejandro Lerroux, *Mis Memorias* (Madrid: Afrodisio Aguado, 1963), 15 & José Álvarez Junco, *El Emperador del Paralelo. Lerroux y la demagogia populista* (Madrid: Alianza, 1990), 46.
3 Lerroux, *Mis Memorias*, 613 & 'Mi Canto a Teresa', *Boletín de la Real Academia de la Historia*, Vol. 102 (3), 2005, 359–384.
4 Ibid., 362 & Lerroux, *Mis Memorias*, 37–38; 612–616.
5 Instituto Provincial de Cádiz, *Homenage a Calderón* (Cádiz: Imp. de la Rev. Médica de D. Federico Joly, 1881), 25–28 & Lerroux, *Mis Memorias*, 50 & 594.
6 Ibid., 83–87 & 600.
7 *Gaceta de Madrid*, 30 December 1884 & 11 January 1885; Lerroux, *Mis Memorias*, 91–92.
8 Lerroux, 'Mi Canto a Teresa', 382; *Mis Memorias*, 133.
9 Álvarez Junco, *El Emperador*, 203–208; Demetrio Castro Alfín, 'Orígenes y primeras etapas del republicanismo en España', in Nigel Townson (ed.), *El republicanismo en España (1830–1977)*, (Madrid: Alianza, 1994), 33–57 &

Manuel Álvarez Tardío, 'La democracia de los radical-socialistas' in Fernando del Rey (ed.), *Palabras como puños. La intransigencia política en la Segunda República española* (Madrid: Tecnos, 2011), 229–287.

10 Carlos Dardé, 'La larga noche de la Restauración, 1875–1900' in Townson (ed.), *El republicanismo*, 113–135.

11 Lerroux, *Mis Memorias*, 20; 517–518; 611; Alejandro Lerroux, *La Pequeña Historia* (Buenos Aires: Cimera, 1937), 59; Ruiz Manjón, *El Partido Republicano Radical*, 21–22.

12 Lerroux, *Mis Memorias*, 181; 218; 551–552; Álvarez Junco, *El Emperador*, 68.

13 Lerroux, *La Pequeña Historia*, 328–329 & *Mis Memorias*, 238; 247–248 & 603; Carlos Seco Serrano, *Alfonso XIII y la crisis de la Restauración* (Madrid: Rialp. 1979), 71; Álvarez Junco, *El Emperador*, 61.

14 *El País*, 14 February & 6 December 1895; Lerroux, *Mis Memorias*, 570–571; Miguel Artola, *Partidos y programas políticos (1808–1936)* (Madrid: Aguilar, 1974), 391–392; Álvarez Junco, *El Emperador*, 117.

15 Lerroux, *Mis Memorias*, 207; 434; 554–556; Álvarez Junco, *El Emperador*, 145–146.

16 *La Época & El Imparcial*, 7 & 8 February 1896; *El Progreso*, 2 July 1899; César Jalón, *Memorias políticas* (Madrid: Guadarrama, 1973), 25; Álvarez Junco, *El Emperador*, 170.

17 *La Correspondencia de España*, 12 December 1887; Lerroux, *Mis Memorias*, 387 & 644.

18 Ibid., 212–213; 243; 273 & 277.

19 *La Época & El Imparcial*, 2 & 3 July 1899; *El Progreso*, 9 July 1899; Lerroux, *Mis Memorias*, 355; Álvarez Junco, *El Emperador*, 170.

2 Revolutionary Organiser (1899–1909)

1 *DSC*, 13 July 1901, 580–581 & 589.
2 *DSC*, 15 July 1901; Álvarez Junco, *El Emperador*, 161.
3 Fernando Soldevilla, *El año político 1901* (Madrid: Imprenta de Ricardo Rojas, 1902), 40; Romero Maura, «*La rosa de fuego*», 116; & Luis Arranz Notario, *Silvela. Entre el liberalismo y el regeneracionismo* (Madrid: Gota a Gota, 2013), 144–145.
4 Romero Maura, «*La rosa de fuego*», 65, 70–71 & 84–85; Ángel Duarte, *El republicanisme català a la fi del segle XIX* (Vic: Eumo, 1987), 141–146.
5 ACD, Leg.115; Lerroux, *Mis Memorias*, 410–411 & 424; Romero Maura, «*La rosa de fuego*», 118 & 186.
6 Ángel Duarte, 'Salmerón y Lerroux. Consideraciones sobre liderazgos en transición (1890–1906)', in Demetrio Castro (ed.), *Líderes para el pueblo republicano* (Pamplona: UPNA, 2015), 196–197.
7 Lerroux, *Mis Memorias*, 38–39.
8 *DSC*, 15 July 1910, 656.
9 Alejandro Lerroux, *Trayectoria política* (Madrid: n.p., 1932), 41.

186 Notes to Chapter 2

10 Duarte, *El republicanisme català*, 145.
11 Lerroux, *La Pequeña Historia*, 266–267 & Romero Maura, «*La rosa de fuego*», 179.
12 AHN, Leg. 20A & Lerroux, *Mis Memorias*, 223 & 558–559.
13 *DSC*, 27 June 1916, 908; AHN, Leg. 44A; Lerroux, *Mis Memorias*, 422.
14 Ramiro Reig, *Blasquistas y clericales. La lucha por la ciudad en la Valencia de 1900* (Valencia: Alfons el Magnànim, 1986) & Alejandro Martínez Relanzón, *Elecciones y modernización política en Valencia (1890–1923)* (Castellón: Sace, 2017).
15 *DSC*, 14. July 1910, 626.
16 Angelo Panebianco, *Modelos de partido* (Madrid: Alianza, 1990), 267–275 & Valdimer Key Jr., *Política, partidos y grupos de presión* (Madrid: Instituto de Estudios Políticos, 1962), 527–537.
17 Lerroux, *Mis Memorias*, 519; Antonio Marsá & Bernardo Izcaray, *Libro de oro del Partido Republicano Radical* (Madrid: Sucesores de Rivadeneyra, 1935), 26–27.
18 ACD, Legs. 117 & 119; Romero Maura, «*La rosa de fuego*», 306, 339 & 352.
19 *DSC*, 20 July 1901, 727 & Lerroux, *Mis Memorias*, 369.
20 Ibid., 408.
21 Ibid., 478, 522 & 534–535.
22 *DSC*, 28 November 1901, 1939; *La Época*, 29 July 1903; Lerroux, *Mis Memorias*, 527–528 & Romero Maura, «*La rosa de fuego*», 214 & 233.
23 Lerroux, *Mis Memorias*, 463 & Juan Avilés Farré, *Francisco Ferrer y Guardia: pedagogo, anarquista y mártir* (Madrid: Marcial Pons, 2006), 160–162 & 190–193.
24 Lerroux, *Mis Memorias*, 439.
25 *DSC*, 15 July 1910, 646 & Ruiz Manjón, *El Partido Republicano Radical*, 53–54.
26 Lerroux, *Mis Memorias*, 223 & 568 & Álvarez Junco, *El Emperador*, 326.
27 ACD, Leg. 121; *DSC*, 14 December 1910, 627; *ABC* & *El Imparcial*, 15. February 1908 & 13–14 December1908; Lerroux, *Mis Memorias*, 581–582; Ruiz Manjón, *El Partido Republicano Radical*, 69 & José María Marco, *Maura. La política pura* (Madrid, Gota a Gota, 2013), 100–103.
28 Lerroux, *Mis Memorias*, 306–307, 315 & 318 & Romero Maura, «*La rosa de fuego*», 460.
29 Melchor Fernández Almagro, *Historia del reinado de D. Alfonso XIII* (Madrid, Sarpe, 1986), 119 & Lerroux, *Mis Memorias*, 320–322.
30 *DSC*, 15 July 1910, 654 & Lerroux, *Mis Memorias*, 327, 467 & 644.
31 *ABC* & *El Imparcial*, 31 October 1909 & 1 November 1909; Lerroux, *Mis Memorias*, 644; Álvarez Junco, *El Emperador*, 385 & Romero Maura, «*La rosa de fuego*», 541.
32 *DSC*, 15 October 1910, 656–657.

3 The Respectable Republican (1909–1923)

1. Fernando Soldevilla, *El año político 1922* (Madrid Imprenta y Encuadernación de Julio Cosano, 1923), 316–317 & Natalio Rivas, *Retazos de Historia* (Madrid: Editora Nacional, 1952), 232–233.
2. *La Época* & *El Imparcial*, 15 September 1922.
3. *La Época*, 28 September 1922 & Manuel Azaña, *Obras completas*. Vol. II. (Madrid: CEPC, 2007), 120.
4. DSC, 27 June 1916 & Joan B. Culla *El republicanisme lerrouxista a Catalunya (1901–1923)* (Barcelona: Edicions Curial, 1986), 221–223, 246–250 & 307–310.
5. *El Imparcial*, 25 September 1922.
6. Lerroux, *Mis Memorias*, 216–217.
7. Ibid., 570.
8. Ibid., 627 & 637; Jalón, *Memorias políticas*, 246.
9. ACD, Leg. 123; *El Imparcial* & *ABC*, 10 February 1911 & 3 December 1912; Lerroux, *Mis Memorias*, 468.
10. DSC, 17 December 1910, 3060–3068 & 20 December 1910, 3142–3143.
11. Lerroux, *Mis Memorias*, 589–591.
12. Gabriel Maura, *Historia crítica del reinado de don Alfonso XIII durante su menoridad bajo la regencia de su madre doña María Cristina de Austria* (Barcelona: Montaner y Simón, 1919), 248–249.
13. DSC, 8 April 1911, 654; & 30 May 1914, 997–1008; Lerroux, *La Pequeña Historia*, 24–25.
14. DSC, 2 July 1912, 4415 & Lerroux, *Mis Memorias*, 441.
15. ACD, Leg. 125. Lerroux, *La Pequeña Historia*, 46–49.
16. *El Imparcial*, 26 August 1914 & Alejandro Lerroux, *La verdad a mi país. España y la guerra* (Madrid: Librería de la Viuda de Pueyo, 1915).
17. *El Imparcial* & *ABC*, 7 September 1914; Lerroux, *La Pequeña Historia*, 27–29.
18. AHN (Fondos Contemporáneos, Tribunal Supremo), Leg. 4 & TNA, FO 371/3034: Hardinge to Balfour, 8 September 1917; Ruiz Manjón, *El Partido Republicano Radical*, 116.
19. ACD, Legs. 127 & 129; Luis Arranz Notario, Luis Elorza & Fernando Rey Reguillo, 'Liberalismo y corporativismo en la crisis de la Restauración' in José Luis García Delgado (ed.), *La crisis de la Restauración. España entre la Primera Guerra Mundial y la II República* (Madrid: Siglo XXI, 1986), 5–50 & Lerroux, *Mis Memorias*, 536.
20. ACD, Legs. 131, 133 y 135; Marsá e Izcaray, *Libro de oro*, 105–125 & *El Imparcial* & *ABC*, 16 November 1920 & 30 April 1923.
21. DSC, 14 January 1920, 1782–1786.
22. DSC, 10 January 1920, 1674–1685 & 1786–1793; *El Sol*, 21 October 1919 & 29 December 1919 & *El Imparcial* & *La Época*, 29 May 1920.
23. ARH, N. Rivas, 11/8910; Jalón, *Memorias políticas*, 51; Lerroux, *Mis Memorias*, 490–492; Javier Tusell & Genoveva García Queipo de Llano, *Alfonso XIII: el rey polémico* (Madrid: Taurus, 2001), 356.

24 Lerroux, *La Pequeña Historia*, 405, 443 & 495.
25 *DSC*, 29 November 1921, 4448–4459; Fernando Soldevilla, *El año político 1921* (Madrid: Imprenta y Encuadernación de Julio, 1922), 301–302 & *El Socialista*, 1 October 1921.
26 TNA-FO 371/9389: Wingfield to Curzon, 21 December 1922; *El Imparcial* & *ABC*, 10 November 1922; 6 & 18 December 1922; 15 January 1923; 7 April 1923; Panebianco, *Modelos de Partido*, 51–52 & Lerroux, *Mis Memorias*, 492–493.

4 From Sceptical Conspirator to Minister of the Republic (1923–1931)

1 Niceto Alcalá-Zamora, *La victoria republicana, 1930–1931* (Madrid: La Esfera de los Libros, 2012), 82–83.
2 Lerroux, *Pequeña Historia*, 34 & 165–166.
3 Fernando Soldevilla, *El año político 1923* (Madrid Imprenta y Encuadernación de Julio Cosano, 1924), 374 & Lerroux, *Mis Memorias*, 169 & 285.
4 *El Imparcial* & *La Época*, 15 & 17 June 1924; 1 July 1924; *El Noticiero Universal*, 13 January 1925; Melchor Fernández Almagro, *Historia del reinado de D. Alfonso XIII*. (Madrid: Sarpe, 1986 (original 1933)), vol. 2, 139 & 157 & Lerroux, *Mis Memorias*, 608–609.
5 *ABC*, 5. November 1926 & Lerroux, *Mis Memorias*, 537.
6 Ruiz Manjón, *El Partido Republicano Radical*, 139 & 144.
7 AGGCE, P-S Madrid, Leg. 704 & 723. *El Imparcial*, 6 & 11 November 1926 & Lerroux, *Mis Memorias*, 330.
8 *Ahora*, 2 August 1931; Lerroux to Ángel Rizo, 26 August 1930; Lerroux, *Pequeña Historia*, 62 & 71–72; Ruiz Manjón, *El Partido Republicano Radical*, 149 & Niceto Alcalá-Zamora, *Memorias (segundo texto de mis Memorias)* (Barcelona: Planeta, 1977), 144.
9 Lerroux, *Pequeña Historia*, 72–73 & 85.
10 TNA, FO 371/15042: Grahame to Henderson, December 1930; Emilio Mola Vidal, *Memorias* (Barcelona: Planeta, 1977), 303 & Lerroux, *Pequeña Historia*, 81.
11 *DSC*, 24 September 1931, 1140–1146.
12 *El Sol*, 7 June 1931 & Lerroux, *Mis Memorias*, 174.
13 *ABC*, 16 April 1931; Lerroux, *Pequeña Historia*, 90–91 & 144; & Alcalá-Zamora, *Memorias*, 161.
14 *El Progreso*, 7 June 1930 & Marsá e Izcaray, *Libro de oro*, 123–125.
15 Shlomo Ben Ami, *Los orígenes de la Segunda República: anatomía de una transición* (Madrid: Alianza, 1990), 434–445.
16 *El Sol*, 5 May 1931; Jalón, *Memorias políticas*, 52 & Lerroux, *Pequeña Historia*, 18–19.
17 *ABC*, 5 June 1931 & Salvador de Madariaga, *Memorias (1921–1936)* (Madrid: Espasa-Calpe, 1974), 273–275.
18 Lerroux, *Pequeña Historia*, 102–103 & 248; Manuel Álvarez Tardío, *Anticlericalismo y libertad de conciencia* (Madrid: Centro de Estudios

Políticos y Constitucionales, 2002), 76; & Alcalá-Zamora, *Memorias*, 183.
19   *ABC*, 23 June 1931; Marsá e Izcaray, *Libro de oro*, 556 & Lerroux, *Pequeña Historia*, 47.
20   Santos Juliá, 'La experiencia del poder: la izquierda republicana, 1931–1933', in Nigel Townson (ed.), *El republicanismo en España (1830–1977)* (Madrid: Alianza, 1994), 173–174.
21   Santos Juliá, *Los socialistas en la política española* (Madrid: Taurus, 1997), 167–169; José Manuel Macarro, *Socialismo, República y Revolución en Andalucía* (Seville: Universidad de Sevilla, 2000) & Fernando del Rey Reguillo, 'La República de los socialistas', in Fernando del Rey Reguillo (ed.), *Palabras como puños. La intransigencia política en la Segunda República española* (Madrid: Tecnos, 2011), 158–225.
22   AGGCE, P-S Madrid, Legs. 621, 853 & 1161.
23   ACD, Leg. 137; TNA, FO 371/15774: Grahame to Henderson, 9 July 1931 & Lerroux, *Mis Memorias*, 404.
24   *Gaceta de Madrid*, 26 May 1931; Roberto Villa García, *La República en las Urnas. El despertar de la democracia en España* (Madrid: Marcial Pons, 2011), 77–81 & Alcalá-Zamora, *La victoria republicana*, 246.
25   Alcalá-Zamora, *Memorias*, 210.
26   Lerroux, *Pequeña Historia*, 114 & 363 & Marsá e Izcaray, *Libro de oro*, 555.
27   *DSC*, 13 October 1931, 1719–1720; *El Sol*, 20 October 1931; Nigel Townson, *La República que no pudo ser. La política de centro en España (1931–1936)* (Madrid: Taurus, 2002), 105; Alcalá-Zamora, *Memorias*, 191–192 & Manuel Álvarez Tardío & Roberto Villa García, *El Precio de la Exclusión. La política durante la Segunda República* (Madrid: Encuentro, 2010), 155–202.
28   *DSC*, 27 October 1931, 1945–1947; 29 October 1931, 2022–2023; & 4 November 1931, 2119–2120; *Ahora*, 15 November 1931; Lerroux, *Pequeña Historia*, 35 & Jesús Pabón, *Cambó, 1930–1947* (Barcelona: Alpha, 1969), 222.
29   *DSC*, 14 October 1931, 1725–1726; Lerroux, *Pequeña Historia*, 112–113 & Manuel Azaña, *Memorias políticas y de guerra* (Madrid: Afrodisio Aguado, 1976), Vol. 1, 14 October 1931.
30   *Ahora*, 15 November 1931.
31   Antonio Royo-Villanova, *La Constitución española de 9 de diciembre de 1931* (Valladolid: Imprenta Castellana, 1934), 9; Lerroux, *Pequeña Historia*, 404 & Alcalá-Zamora, *Memorias*, 502.
32   *DSC*, 17 December 1931, 2940; *Ahora*, 10, 13 & 16 December 1931 & 23 February 1932; *El Sol*, 10 & 13 December 1931. Alcalá-Zamora, *Memorias*, 210 & Lerroux, *Pequeña Historia*, 127.
33   *DSC*, 17 December 1931, 2941–2942.

5 Leader of the Republican Opposition (1932–1933)

1   Manuel Azaña, *Diarios 1932–1933. «Los cuadernos robados»* (Barcelona: Crítica, 1997), 139 & 313.

190   Notes to Chapter 5

2   Ibid., 36 & Joaquín del Moral, *Oligarquía y enchufismo. Escarceos críticos sobre la actual política española* (Madrid: CIAP, 1933).
3   TNA, FO 371/16506: Grahame to Simon, 3 March 1932; Alcalá-Zamora, *Memorias*, 211–212 & 508–510; Joaquín Tomás Villarroya, *La destitución de Alcalá-Zamora* (Valencia: CEU, 1988), 57–59 & Villa García, *La República*, 90–95.
4   TNA, FO 371/16506: Grahame to Simon, 3 March 1932; *Ahora* & *ABC*, 23 February 1932.
5   TNA, FO 371/16506: Grahame to Simon, 3 March 1932; *ABC*, 5 December 1931; *Ahora* & *El Sol*, 28 February & 12 April 1932.
6   TNA, FO 371/16506: Grahame to Simon, 3 March 1932 & Lerroux, *Pequeña Historia*, 224.
7   *DSC*, 20 May 1932, 5717–5726; *Ahora*, 12 July 1932 & *El Liberal*, 8 August 1932.
8   Lerroux, *Pequeña Historia*, 131–132.
9   AGGCE, P-S Madrid, Leg. 672; *DSC*, 19 July 1932, 7142–7143; *Ahora*, 28 August 1932; Lerroux, *Pequeña Historia*, 133–134 & 138; Azaña, *Memorias políticas*, 491; Martínez Barrio, *Memorias* (Barcelona: Planeta, 1983), 132–133 & 137 & Ruiz Manjón, *El Partido Republicano Radical*, 325.
10   *Ahora* & *El Sol*, 12 July 1932.
11   *DSC*, 19 July 1932, 7155–7158.
12   Ruiz Manjón, *El Partido Republicano Radical*, 325–328.
13   Lerroux, *Pequeña Historia*, 137 & Juan Avilés Farré, *La izquierda burguesa y la tragedia de la II Segunda República* (Madrid: Comunidad de Madrid, 2006), 218–222.
14   Partido Republicano Radical, *Asamblea nacional extraordinaria* [October 1932] (Madrid: Imprenta de Zoila Ascasíbar, 1932), 150–152; Marsá e Izcaray, *Libro de oro*, 226–232 & Ruiz Manjón, *El Partido Republicano Radical*, 632–637.
15   Roberto Villa García, 'El ocaso del republicanismo histórico: lerrouxistas y blasquistas ante las elecciones de 1936' in *Anales de la Real Academia de Cultura Valenciana* nº 87 (2012), 85–98; Luis Arranz Notario, 'Modelos de partido', in Santos Juliá (ed.), *Política en la Segunda República* (Madrid: Marcial Pons, 1995), 100–104 & Ruiz Manjón, *El Partido Republicano Radical*, 590.
16   AGGCE, P-S Madrid, Leg. 694 & TNA, FO 371/17426: Grahame to Simon, 17 March 1933.
17   *DSC*, 3 February 1933, 10919, 10921 & 10928 & 23 February 1933, 11421 & Lerroux, *Pequeña Historia*, 140.
18   TNA, FO 371/17426: Grahame to Simon, 17 March 1933; Ruiz Manjón, *El Partido Republicano Radical*, 358; Álvarez Tardío, *Anticlericalismo*, 261–262 & 268–269 & Lerroux, *Pequeña Historia*, 149.
19   *El Sol*, 13 June 1933; Lerroux, *Pequeña Historia*, 139; Azaña, *Diarios 1932–1933*, 345 & Alcalá-Zamora, *Memorias*, 241–242.
20   *El Socialista*, 15 July 1932 & *DSC*, 19 July 1932, 7160–7161.

21 AHN, Leg. 31A; Roberto Villa García, 'Burgos podridos y democratización. Las elecciones municipales de abril de 1933' in *Hispania* nº 240 (2012), 166–168 & Ruiz Manjón, *El Partido Republicano Radical*, 363.
22 *DSC*, 6 September 1933, 15316–15324 & Villa García, *La República*, 107–108.

6 Prime Minister (1933–1934)

1 José María Gil-Robles, *No fue posible la paz. Memorias* (Barcelona: Planeta, 1998), 159.
2 *DSC*, 2 October 1933, 15401 & 15408; TNA, FO 371/17427: Grahame to Simon, 14 September 1933; Lerroux, *Pequeña Historia*, 152–153 & Alcalá-Zamora, *Memorias*, 244.
3 *DSC*, 2 October 1933, 15391–15398 & Lerroux, *Pequeña Historia*, 154.
4 *DSC*, 2 October 1933, 15412 & 3 October 1933, 15432 & 15442–15447; Lerroux, *Pequeña Historia*, 158 & Alcalá-Zamora, *Memorias*, 244.
5 *DSC*, 2 October 1933, 15401; Joaquín Tomás Villarroya, 'El voto de desconfianza en la II República', *Cuadernos de la Cátedra Fadrique Furio Ceriol* nº 3 (1981), 3–5 & Juan Francisco Fuentes, *Largo Caballero* (Madrid: Síntesis, 2005), 225–232.
6 TNA, FO 371/17434: Grahame to Simon, 11 October 1933 & Jalón, *Memorias políticas*, 73–74.
7 Lerroux, *Pequeña Historia*, 176.
8 AHN, Leg. 38A; TNA, FO 371/17427: Grahame to Simon, 9 November 1933; *Ahora* & *El Sol*, 19 November 1933 & 3 April 1934; Lerroux, *Pequeña Historia*, 174–176 & 190–191; Martínez Barrio, *Memorias*, 207; Rafael Salazar Alonso, *Bajo el signo de la revolución* (Astorga (León): Akrón, 2007), 84–85; Jalón, *Memorias políticas*, 80–81; Villa García, *La República en las Urnas*, 309 & Ruiz Manjón, *El Partido Republicano Radical*, 387.
9 ACD, Leg. 139.
10 *Ahora* & *El Sol*, 21 December 1933; Lerroux, *Pequeña Historia*, 191 & 238 & Manuel Álvarez Tardío, *Gil-Robles. Un conservador en la República* (Madrid: Gota a Gota, 2016), 122–124.
11 *ABC*, *Ahora*, *El Sol* & *ABC*, 21, 22 & 23 November 1933 &Villa García, *La República en las Urnas*, 437–438.
12 Roberto Villa García, 'La CNT contra la República: la insurrección revolucionaria de diciembre de 1933' in *Historia y Política* nº 25 (2011), 203; Villa García, *La República en las Urnas*, 439–44; Alcalá-Zamora, *Memorias*, 259–260 & *Ahora*, 6 December 1933.
13 Martínez Barrio, *Memorias*, 213 & Jalón, *Memorias políticas*, 88.
14 Lerroux, *Pequeña Historia*, 197–198 & 238–239.
15 *Ahora* & *El Sol*, 23 January 1934.
16 *DSC*, 20 December 1933, 125; *El Socialista*, 26, 29 & 30 November 1933; *ABC*, 6 February 1934; Juliá, *Los socialistas*, 202–203 & Lerroux, *Pequeña Historia*, 209–210.

192 Notes to Chapter 7

17 AGGCE, P-S Madrid, Leg. 696; TNA, FO 371/17427: Grahame to Simon, 2 March 1934 & *Gaceta de Madrid*, 10 April 1934.
18 AGGCE, P-S Madrid, Leg. 696; TNA, FO 371/18595: Grahame to Simon, 23 May 1934; *Ahora* & *El Sol*, 18 May 1934; Lerroux, *Pequeña Historia*, 249–250 & Townson, *La República*, 268–269.
19 Lerroux, *Pequeña Historia*, 213–214 & Stanley G. Payne, *Alcalá-Zamora. El fracaso de la República conservadora* (Madrid: Gota a Gota), 163–164.
20 *DSC*, 19 December 1933, 73.
21 Alcalá-Zamora, *Memorias*, 271–272.
22 Ibid., 275–276 & 518; Lerroux, *Pequeña Historia*, 228–229.
23 Álvarez Tardío, *Anticlericalismo*, 300–301, 303–307 & 317–318 & Lerroux, *Pequeña Historia*, 323–325.
24 Ibid., 226 & 255.
25 TNA, FO 371/18595: Grahame to Simon, 27 April 1934 & Alcalá-Zamora, *Memorias*, 315.
26 *DSC*, 6 June 1934, 3452–3467 & 7 June 1934, 3491–3494. Lerroux, *Pequeña Historia*, 233–234.
27 TNA, FO 371/18596: Grahame to Simon, 26 September 1934; *ABC*, *Ahora* & *El Sol*, 15 September 1934; Salazar Alonso, *Bajo el signo*, 295–297 & Alcalá-Zamora, *Memorias*, 287.
28 AGGCE, P-S Madrid, Leg. 696; TNA, FO 371/18596: Grahame to Simon, 30 August 1934; *DSC*, 4 July 1934, 4461–4463; & Lerroux, *Pequeña Historia*, 255 & 277.
29 Ibid., 261.

7 A Conservative against Anarchy (1934–1935)

1 Jalón, *Memorias políticas*, 136.
2 TNA, FO 371/18596: Grahame to Simon, 10 October 1934.
3 *DSC*, 20 November 1933, 4884–4885; Juan José Linz, 'De Grandes Esperanzas a la Guerra Civil: la quiebra de la democracia en España' in *Obras Escogidas*, Vol. 4 (Madrid, CEPC: 2009), 139; Martínez Barrio, *Memorias*, 228–234 & 246–247 & Alcalá-Zamora, *Memorias*, 277–278 & 287.
4 Lerroux, *Pequeña Historia*, 216, 262, 278 & 300–301.
5 TNA, FO 371/18596: Grahame to Simon, 8 October 1934 & Sandra Souto, *¿Y Madrid? ¿Qué hace Madrid?* (Madrid: Siglo XXI, 2004), 243.
6 *Gaceta de Madrid*, 7 October 1934.
7 TNA, FO 371/18596: Grahame to Simon, 8 October 1934; *ABC*, 7 & 9 October 1934; *El Sol*, 14 October 1934 & Lerroux, *Pequeña Historia*, 271–273.
8 *DSC*, 9 October 1934, 4490–4491; TNA, FO 371/18596: Grahame to Simon, 10 October 1934; Jalón, *Memorias políticas*, 144 & Lerroux, *Pequeña Historia*, 304.
9 Alcalá-Zamora, *Memorias*, 299; Lerroux, *Pequeña Historia*, 276; & Avilés, *La izquierda burguesa*, 350–353 & 436.
10 AGGCE, P-S Madrid, Leg. 749; TNA, FO 371/18597: Grahame to Simon, 25

Notes to Chapter 8   193

October 1934; *ABC*, 12 October 1934; *Ahora* & *El Sol*, 6 November 1934; Lerroux, *Pequeña Historia*, 283, 309–310 & 313–315. Alcalá-Zamora, *Memorias*, 292–294 & 521 & Jalón, *Memorias políticas*, 145–149.

11 Lerroux, *Pequeña Historia*, 302, 317 & 500 & Alcalá-Zamora, *Memorias*, 294, 301 & 524–525.
12 TNA, FO 371/18597: Grahame to Simon, 25 October 1934; Ruiz Manjón, *El Partido Republicano Radical*, 463 & Lerroux, *Pequeña Historia*, 193.
13 Ibid., 295–296; Linz, 'De Grandes Esperanzas', 183 & Stanley G. Payne & Jesús Palacios, *Franco* (Barcelona: Espasa, 2014), 120.
14 Lerroux, *Pequeña Historia*, 25 & 368–370 & Alcalá-Zamora, *Memorias*, 526–527.
15 *Gaceta de Madrid*, 3 January 1935 & *DSC*, 11 December 1934, 5381–5385.
16 Lerroux, *Pequeña Historia*, 307.
17 TNA, FO 371/19736: Grahame to Simon, 9 May 1935; *Ahora* & *El Sol*, 18 July 1934 & 9 July 1935; Lerroux, *Pequeña Historia*, 332–333 & Jalón, *Memorias políticas*, 210–212.
18 *DSC*, 5 July 1935, Ap. 4; TNA, FO 371/19736: Grahame to Hoare, 2 July 1935 & *Gaceta de Madrid*, 3 November 1935.
19 AGGCE, P-S Madrid, Leg. 1860 & TNA, FO 371/19736: Grahame to Hoare, 2 July 1935 & *ABC* & *Ahora*, 25 June 1935.
20 Lerroux, *Pequeña Historia*, 331–335 & Jalón, *Memorias políticas*, 205–206.
21 *El Sol*, 27 August 1935; *Ahora*, 27 August 1935 & 10 September 1935; *ABC*, 10 September 1935; Lerroux, *Pequeña Historia*, 341 & 344; Alcalá-Zamora, *Memorias*, 338–339 & Gil-Robles, *No fue posible*, 309–310.
22 Lerroux, *Pequeña Historia*, 346 & Gil-Robles, *No fue posible*, 158 & 284.

8 Much Ado About Nothing (1935–1936)

1 Miguel Maura, *Así cayó Alfonso XIII. De una Dictadura a otra* (Madrid: Marcial Pons, 2007), 184–185. The most complete biography of Miguel Maura is Antonio Cañellas Mas, *Miguel Maura, La Derecha Republicana* (Madrid: Gota a Gota, 2018).
2 *ABC*, 11 September 1933 & Villa García, *La República en las Urnas*, 174.
3 Max Weber, *El político y el científico* (Madrid: Alianza, 2009), 88–96; *Diario de la Marina*, 3 January 1937; Alcalá-Zamora, *Memorias*, 488; Indalecio Prieto, *De mi vida: recuerdos, estampas, siluetas, sombras*. Vol. 1 (Mexico D.F., Oasis: 1968), 44 & Lerroux, *Pequeña Historia*, 269–270.
4 Gil-Robles, *No fue posible*, 158 & 284 & Lerroux, *Pequeña Historia*, 105 & 166–167.
5 ACTS, Leg. 6239; *ABC*, 11 March 1936 & Salazar Alonso, *Bajo el signo*, 337.
6 *DSC*, 22 October 1935, 10024 & Lerroux, *Pequeña Historia*, 327.
7 Ibid., 339–340 & Alcalá-Zamora, *Memorias*, 312.
8 *DSC*, 22 October 1935, 10013; Alcalá-Zamora, *Memorias*, 312; Joaquín Chapaprieta, *La paz fue posible. Memorias de un político* (Barcelona: Ariel, 1971), 267–268; Juan Simeón Vidarte, *El bienio negro y la insurrección de*

Notes to Chapter 8

Asturias (Barcelona: Grijalbo, 1978), 455–456 & Andrés de Blas, 'El Partido Radical', 158–160.
9 Lerroux, *Pequeña Historia*, 353–360 & Payne, *Alcalá-Zamora*, 172–173.
10 *Ahora* & *El Sol*, 21 & 26 September 1935; Chapaprieta, *La paz fue posible*, 215–21 & Lerroux, *Pequeña Historia*, 365–366.
11 *ABC* & *Ahora*, 26 & 27 September 1935; Jalón, *Memorias políticas*, 51, the emphasis is in the original & Payne, *Alcalá-Zamora*, 257.
12 *DSC*, 1 October 1935, 9541 & 9549; & 22 October 1935, 10009; Lerroux, *Pequeña Historia*, 368; Gil-Robles, *No fue posible*, 284; Chapaprieta, *La paz fue posible*, 207–208, 214, 243 & 254–256 & Jalón, *Memorias políticas*, 219–222.
13 *Ahora* & *El Sol*, 10 October 1935; Gil-Robles, *No fue posible*, 286–287; Chapaprieta, *La paz fue posible*, 258–259 & Lerroux, *Pequeña Historia*, 372–373.
14 Alcalá-Zamora, *Memorias*, 312, 341 & 533. Gil-Robles, *No fue posible*, 287–288 & Chapaprieta, *La paz fue posible*, 262–267 & Lerroux, *Pequeña Historia*, 377.
15 *DSC*, 22 October 1935, 10020. & Álvarez Tardío, *Gil-Robles*, 188–189.
16 *DSC*, 22 October 1935, 10022; 23 October 1935, 10037; 25 October 1935, Ap. 7; & 28 October 1935, 10164; Lerroux, *Pequeña Historia*, 379 & Chapaprieta, *La paz fue posible*, 267–269.
17 *DSC*, 28 October 1935, 10168 & 10179–10180; Lerroux, *Pequeña Historia*, 269–270 & 384–385 & Chapaprieta, *La paz fue posible*, 276–278.
18 AGA (Fondo Juzgados Especiales), Legs. 43/4092–4096; *DSC*, 25 October 1935, Ap. 7; & 28 October 1935, 10161–10163 & 10168; *ABC*, 11 March 1936; Chapaprieta, *La paz fue posible*, 268; Salazar Alonso, *Bajo el signo*, 336 & Gil-Robles, *No fue posible*, 289.
19 AHN (Fondos Contemporáneos-Tribunal Supremo), Exp. 52; *Gaceta de Madrid*, 10 March 1931 & 4 May 1935 & Lerroux, *Pequeña Historia*, 387–389.
20 *DSC*, 5 December 1935, Ap. 18 & Chapaprieta, *La paz fue posible*, 249–250.
21 *Gaceta de Madrid*, 20 July 1934; *DSC*, 7 December 1935, 11218 & Lerroux, *Pequeña Historia*, 293–294 & 348.
22 *DSC*, 5 December 1935, Ap. 18 & 7 December 1935, 11201; *Gaceta de Madrid*, 18 July 1935; Lerroux, *Pequeña Historia*, 394–395 & Gil-Robles, *No fue posible*, 325–326. Chapaprieta, *La paz fue posible*, 250–251 & Alcalá-Zamora, *Memorias*, 310–311 & 528.
23 *DSC*, 29 November 1935, 10993–10994; Gil-Robles, *No fue posible*, 328 & 333; Chapaprieta, *La paz fue posible*, 305–307 & Pabón, *Cambó, 1930–1947*, 456–457.
24 *DSC*, 7 December 1935, Ap. 18 & *Ahora*, 30 November 1935.
25 AGGCE, DNSD-Secretaría, nº 27; *DSC*, 7 December 1935, Ap. 18 & 11286–11288; *ABC* & *Ahora*, 29 November & 3 December 1935; Lerroux, *Pequeña Historia*, 400–401; Gil-Robles, *No fue posible*, 345–346; Antonio Royo-Villanova, *Treinta años de política antiespañola* (Valladolid: Librería

Santarén, 1940), 258–259. Pabón, *Cambó, 1930–1947*, 455 & Álvarez Tardío, *Gil-Robles*, 190–191.
26 Stanley G. Payne, *El colapso de la República. Los orígenes de la Guerra Civil (1933–1936)* (Madrid: La Esfera de los Libros, 2005), 530 & Manuel Álvarez Tardío & Roberto Villa García, *Fraude y violencia en las elecciones del Frente Popular* (Madrid: Espasa, 2017), 163–169.
27 *Ahora* & *El Sol*, 22 & 24 December 1935; *ABC*, 10 December 1935; Chapaprieta, *La paz fue posible*, 342 & Ruiz Manjón, *El Partido Republicano Radical*, 532–535 & 548–551.
28 Pabón, *Cambó, 1930–1947*, 429; Payne, *El colapso de la República*, 187 & Lerroux, *Pequeña Historia*, 418 & 422.
29 Ibid., 424 & Stanley G. Payne, *Unión Soviética, comunismo y revolución en España (1931–1939)* (Barcelona: Plaza y Janés, 2003), 136 & 139.
30 ACD, Leg. 141; *ABC* & *Ahora*, 14 January 1936 & Villa García, 'El ocaso del republicanismo histórico', 108.
31 Lerroux, *Pequeña Historia*, 435 & Álvarez Tardío & Villa García, *Fraude y violencia*, 200 & 226.
32 Lerroux, *Pequeña Historia*, 412, 426 & 447 & Álvarez Tardío & Villa García, *Fraude y violencia*, 284–307.
33 Lerroux, *Pequeña Historia*, 425–426, 431–432 & 451.
34 ACD, Leg. 141. Lerroux, *Pequeña Historia*, 411 & 445–446 & Villa García, 'El ocaso del republicanismo histórico', 109–117.
35 ADF, Vol. 167, Marcassin to Flandin, 2 May 1936; AGF, DP-C, Romero to Giménez Fernández, March 1936 & Ruiz Manjón, *El Partido Republicano Radical*, 577–582.
36 AGGCE, P-S Madrid, Leg. 694 & Lerroux, *Pequeña Historia*, 412, 455–463, 479 & 484.

Epilogue: Exile and Return (1936–1949)
1 *ABC* & *La Vanguardia*, 28 Jun. 1949 & Juan Ignacio Luca de Tena, *Mis amigos muertos* (Barcelona: Planeta, 1971), 192–193.
2 *Diario de la Marina*, 3 Jan. 1937 & Lerroux, *Pequeña Historia*, 485, 490 & 492–494.
3 Ibid., 446, 490, 494–496 & 514–516.
4 Ibid., 497–499.
5 Ibid., 511–513 & 516–519.
6 Álvarez Junco, *El Emperador*, 439–441.
7 Payne, *El colapso*, 82.
8 Manuel Portela, *Memorias* (Madrid: Alianza, 1988), 149 & 154.
9 Linz, 'De Grandes Esperanzas', 146 & Ruiz Manjón, *El Partido Republicano Radical*, 680.
10 Lerroux, *Mis Memorias*, 249 & 511; Francisco Franco Salgado, *Mis conversaciones privadas con Franco* (Barcelona: Planeta, 2005), 273. & Julius Ruiz, *El Terror Rojo* (Barcelona: Espasa, 2012), 88.

11 *Boletín Oficial del Estado*, 13 Feb. 1939 & Lerroux, *Mis Memorias,* 511 & 513.
12 AGGCE, TERMC, Fichero 77 & SE-Masonería A, Leg. 14 & Lerroux, *Mis Memorias*, 251–252.

Primary Sources and Bibliography

Archives and Parliamentary Papers
ARCHIVO GENERAL DE LA ADMINISTRACIÓN (AGA)
ARCHIVO DEL CONGRESO DE LOS DIPUTADOS (ACD)
ARCHIVES DIPLOMATIQUES – FRANCE DIPLOMATIE (ADF)
ARCHIVO GENERAL DE LA GUERRA CIVIL ESPAÑOLA (AGGCE)
ARCHIVO MANUEL GIMÉNEZ FERNÁNDEZ (AGF)
ARCHIVO HISTÓRICO NACIONAL (AHN)
ARCHIVO DE LA REAL ACADEMIA DE LA HISTORIA (ARH)
DIARIO DE SESIONES DEL CONGRESO DE LOS DIPUTADOS (DSC)
THE NATIONAL ARCHIVES (LONDON) – FOREIGN OFFICE (TNA-FO)

Lerroux's Writings & Radical Party Documents (Selection)
INSTITUTO PROVINCIAL DE CÁDIZ. *Homenage a Calderón* (Cadiz: Imp. de la Rev. Médica de D. Federico Joly, 1881).
LERROUX, ALEJANDRO. *La verdad a mi país. España y la guerra* (Madrid: Librería de la Viuda de Pueyo, 1915).
—— *Al servicio de la República* (Madrid: Javier Morata, 1930).
—— *Las pequeñas tragedias de mi vida* (Madrid: Editorial Zeus, 1930).
—— *Trayectoria política* (Madrid: S.E., 1932).
—— *La Pequeña Historia* (Buenos Aires: Cimera, 1937).
—— *Mis Memorias* (Madrid: Afrodisio Aguado, 1963).
—— 'Canto a Teresa', *Boletín de la Real Academia de la Historia*, Vol. 102 (3), 2005, 359–384.
MARSÁ, ANTONIO E IZCARAY, BERNARDO. *Libro de oro del Partido Republicano Radical* (Madrid: Sucesores de Rivadeneyra, 1935).
PARTIDO REPUBLICANO RADICAL. *Asamblea nacional extraordinaria* (octubre de 1932) (Madrid: Imprenta de Zoila Ascasíbar, 1932).

Cited Bibliography
ALCALÁ-ZAMORA, NICETO. *Memorias (segundo texto de mis Memorias)* (Barcelona: Planeta, 1977).
—— *La victoria republicana, 1930–1931* (Madrid: La Esfera de los Libros, 2012).
ÁLVAREZ JUNCO, JOSÉ. *El Emperador del Paralelo. Lerroux y la demagogia populista* (Madrid: Alianza, 1990).

ÁLVAREZ TARDÍO, MANUEL. *Anticlericalismo y libertad de conciencia* (Madrid: Centro de Estudios Políticos y Constitucionales, 2002).

—— 'La democracia de los radical-socialistas', in Fernando del Rey Reguillo (ed.), *Palabras como puños. La intransigencia política en la Segunda República española* (Madrid: Tecnos, 2011), 229–287.

—— *Gil-Robles. Un conservador en la República* (Madrid: Gota a Gota, 2016).

ÁLVAREZ TARDÍO, MANUEL & VILLA GARCÍA, ROBERTO. *El Precio de la Exclusión. La política durante la Segunda República* (Madrid: Encuentro, 2010).

—— *Fraude y violencia en las elecciones del Frente Popular* (Madrid: Espasa, 2017).

ANON. *Estado del Cuerpo de Ingenieros del Ejército en 1876.* Madrid, Imprenta del Memorial de Ingenieros, 1876.

ARRANZ NOTARIO, LUIS. 'Modelos de partido', in Santos Juliá (ed.), *Política en la Segunda República* (Madrid: Marcial Pons, 1995), 81–110.

—— *Silvela. Entre el liberalismo y el regeneracionismo* (Madrid: Gota a Gota, 2013).

ARRANZ NOTARIO, LUIS; ELORZA, ANTONIO; & REY REGUILLO, FERNANDO. 'Liberalismo y corporativismo en la crisis de la Restauración', in José Luis García Delgado, *La crisis de la Restauración. España entre la Primera Guerra Mundial y la II República* (Madrid: Siglo XXI, 1986), 5–50.

ARTOLA, MIGUEL. *Partidos y programas políticos (1808–1936)* (Madrid: Aguilar, 1974).

AVILÉS FARRÉ, JUAN. *La izquierda burguesa y la tragedia de la II Segunda República* (Madrid: Comunidad de Madrid, 2006).

—— *Francisco Ferrer y Guardia: pedagogo, anarquista y mártir* (Madrid: Marcial Pons, 2006).

AZAÑA, MANUEL. *Memorias políticas y de guerra.* Vol. 1. (Madrid: Afrodisio Aguado, 1976).

—— *Diarios 1932–1933. "Los cuadernos robados"* (Barcelona: Crítica, 1997).

—— *Obras completas.* Vol. II. (Madrid: CEPC, 2007).

BAROJA, PÍO. *Galería de tipos de la época* (Madrid: Biblioteca Nueva, 1952).

BEN AMI, SHLOMO. *Los orígenes de la Segunda República: anatomía de una transición* (Madrid: Alianza, 1990).

CASTRO ALFÍN, DEMETRIO. 'Orígenes y primeras etapas del republicanismo en España', in Nigel Townson (ed.): *El republicanismo en España (1830–1977)* (Madrid: Alianza, 1994), 33–57.

CHAPAPRIETA, JOAQUÍN. *La paz fue posible. Memorias de un político* (Barcelona: Ariel, 1971).

CULLA, JOAN B. *El republicanisme lerrouxista a Catalunya (1901–1923).* (Barcelona: Edicions Curial, 1986).

DARDÉ, CARLOS. 'La larga noche de la Restauración, 1875–1900', in Nigel Townson (ed.), *El republicanismo en España (1830–1977)* (Madrid: Alianza, 1994), 113–135.

DE BLAS, ANDRÉS. 'El Partido Radical en la política española de la Segunda República', *Revista de Estudios Políticos* nº 31–32, 1983, 137–164.

DE MADARIAGA, SALVADOR. *Memorias (1921–1936)* (Madrid: Espasa-Calpe, 1974).
DEL MORAL, JOAQUÍN. *Oligarquía y enchufismo. Escarceos críticos sobre la actual política española* (Madrid: CIAP, 1933).
DEL REY REGUILLO, FERNANDO. 'La República de los socialistas', in Fernando del Rey Reguillo (ed.), *Palabras como puños. La intransigencia política en la Segunda República española* (Madrid: Tecnos, 2011), 158–225.
DUARTE, ÁNGEL. *El republicanisme català a la fi del segle XIX* (Vic: Eumo, 1987).
—— 'Salmerón y Lerroux. Consideraciones sobre liderazgos en transición (1890–1906)' in Demetrio Castro (coord.), *Líderes para el pueblo republicano* (Pamplona: UPNA, 2015), 179–204.
FERNÁNDEZ ALMAGRO, MELCHOR. *Historia del reinado de D. Alfonso XIII* (Madrid, Sarpe: 1986 (or. 1933)), 2 Vols.
FRANCO SALGADO-ARAUJO, FRANCISCO. *Mis conversaciones privadas con Franco* (Barcelona: Planeta, 2005).
FUENTES, JUAN FRANCISCO. *Largo Caballero* (Madrid: Síntesis, 2005).
GIL-ROBLES, JOSÉ MARÍA. *No fue posible la paz. Memorias* (Barcelona: Planeta, 1998).
JALÓN, CÉSAR. *Memorias políticas* (Madrid: Guadarrama, 1973).
JULIÁ, SANTOS. 'La experiencia del poder: la izquierda republicana, 1931–1933', in Nigel Townson (ed.), *El republicanismo en España (1830–1977)* (Madrid: Alianza, 1994), 165–192.
—— *Los socialistas en la política española* (Madrid: Taurus, 1997).
KEY JR., VALDIMER O. *Política, partidos y grupos de presión* (Madrid: Instituto de Estudios Políticos, 1962).
LINZ, JUAN JOSÉ. 'De Grandes Esperanzas a la Guerra Civil: la quiebra de la democracia en España', in *Obras Escogidas*, Vol. 4 (Madrid: CEPC, 2009), 119–188.
LUCA DE TENA, JUAN IGNACIO. *Mis amigos muertos* (Barcelona: Planeta, 1971).
MACARRO, JOSÉ MANUEL. *Socialismo, República y Revolución en Andalucía* (Seville: Universidad de Sevilla, 2000).
MARCO, JOSÉ MARÍA. *Maura. La política pura* (Madrid: Gota a Gota, 2013).
MARTÍNEZ BARRIO, DIEGO. *Memorias* (Barcelona: Planeta, 1983).
MARTÍNEZ RELANZÓN, ALEJANDRO. *Elecciones y modernización política en Valencia (1890–1923)* (Castellon: Sace, 2017).
MAURA, GABRIEL. *Historia crítica del reinado de don Alfonso XIII durante su menoridad bajo la regencia de su madre doña María Cristina de Austria* (Barcelona: Montaner y Simón, 1919).
MAURA, MIGUEL. *Así cayó Alfonso XIII. De una Dictadura a otra* (Madrid: Marcial Pons, 2007).
MOLA VIDAL, EMILIO. *Memorias* (Barcelona: Planeta, 1977).
PABÓN, JESÚS. *Cambó, 1876–1918* (Barcelona: Alpha, 1952).
—— *Cambó, 1930–1947* (Barcelona: Alpha, 1969).
PANEBIANCO, ANGELO. *Modelos de partido* (Madrid: Alianza, 1990).
PAYNE, STANLEY G. *Unión Soviética, comunismo y revolución en España (1931–1939)* Barcelona: Plaza y Janés, 2003).

―――― *El colapso de la República. Los orígenes de la Guerra Civil (1933–1936)* (Madrid: La Esfera de los Libros, 2005).

―――― *Alcalá-Zamora. El fracaso de la República conservadora* (Madrid: Gota a Gota, 2016).

PAYNE, STANLEY G. & PALACIOS, JESÚS. *Franco* (Barcelona: Espasa, 2014).

PRIETO, INDALECIO. *De mi vida: recuerdos, estampas, siluetas, sombras.* Vol. 1. (Mexico D.F: Oasis, 1968).

PORTELA, MANUEL. *Memorias* (Madrid: Alianza, 1988).

PRESTON, PAUL. *A People Betrayed: A History of Corruption, Political Incompetence and Social Division in Modern Spain* (London: William Collins, 2020).

REIG, RAMIRO. *Blasquistas y clericales. La lucha por la ciudad en la Valencia de 1900* (Valencia: Alfons el Magnànim, 1986).

RIVAS, NATALIO. *Retazos de Historia* (Madrid: Editora Nacional, 1952).

ROMERO MAURA, JOAQUÍN. *«La rosa de fuego». El obrerismo barcelonés de 1899 a 1909* (Madrid: Alianza, 1989 (or. 1975)).

ROYO-VILLANOVA, ANTONIO. *La Constitución española de 9 de diciembre de 1931* (Valladolid: Imprenta Castellana, 1934).

―――― *Treinta años de política antiespañola* (Valladolid: Librería Santarén, 1940).

RUIZ, JULIUS. *El Terror Rojo* (Barcelona: Espasa, 2012).

RUIZ MANJÓN, OCTAVIO. *El Partido Republicano Radical (1908–1936)* (Madrid: Tebas, 1976).

SALAZAR ALONSO, RAFAEL. *Bajo el signo de la revolución* (Astorga (Leon): Akrón, 2007).

SECO SERRANO, CARLOS. *Alfonso XIII y la crisis de la Restauración* (Madrid: Rialp. 1979).

SOLDEVILLA, FERNANDO. *El año político 1901* (Madrid: Imprenta de Ricardo Rojas, 1902).

―――― *El año político 1921* (Madrid: Imprenta y Encuadernación de Julio Cosano, 1922).

―――― *El año político 1922* (Madrid: Imprenta y Encuadernación de Julio Cosano, 1923).

―――― *El año político 1923* (Madrid: Imprenta y Encuadernación de Julio Cosano, 1924).

SOUTO, SANDRA. *¿Y Madrid? ¿Qué hace Madrid?* (Madrid: Siglo XXI, 2004).

TOMÁS VILLARROYA, JOAQUÍN. 'El voto de desconfianza en la II República', *Cuadernos de la Cátedra Fadrique Furio Ceriol* nº 3, 1981, 1–10.

―――― *La destitución de Alcalá-Zamora* (Valencia: CEU, 1988).

TOWNSON, NIGEL. *The Crisis of Democracy in Spain: Centrist politics under the Second Republic, 1931–1936* (Portland: Sussex Academic Press, 2000).

―――― *La República que no pudo ser. La política de centro en España (1931–1936)* (Madrid: Taurus, 2002).

TUSELL, JAVIER & GARCÍA QUEIPO DE LLANO, GENOVEVA. *Alfonso XIII: el rey polémico* (Madrid: Taurus, 2001).

VIDARTE, JUAN SIMEÓN. *El bienio negro y la insurrección de Asturias* (Barcelona: Grijalbo, 1978).

Villa García, Roberto. *La República en las Urnas. El despertar de la democracia en España* (Madrid: Marcial Pons, 2011).

—— 'La CNT contra la República: la insurrección revolucionaria de diciembre de 1933', *Historia y Política* nº 25, 2011, 177–205.

—— 'Burgos podridos y democratización. Las elecciones municipales de abril de 1933', *Hispania* nº 240, 2012, 147–176.

—— 'El ocaso del republicanismo histórico: lerrouxistas y blasquistas ante las elecciones de 1936', *Anales de la Real Academia de Cultura Valenciana* nº 87, 2012, 75–120.

Weber, Max. *El político y el científico* (Madrid: Alianza, 2009).

Index

Africa, 17, 50, 53, 127, 142, 159–61
Agrarian Party, 119, 121, 127, 135, 153, 155, 164, 166, 173, 180
Agrarian reform, 76, 80, 100, 102–6, 112–14
Aguirre, Antonio, 56
Aizpuru, Luis, 68
Alba, Santiago, 63–4, 71, 73, 121, 127, 153, 164, 166–7, 179
Alcalá-Zamora, Niceto, 2, 6–8, 59
　attempts to discredit Lerroux, 146, 152–3, 179, 181
　becoming President of the Republic, 84–8
　head of Republican Provisional Government, 67–8, 72–5
　involvement with constitutional crises, 121–34
　involvement with Cortes as President, 101, 105, 108–11, 113–17, 121–34, 139–171
Alfonso XIII, 4–5, 17, 46–47, 58–65, 68–73
Almirall, Valentin, 40
Álvarez, Melquíades, 28, 53, 55, 58, 61, 63, 72, 101, 173, 178–9
　alliance with Lerroux, 61, 72, 101, 121
　as a liberal reformist, 53, 54, 58, 178–9
Anarchism, 4, 8, 26–30, 33–4, 39, 42, 45–7, 50–1, 60, 114
　insurrections and punishments, 34, 50, 58, 63–64, 108, 121, 129
　relationship with Lerroux, 45–7, 50–1, 58, 132
　writers and propaganda, 26–30, 33, 39
Anarchosyndicalism, 80, 121, 125, 129, 181
Anaya, Federico, 52
Andalusia, 22, 55, 60, 71, 106, 124, 136
Anglés, Juan, 43
Anti-revolutionary Bloc, 166–168

Anticlericalism, 2, 4, 35–7, 40, 100–1, 109, 138, 144
Asturian Revolt, 132–42
Asturias, 17, 22, 55, 129, 132–42
Athenaeum, 61, 70
Azaña, Manuel, 1–2, 5–6, 8, 53, 70, 78, 81, 130–4, 148–51, 156–9
　after February 1936 election, 170, 179–81
　as prime minister 1931–33, 85–8, 98–119
　attitude to Lerroux, 133, 139–42
Azpiazu, Ubaldo, 75, 104

Baguenas, Martin, 174
Barcelona, 1, 26, 74, 107, 130, 135, 139, 143, 146, 148, 167
　as original seat of Radical Party, 4, 8, 10, 29–51, 62, 74, 101
　Radical Party scandals in Barcelona, 55–62
Baroja, Pio, 10, 11, 12
Basque Nationalist Party (PNV), 129, 162
Basque Nationalism, 114, 129–130, 181
Batet, Domingo, General, 135, 142
Bautista Aznar, Juan, 74
Bellon, Ildefonso, 158
Berenguer, Dámaso, 5, 71, 73–4, 84, 125–6
Bergamín, Francisco, 72
Besteiro, Julián, 73, 85, 115–6, 138
Blanco y Negro (newspaper), 124
Blasco Ibáñez, Sigfrido, 157–8
Blasco Ibáñez, Vicente, 40, 43, 69, 102, 124, 128,
Burgos y Mazo, Manuel, 72

Cadiz, 12, 15, 21–2, 58, 108
Calle O'Donnell, (Madrid home of Lerroux), 54–5, 110, 148, 172, 182
Calvo Sotelo, José, 110, 125, 141, 157, 174

Cambo, Francesc, 48, 85, 119, 127, 156, 165, 167
Campoamor, Clara, 85, 175
Canalejas, José, 28, 58
Cánovas, Antonio, 25, 58
Carabineros, 104
Carlism, 13–4, 25, 29, 32–3, 36, 39, 47–8, 172, 177
Casa del Pueblo (House of the People), 4, 41, 129
Casanas y Pages, Salvador, 37
Casanueva, Cándido, 120, 127, 163
Casas Viejas, 108
Castelar, 11, 19, 21–2, 29
Catalan Nationalism, 2, 4, 8, 52, 57–8, 61–3, 68, 70–4, 100–6, 122, 150, 167, 181
 administrations, *see Generalidad, Mancomunidad,*
 solidarity crisis 1906–7, 31–44, 47–50
Catalan Republican Left (ERC), 86, 103–4, 107, 110
Catalan Solidarity, 34, 42, 47–9
Catalan Statute, 72, 102–3, 106, 143
Catena, Antonio, 23, 24, 27
Catholic Right, 2, 134, 143, 145, 166–7, 181
Cavalcanti, Jose General, 70, 172, 175
CEDA, *see Spanish Confederation of Autonomous Right-Wing Groups*
Centeno, José, 151–2
Chapaprieta, Joaquín, 43, 153–7, 160–6
Church, 1, 19, 35–7, 76–9, 83–4, 105–9, 172
Cid y Ruiz-Zorrilla, José María, 121
Circulo de Bellas Artes, 101
CNT, *see National Confederation of Labour*
Cohen, Gastón, 151
Communism, 2, 46, 80, 129 165, 167, 170, 176, 183
Companys, Luis, 130, 135, 139
Conservatism, 11, 132–3, 166–8, 179–80
 conservatives in government, 25, 31–2, 35–9, 42, 48–9, 53, 57–9, 61, 64–5, 69,
 conservatives within the Republic, 76–7, 84, 86, 101, 106, 112, 118–22, 126–7
 the Radical Party as Conservative, 138, 143, 146, 148–9, 167–8, 180

Constitution, 2, 4, 6, 9, 11, 26, 29, 35–6, 38, 48–9, 41, 112–6, 130, 134, 136, 170–3, 176, 178–81
 constitutional crisis after October 1934 revolution, *see October Revolution of 1934*
 constitutional reform, 61–62, 113, 120–7, 140, 145
 development of 1931 constitution, 76, 81, 82–7, 98–110
 suspension during dictatorship, 1923–30, 68–69
Constitutional Guarantees Court, 100, 109–10
Constitutional Monarchy, 18, 21, 35–8, 41, 45–51, 53, 62–4, 68, 77, 114, 126,
Corominas, Eusebio, 33, 48
Corominas, Pedro, 57
Cortes (Spanish Parliament), 82, 85–9, 100–3, 106, 125–6, 130–1, 133–4, 137, 149, 162, 165, 172
 during Constitutional Monarchy, 44, 49–50, 59, 65
 threats of dissolution, 108–10, 113–17, 121, 155–7
Costa, Joaquín, 53, 69
Cu-Cut (satirical magazine), 47

Dato, Eduardo, 25, 42, 49, 53, 59, 61, 64
De Albornoz, Álvaro, 71, 83, 107, 109
De Castro, José Antonio, 160–2
De Unamuno, Miguel, 120
Defence Councils, 60, 61, 63
Dencás, Josep, 138–9
Despujol, Ignacio, Captain General, 74
Dictatorship, 1923–30, 5, 11, 68
DLR, *see Liberal Republican Right*
Domingo, Marcelino, 3, 61, 63, 65, 68, 70–1, 83, 107, 109, 114, 116, 118
Dualde, Joaquín, 144

Elections
 election of June 1931, 6, 82
 election of November 1933, 2, 101, 117
 election of February 1936, 167–75
El Imparcial (newspaper), 21
El Pais (newspaper), 4, 23–7, 46, 55
El Progreso (newspaper), 27–30, 48, 55
El Radical (newspaper), 10, 12, 55–6, 60
Enchufismo, 3, 99

ERC, see Catalan Republican Left
Escamots (Esquerra militia), 130
Escuela Nueva (republican intellectual group) 70
Españolismo (Spanishness), 9, 38–9, 54, 57, 77–9, 120, 132, 173, 175–7, 182
Esplá, Carlos, 139
Esquerdo, José María, 26–7, 29, 32
Esquerra, 57, 130, 134, 138, 140, 143
Estraperlo, 7, 9, 150–62, 181
Extremadura, region of, 55, 106, 136

Factionalism, 11, 24, 33, 42, 55, 70, 125
Falangism, 128, 137, 171, 174, 177, 182
Federalism, 21, 27, 31–3, 38, 40, 45, 57, 70 75, 135, 159
Ferrer Guardia, Francisco, 4, 26, 29, 46, 50
FIRPE, see Spanish Left Republican Parliamentary Federation
First Republic (1873–4), 8, 11–12, 18–20, 41, 121, 127, 139
Franco, Francisco, 2, 7, 12, 59, 60, 142, 172–7, 182–183
Fraternities, 41, 46
Freemasonry, 22, 124, 182–3
Fuente, Ricardo, 55

Galán, Fermín, 73, 129, 140
Garcia Hernandez, Angel, 73, 129, 140
Garcia Prieto, Manuel, 61–2, 69, 72, 79, 109, 114, 123, 129, 148, 151–152, 155
Gasset, Fernando, 43
General Workers' Union (UGT), 27–8, 61, 73, 80, 82, 102, 104, 106–7, 123, 129
Generalidad (Catalan administration), 57, 102–3, 130, 132, 135–6, 143
Giménez Fernández, Manuel, 131, 145
Ginard de la Rosa, Rafael, 23
Giral, José, 70–1, 137
Goded Llopis, Manuel, General, 71
Goicoechea, Antonio, 154
Gordon Ordas, Felix, 7, 124
Guadarrama, 5, 54, 175
Guerra del Río, Rafael, 55, 108, 163, 172
Guzmán, Martín Luis, 151–2, 157

Herrero, Emilio, 155
Himno de Riego (republican anthem), 75

Iglesias, Pablo, 2, 26–8, 56–7, 74, 133

Jalón, César, 132, 154, 172
Jaurès, Jean, 10
Junoy, Emilio, 33, 43
Jurisdictions Law, 47–8

La Publicidad (republican newspaper), 33, 35, 40, 48
La Rambla (home village of Lerroux), 12, 59
League of Nations, 6, 78, 84
Lerroux y Rodriguez, Alejandro (father of Lerroux), 13–17, 21–2
Lerroux, Adriana (sister of Lerroux), 13, 182
Lerroux, Alejandro
  accepting illicit payments, 24–25
  accusations of corruption, 28, 57, 60, 147–50, 163, 181
  as a lawyer, 16, 18, 54, 69
  attitude to paramilitaries, 27, 137, 171
  attitude to Africa, 52–3, 58, 63, 65, 127
  attitude to Civil War, 175–6
  attitude to First World War, 5, 59–60
  attitude to leftist critics, 152, 156–7, 169, 171, 173, 175
  attitude to military, 15–18, 141–2, 175–7
  attitude to monarchy, 52–3, 60, 63–5
  attitude to religion, 15, 35–7, 59, 75–76, 78–9, 84, 101, 109, 127, 167, 172
  character, 16, 31, 148–9, 173
  controversy over death sentences, 139–41
  education, 16–18, 54–5
  'Emperor of Paralelo', 30, 39, 48, 56, 59
  foreign minister, 13, 72, 75, 78, 81, 84, 154
  in Argentina, 5, 49–51
  in opposition, 100
  in Paris, 10, 21, 28, 47, 49–50, 69, 71
  in prison, 5, 33, 49, 71
  political ability, 10, 11, 44
  political views and ability, 10–1, 40–1, 44–6, 99, 107–8, 117, 167–9, 181
  prime minister, 112, 121–6, 131–6
  reputation, 1–7, 99, 110, 132–3, 137–8, 147, 162, 164, 166, 170, 173, 178, 181

San Rafael estate, 5, 54, 106, 147, 152, 171, 174
speaking ability, 26, 29, 44, 52, 132, 135
views of Catalan nationalism, 38–39, 52, 101–3, 143
views of corruption, 117–18
views of dictatorship, 69
views of patriotism, 38, 77–9, 98, 100, 111, 132, 136, 155, 176–7
views of reform, 76–77, 80–4
views of republic, 75–76, 98, 113, 178
views of revolution, 45–7, 51–2, 61, 63–4, 68–9, 105, 132–3, 173, 175–6
views of rural affairs, 80–1, 100–2
vote of no confidence, 114–5
war minister, 141
writing and journalism, 11–12, 23–5, 55
(*see also Alcalá-Zamora, Niceto, Álvarez, Melquíades, Anarchism, Azaña, Manuel, Calle O'Donnell, La Rambla, Madrid, Radical Party, Socialists*)
Lerroux, Arturo (brother of Alejandro), 13–18, 22–4
Lerroux, Aurelio (brother of Alejandro), 13–14, 30
Lerroux, Aurelio (nephew of Alejandro), 14, 54, 150–2, 157–8, 172, 174
Lerroux, Teresa (wife of Alejandro), 24, 172–4, 182–3
Liberal Democrats, 162, 164, 166
Liberal Party, 31–2, 36, 47–52, 56, 58–61, 63–5, 69, 71, 73, 112
Liberal Republican Right (DLR), 79, 82, 83, 86
Liberalism, 28–32, 36–40, 47–52, 56, 58–9, 61–73, 81–3, 98 100–1, 117, 119, 125–6, 135, 142–8
liberal democracy, 81, 98, 100, 112, 117, 126, 133, 145, 146, 167, 173–83
traditions of, 2, 3, 5, 10, 19–21, 76, 173
Lliga, 31–2, 35–43, 47, 54, 57–9, 62, 74, 85, 127, 130, 156
(*see also Catalan Nationalism*)
Local Administration Law, 43
López Ochoa, Eduardo, General, 74, 142
Luca de Tena, Juan Ignacio, 172–3
Lucia, Luis, 161–3

Macia, Francesc, 74, 102, 139
Madrid, 4–5, 61, 82, 106, 108, 151, 155
headquarters of Radical Party, 55, 58
importance to Lerroux, 10–18, 21–3, 26, 28, 31, 41, 54–5
political events in Madrid, 61, 73–4, 77, 100, 102, 106, 119–122, 130, 132–6, 150, 174, 182
Mancomunidad (Catalan administration), 54, 57–58, 130–43
March, Juan, 3, 6, 111, 125
Marraco, Manuel, 128–9
Marsá, Antonio, 70
Martínez Barrio, Diego, 2, 71–2, 104–8, 116–24, 133–4, 144–5, 180–1
Martínez Campos, Arsenio, 28
Martínez de Velasco, José, 113, 127, 131, 135, 156, 163, 173
Maura, Antonio, 1, 7, 38, 42–3, 48–51, 56–9, 77, 82, 85, 155
Maura, Miguel, 72, 75, 101, 105, 126, 133, 147–149, 164
Millán Astray, José, 141
Mines, 44
Mir y Miró, José, 33
Mixed labour boards (*jurados mixtos*), 80
Monarchy, 1, 5, 8, 11, 98–9, 105, 110, 112, 117, 119, 140, 173, 176
rejection of the monarchy, 29, 60–65, 71–81, 96, 178–9
(*see also Constitutional Monarchy*)
Montero Ríos, Eugenio, 21, 42, 47
Moreno Espinosa, Adolfo, 21–22
Moreno, Guillermo, 159–163
Moret, Segismundo, 25, 28, 31, 42, 50–51, 56, 155
Morgades, José, 37
Morocco, 58, 63, 65, 69, 78, 127, 159–161, 174

National Assembly, 70
National Confederation of Labour (CNT), 54, 61–2, 80–1, 108
Nombela scandal, 7, 9, 12, 159–166, 181
Nombela, Antonio, 160–3

October Revolution of 1934, 133–141
Ordas, Felix Gordon, 7, 124

Patriotic Union (UP), 70
Peire, Tomás, 81

Index

Pérez Farrás, Enrique, 139–41
Pi y Margall, Francisco, 11, 20–1, 31–3, 38, 159
Pich y Pon, Juan, 150, 157
Planas, Manuel, 39
Polavieja, Camilo de, General, 28, 35, 39
Popular Front, 166–71, 173–5
Portela Valladares, Manuel, 143, 164
Posadas, 59
Prat de la Riba, Enric, 38
Prieto, Indalecio, 3, 65, 68, 138
Primo de Rivera, José Antonio, 137, 149, 157
Primo de Rivera, Manuel, 5, 8, 11, 60, 65–6, 68–72, 80, 148, 176, 179
Pronunciamientos, 6, 21, 29, 45–6 69, 104, 106
   pronunciamiento of 1868, 29, 46
   pronunciamiento of 1887, 21
   pronunciamiento of 1923, 104, 179
   pronunciamiento of 1932, 6, 106
Provisional Government of 1931, 5, 67, 72–9, 84
PSOE, *see Spanish Socialist Workers' Party*

Quiroga, Casares, 108

Radical Democratic Party, 124
Radical Party, 1–13, 42, 48–65, 67–88, 98–133, 137–152, 155–7, 160–70, 173–5, 178–82
   as centre-right, *see Republicans, centre-right*
   as Conservative, *see Conservatism*
   as left-republicans, *see Republicans, left*
Radical Republican Party, *see Radical Party*
Reptile Fund (*fondo de reptiles*), 24
'Republic of all Spaniards', 77, 79
Republican Action, 70
Republican Alliance, 70–1, 82, 88, 98, 179–80
Republican Federation, 41, 43, 62
Republican National Federal Union (UFNR), 57, 59, 61
Republican Progressive Party, 17, 20–1, 23, 161
Republican Union, 41–4, 47–8, 55–6
Republican unity (concept), 21, 26, 62, 71, 113
Republican Unity (faction), 33–34
Republican-Socialist Alliance, 2, 56, 67, 72–7, 82, 86–8, 99, 105–7, 112, 126, 147, 159, 165–71, 179–81
   (*see also Popular Front*)
Republicanism, 1, 4, 8, 10–12, 18–19, 21–2, 33, 39–40, 44–5, 52–5, 62–3, 70, 76–7, 107, 125
Republicans, centre-right, 2, 8, 9, 75, 77, 110, 112, 119–25
   centre-right coalition, 121, 124, 130–40, 144, 146, 153–7, 163–7, 170, 179–81
   Radical Party becoming centre-right, 8, 9, 77, 110, 119–30
Republicans, left, 2, 3, 6, 9–10, 20–1, 36, 40, 56, 81–88, 99, 101–23, 130, 151, 159, 164–6, 169–71, 175, 179–81
   attempts to destabilise Radical government, 152–7
   collapse of vote and withdrawal from politics, 118–30, 133–7
   formation of FIRPE, *see Spanish Left Republican Parliamentary Federation*
   many Radical as left Republicans, 76–9, 81, 102
   (*see also Republican-Socialist Alliance*)
Republicans, right, 8, 9, 79, 83, 86, 110, 113–31, 164–6, 170, 173, 179–81
Restoration of Spanish monarchy 1874, 11, 20–1, 62, 70–1, 77, 98–9, 105, 117–8, 125
Revolutionary Committee, 5, 72, 75, 138
Rico-Avello, Manuel, 117
Rico, Gumersindo, 132
Rico, Pedro, 135
Río Rodríguez, Cirilo del, 121, 172
Rocha, Juan José, 152, 158, 182
Romanones, Count of [Álvaro de Figueroa y Torres-Sotomayor], 28, 58, 61, 70, 73, 154, 172, 179
Romero Robledo, Francisco, 11, 31–2, 155
Romero, Pita, 121
Royo-Villanova, Antonio, 153, 155, 160–3
Ruiz Zorrilla, Manuel, 17, 20–24, 26, 29, 32, 46, 48

Sagasta, Práxedes Mateo, 21, 29, 31–2
Salamanca, 52, 145–6

Salazar Alonso, 109, 128–9, 131, 151, 157–8
Salmeron, Nicolas, 11, 21, 28, 32–3, 43, 45, 47–9, 53, 55–7
Samper, Ricardo, 128–33, 140–1, 150–2, 160
San Rafael estate, *see Lerroux, Alejandro*
San Sebastian Pact August 1930, 72, 82, 103
Sánchez Fuster, Antonio, 56, 174, 182
Sánchez Roman, Felipe, 105, 115, 124, 133
Sanjurjo, Jose, General, 6, 73, 75, 103–6, 125–6, 140, 171
Savonarola, Girolamo, 36
Second Republic (1931–9), 1, 3, 5, 6–8, 10, 12, 62, 64, 179
Silvela, Francisco, 28, 32, 35–36, 39
Social Popular Party, 112
Socialist insurrection, 11–12, 108, 123, 129–32, 138–41, 170, 180
Socialists, 9–10, 12, 35, 48, 50, 57–60, 63–88, 98–110, 112–20, 122–41, 146–51, 159, 165, 179–82
(*see also Spanish Socialist Workers' Party*)
accusations of corruption, 118, 149, 175
attitude to Lerroux, 2, 6, 27–8, 44, 56, 81, 115, 128–33, 138, 170
support for insurrection, 130–1, 138
(*see also Republican-Socialist Alliance*)
Sol y Ortega, Juan, 32, 34
Spanish Socialist Workers' Party (PSOE), 2, 4, 61, 86–8, 105, 107, 109–110, 153, 178–9, 182
alliance with Trade Unions, 27–28, 58, 80–82, 129, 138
as opposition, 114–19
as ruling party, 63, 70–1, 80–82
hostility towards Radical Party, 6, 9, 123
power sharing with Patriotic Union, 70

Spanish Confederation of Autonomous Right-Wing Groups (CEDA), 112–13, 117–24, 127, 130–1, 134, 139, 141–6, 150, 154–7, 161–73, 180–1
Spanish Left Republican Parliamentary Federation (FIRPE), 107–8
Strauss scandal, 12, 150–8, 164, 166
Strauss, Daniel, 12, 150–9
Syndicalism, 27, 30

Tayá-Nombela scandals, 7, 9, 12, 59–63, 159–66, 181
Tayá, Antonio, 159–63
Telefonica, 132
Torres, Henri, 151
Trade unions, 27, 29, 32–5, 41–6, 50, 60, 61, 71, 80–1, 102, 114, 175
increasing militancy, 81, 102, 175
relationship with politics, 32–5, 43, 46, 50, 60, 175
Tragic Week, 1909, 1, 4, 8, 37, 43, 50, 51, 53

UFNR, *see Republic National Federal Union*
UGT, *see General Workers' Union*
UP, *see Patriotic Union*

Valdivia, José, 106, 157
Valencia, 40, 55, 65, 71, 83, 102, 124, 128, 136, 182
Vallés y Ribot, José María, 33
Vaquero, Eloy, 133, 151
Vélez, Dámaso, 54, 69, 73, 75, 151
Vila, Joaquín, 149
Villacampa, Manuel, 21

Womens' Suffrage, 85, 100, 117
Workers' Alliance, 129, 133, 138
Workers' Solidarity, 50

Yébenes, Pareja, 123